WHISKEY REBELS

WHISKEY REBELS

The Story of
A Frontier Uprising

By

LELAND D. BALDWIN

**DECORATIONS BY
WARD HUNTER**

UNIVERSITY OF PITTSBURGH PRESS

This Book is one of a series relating Western Pennsylvania history, written under the direction of the Western Pennsylvania Historical Survey sponsored jointly by The Buhl Foundation, the Historical Society of Western Pennsylvania and the University of Pittsburgh.

Published by the University of Pittsburgh Press, Pittsburgh, Pa. 15260
Copyright, 1939, by the University of Pittsburgh Press
Copyright © 1967, by Leland D. Baldwin
All rights reserved
Revised Edition, 1968
Third Printing, 1987
Library of Congress Catalog Card Number 39-11763
ISBN 0-8229-5151-7
Manufactured in the United States of America

Contents

Foreword

THE author desires to express his appreciation of the aid given by the staff members of a number of depositories, particularly the Historical Society of Western Pennsylvania, the Darlington Library of the University of Pittsburgh, the Carnegie Library of Pittsburgh, the Library of Congress, and the Connecticut Historical Society. For editorial assistance he desires to thank Elisabeth M. Sellers, a fellow member of the staff of the Western Pennsylvania Historical Survey, and Dr. Solon J. Buck, former director of the Survey.

There are great gaps in the materials bearing on the Whiskey Insurrection, particularly on the military and statistical aspects, and on the motivations of the inner council of the Federalist party. It is probable that statistics on the distilling business in the United States in the 1790's exist in the Tench Coxe Papers, but unfortunately access could not be obtained to them.

LELAND D. BALDWIN

Preface to the Revised Edition

THIS edition updates the bibliography and corrects certain typographical errors. There are also a few cases in which further light has made it necessary to alter judgments. Of the latter the most notable concern the ratio of grain to proof alcohol in whiskey distilling in the 1790's, and the results of the Congressional elections of 1794 and 1796.

L.D.B.

Fall, 1968

WHISKEY REBELS

Chapter I: *The Monongahela Pioneers*

THE region of which Pittsburg is the center, is one of the most beautiful in the world," wrote a local real estate promoter of the early nineteenth century, without even a conspiratorial wink. "It resembles the vale of Cashmere, the Scripture Eden, or Paradise."[1] In the light of this sweeping assertion the modern romanticist may be forgiven a twinge of nostalgic longing as he stands upon one of the bluffs that border the course of the Monongahela River and visualizes the scene as it was in pioneer days. The vast wrinkled plateau is not scarred and naked, but clad in a mantle of many-shaded green. Here and there is a little field, with its blackened stumps or girdled and dying trees, in the midst of which is set the rude cabin of unsquared logs that is the home of the pioneer. Almost hidden by the overhanging trees are the traces that serve as roads, now and then emerging into a larger clearing where cluster the more pretentious plantation buildings of some local magnate. Far below, the turbid Monongahela coils among its guardian hills, and a flatboat, laden with domestic animals and tousle-headed immigrant children and with a farm wagon perched precariously on the roof, winds its way downstream to "Kaintuck" or even to the fabulously fertile Spanish realm beyond.

Behind the flatboat a long, low keelboat, looking like a Venetian gondola with a freight car amidships, turns toward the shore while the men ship their poles, their red shirts gleaming on the deck. The mellow, haunting strains of the keelboat's horn float through the valley clearings and up to the listening heights. There is a scurry of tiny figures on the little plain at the mouth of the creek toward which the boat is turning; nestled in the shadow of the bluff is a village, only a few cabins and a blockhouse, now used as the village store, but a scant half dozen years ago the haven of refuge for a hundred frightened pioneers. A bale of goods is unloaded, a barrel or two of flour or whiskey taken aboard, and a passenger shipped. The keelboat puts out from shore, the red shirts straining at the poles while the steersman blows another round on the horn to "scare away the devil and secure good luck."

Halfway up the hill on the opposite side of the river there is a cave-like opening that has spewed forth its blackness like the tail of an unsightly comet down to the water's edge. Standing in the mouth of the cave watching the scene below is a silent, gnome-like creature, surely a strange anomaly in these wilds. The keelboat disappears behind a hill and the miner returns to his torch and pick. Consciously or not, miner and keelboatmen are the harbingers of a new age. The ancient forest that has brooded over this wilderness from time immemorial, giving shelter and sustenance to man and beast, is beginning to fall before the woodsman's ax, and the soft, distant notes of the boatman's horn are echoing like a requiem over the brave days that are soon to pass.

There were definite indications in 1794 that western Pennsylvania was beginning to lose its character as a frontier community. The counties of Westmoreland, Fayette, Allegheny, and Washington had been set apart. The Forbes Road had been reopened, and occasional wagons and carriages were finding their way over the mountains. Regular mail connections had been established with the East, and a line of government bateaux plied the Ohio River with mail and passengers. The villages on the Monongahela were served by two private packet boats, each running on a schedule. Merchants at Pittsburgh and Brownsville were already gaining a reputation for gouging the luckless immigrants who tried to outfit at those places for the voyage down river. Boatbuilding flourished at a score or more yards; coal was being mined and shipped to Kentucky; and buhrstone mills to the number of perhaps a dozen had been built in the last three years. General James Wilkinson's coup in opening up a limited trade with New Orleans had redounded to the benefit of the Monongahela country and, together with heavy government purchases of provisions and whiskey, had served to increase the amount of specie in circulation in that region. Three academies and a newspaper had been founded, and the Presbyterian and Lutheran churches had become firmly established among the Scotch, Scotch-Irish, and German settlers.

The Revolution was over, and a federal government was already consolidating the fruits of the victory in the hands of the Eastern moneyed classes. The West, perfectly aware of this fact, complained bitterly that it had been induced to pour out the blood of its men, women, and children simply to enrich speculators and manufacturers. The Indian raids still continued against the outlying settlements; speculators had engrossed the best lands and demanded extravagant prices for them; Providence had provided the rivers as an outlet for the back country produce, but Spain's caprices made that outlet only a little better than none, and the American government even talked of allowing it to be closed altogether.

No, the Monongahela country was not yet a land of ease, nor, indeed, of plenty. The winters, the old inhabitants were later to assert, were longer and colder and the summers shorter and cooler than those a later generation knew. Any clearing was sure to be invaded by a growth of rank weeds infested by veritable clouds of mosquitoes and horseflies. Wolves still lurked in the forests and when plagued by rabies were dangerous to men as well as to stock. Rattlesnakes and copperheads were a continual menace, and it was nothing very uncommon for the men binding wheat to take up a snake along with the sheaf. Fever and ague were universal afflictions, and the lack of waterproof footwear made rheumatism a scourge even among the young men. The rules of sanitation were either unknown or neglected, and in truth the conditions for their observance were unfavorable. Not many persons, even now, would take a daily bath if they had to break the ice over the spring, carry the the water half a mile, and then heat it over an open fire. For the same reasons laundering was a problem and was done as seldom as possible. These conditions, however, promoted the itch and probably laid the basis for the legend that it lasted for seven years.

Among the rank and file, living was still of the plainest. The bill of fare was composed strictly of home products such as corn meal, hominy, pork, a few vegetables, and game. There was no sugar or coffee, and very little fruit, other than berries, for fruit trees had not yet become common. Dishes were usually carved from wood or made from gourds. An iron pot, a frying pan, a few pewter spoons, and a hunting knife completed the culinary equipment. Clothing was homespun and home-fashioned from wool or flax, and the stranger could gauge the economic status of a family by the number of garments hung about the wall. Many of the settlers were actually so poverty-stricken that, even in the days of greatest danger from the Indians, they could not afford to provide themselves with firearms, and when Muster Day arrived they had to appear unarmed or carrying only an ax or a corn cutter.

The Monongahela Pioneers

The condition of many townsmen and of a fairly numerous class of "gentleman farmers" was better. The continued advertisements in the *Pittsburgh Gazette* of shipments of dishes, pictures, ornaments, and clothing of outside manufacture must have appeared in response to an effective demand. General Neville's list of the household goods destroyed in the burning of his country home would have done honor to a gentleman of Philadelphia. Even among the more prosperous yeoman farmers there was more than the beginning of civilized comfort, together with the economic discontent always incident to the attempt to raise the standard of living and at the same time to maintain financial integrity. "A Farmer," writing in the *Pittsburgh Gazette* of November 18, 1786, told how a higher standard of living had stolen up on him and finally threatened to ruin him financially; then, true to the old economics, he proposed to solve the problem by returning to the old standard.

"A short story of myself, will show you how it came hard times—and no money—with me, at the age of 65, who have lived well these forty years. My parents were poor, and they put me at 12 years of age to a farmer, with whom I lived till I was 21; my master fitted me out with two stout suits of homespun, four pair of stockings, four woollen shirts, and two pair of shoes; this was my whole fortune at my setting out in the world, and I thought it a good one: at 22 I married me a wife, and a very working young woman she was: we took a farm of 40 acres on rent, by industry we gained a-head fast; I paid my rent punctually, & laid by money; in 10 years I was able to buy me a farm of 60 acres, on which I became my own tenant. I then in a manner grew rich, and soon added another 60 acres, with which I was content; my estate increased beyond all account: I bought several lots of out-land for my children, which amounted to 7, when I was 45 years old; about this time

I married my oldest daughter to a clever lad, to whom I gave 100 acres of my out-land; this daughter had been a working, dutiful child, and I fitted her out well, and to her mind; for I told her to take of the best of my wool and flax, and to spin herself gowns, coats, stockings and shifts; nay, I suffered her to buy some cotton, and make into sheets, as I was determined to do well by her; at this time my farm gave me and my whole family a good living on the produce of it, and left me one year with another 150 silver dollars, for I never laid out (besides my taxes) more than 10 dollars a year, which was for salt, nails and the like; nothing to wear, eat or drink was purchased, as my farm provided all: with this saving I put money to interest, bought cattle, fatted and sold them, and made great profit: in two years after, my second daughter was courted; my wife says, come, father, you are now rich, you know Molly had nothing but what she spun, and no other cloathing has ever come into our house for any of us. Sarah must be fitted out a little, she ought to fare as well as neighbour N——'s Betty; I must have some money and go to town. Well, wife, it shall be as you think best; I never was stingy, but it seems to me that what we spin at home will do: however, wife goes down in a few days, and returns with a calico gown, a calimanco petticoat, a set of stone teacups, half a dozen pewter tea spoons, and a tea kettle, things that were never seen in my house before; they cost but little, I did not feel it, and I confess I was pleased to see them: Sarah was as well fitted out as any girl in the township: in 3 years more my third daughter had a spark, and wedding being concluded upon, wife comes again for the purse; but when she returned, what did I see! a silken gown, silk for a cloak, looking glass, china tea gear, and a hundred other things, with the empty purse; but this was not the worst of it, Mr. Printer, some time before the marriage of this last daughter, and ever since, this charge increased in my family; besides all sorts of household furniture unknown to us before, cloathing of every sort is bought, and the wheel goes only for the purpose of exchanging our substantial cloath, of flax and wool, for gauze, ribbons, silk, tea, &c. my butter, which uscd to go to market, and brought money, is now expended on the tea-table; my time of breakfast, which used to take ten minutes in eating milk, or pottage made of it, now takes my whole family an hour at tea or coffee; my lambs, which used also to bring cash, are now eaten at home, or if sent to market, are brought back in things of no use; so that, instead of laying up 150 dollars a year, I find now all my loose money is gone, my best debts called in and expended; and being straitened, I can't carry on my farm to so good advantage; that it brings me not near as much; that what it costs me to live (though a less family, and all able to work) is fifty or sixty dollars a year more than what all my farm brings me. Now this has gone on a good many years, and has brought hard times into my family; and if I can't reform it, ruin must follow . . . I am still master of my own house; I am determined to alter my way of living to what it was 20 years ago, when I laid up 150 dollars a year . . . Not one thing to eat, drink or wear shall come into my house, which is not raised on my farm, or in the township, or in the country, except salt and iron work . . . no tea, sugar, coffee or rum. The tea kettle shall be sold. I shall then, Mr. Printer, live and die with a good conscience."

The mode of life the farmer proposed to follow would, of course, if followed by the entire community, have brought consequences that he, being no economist, did not foresee. His was not a voice crying in the wilderness by any means. There were plenty of substantial citizens who agreed with his diagnosis and recommended his remedy, but the Monongahela country as a whole thought otherwise. Expanding business brought visions of even greater expansion, and the region longed to burst the economic and political bands that bound it.

The land policy was the most vital problem before the settlers. The pioneers' land hunger was never satisfied, for there was always a new generation as well as a horde of immigrants ready to swarm into newly opened territory. For this reason the Indians, with a primitive economy that demanded vast hunting preserves, were doomed. The Pittsburgh lawyer, Hugh Henry Brackenridge, sympathized thoroughly with the frontiersman's viewpoint and defended it by voice and pen. He quoted the divine injunction to Adam to till the ground and added: "I consider the earth as given to man in common, and each should use his share, so as not to exclude others, and should be restricted to that mode of using it, which is most favourable to the support of the greatest numbers, and consequently productive of the greatest sum of happiness; that is, the cultivation of the soil. I pay little regard, therefore, to any right which is not founded in agricultural occupancy." He disposed summarily of those easterners who defended the primitive way of life. "To find perfect virtue in the simplicity of the unimproved state . . . in the customs and virtues of the savages," was a "calenture of the intellect." He recommended as a cure for this mawkish sentimentalism a touch of the Indian torture fire such as the whites in the West were getting from time to time.

The conception of the nobility of the red man had small chance of surviving among the westerners, not only because of the land hunger involved but also because of the ridiculous figure cut by the Indians when transplanted from the forest to the towns. Said Brackenridge: "I know a little of the mystery of agent-craft, and the mummery of Indian speechifying. An Indian chief in the hands of a good interpreter and agent, is a more profitable property, than a tame bear or a lion presented for a show. I have seen Indian princes in Pittsburgh, as plenty as in the time of Adonibezek, who had three score and ten kings under his table. Many a chief I have seen driven out of a kitchen by a maid with a broomstick, lest he should steal a tin cup or a table spoon. I have seen a certain blind Sam, so called, because blind of an eye, taken down to this city [*Philadelphia*], passed for a warrior, dining with clubs, and have heard of him presented at a ball, on his way down; the favoured ladies looking upon themselves as beatified in receiving the salute of a king. When he returned with a laced waistcoat, the vulgar Indians, that before thought him one of them, laughed immoderately at the farce."

The cure for Indian troubles favored by the frontiersmen was extermination of the Indians, and from this policy they rarely deviated either in theory or practice. In their minds it was a simple problem of choosing which race should survive, and they did not hesitate to choose. There has never been a time in the westward advance when the pioneers ceased to echo the early cry of the Pennsylvania squatters that "it was against laws of God and nature that so much land should lie idle while so many christians wanted it to work on and to raise their bread."[2]

The land problem was almost as acute from another angle. When the Indians were finally dispossessed, the settler found that he had still to purchase the land from the state government or from individuals or companies who had bought up the claims that Revolutionary veterans and others held. During the Revolutionary period Virginia and Pennsylvania had been at odds over the possession of what is now the southwestern part of Pennsylvania, but in general Virginia had controlled what are now Allegheny, Washington, Greene, and Fayette counties, and Pennsylvania had controlled what is now Westmoreland County. Virginia's land policy was much more liberal than that of Pennsylvania, her selling price being about one-tenth of that demanded by the latter. For that reason immigration, largely from Virginia, had set in most strongly toward the territory under Virginia's jurisdiction, so that, by the time the boundary controversy was settled in 1780, the territory west of the Monongahela held perhaps twice as many people as that between the river and the mountains. The establishment of Pennsylvania's jurisdiction over the Monongahela country validated the claims of a horde of eastern land speculators and raised the price of land out of all reason.

The small farmer, none too capable or thrifty, bartered the bulk of his whiskey and produce to the merchants; and, unless he could wheedle a little cash from them or could manage to make a sale to the army or to a family of immigrants, he could not pay for his land. The merchants, for their part, were not exactly getting rich. The cash they received had to go East to pay for their goods, for there was little else, outside of whiskey and furs, that could be sent in exchange. The West was thus in the position of seeing its cash drained away to the East for the benefit of eastern speculators and manufacturers. If these easterners had been willing to settle in the West and to use their wealth in building up that section, there would have been less complaint, but with very few exceptions they preferred the refinement—and the safety—of the East. One way to nullify this eastern advantage was to lay a tax upon land, thus forcing the speculators to sell at reasonable prices and hastening the development of the West and at the same time laying the greatest burden on the East, where superior improvements and proximity to markets made land more valuable. The political weight of the East, however, made it impossible to put this policy in force, and considerable separatist sentiment was consequently stirred up in the West.

The self-sufficient economy of the frontier simplified the functions of government and fostered within each district a political system that was in many respects a pure democracy. Nearly every man held land—with mortgage attached. Almost all men labored with their hands, and amongst the rank and file of the people there was very little difference in the standards of living. All were subject to militia call, and the man who distinguished himself in war did not need wealth to bolster his social position. The scarcity of cash made it difficult to pay taxes; consequently, salaried offices were not looked upon with favor. Most westerners, moreover, had gained a poor impression of salaried officials in the East or in the old countries and considered them to be instruments of tyranny, and anyhow the duties of government in the West were rarely heavy enough to demand the full time of an official.

There were to be considered, of course, the citizens whose birth or wealth or broad acres enabled them to write "gentleman" after their names. Their political convictions were decidedly aristocratic, and they found themselves heartily in accord with Gouverneur Morris' pronouncement in the constitutional convention: "The Busy haunts of men not the remote wilderness, was the proper school of political Talents. If the Western people get the power into their hands they will ruin the Atlantic interests. The Back members are always most averse to the best measures. . . . The lower part of the State had ye. power in the first instance. They kept it in yr. own hands. & the country was ye. better for it."[3]

The commoners of the West, though they often elected their local aristocrats to high office, were not led around by rings in their noses. Every fall a pack-horse train from each neighborhood went east carrying whiskey, furs, and skins to exchange for salt and iron, and during these trips the men visited their friends and learned the political gossip. Thus the western farmers were perfectly aware of what was going on in the East, even before there was a transmontane mail route or a western paper, and they discussed the issues with interest and intelligence.

The political confusion of the past twenty years, together with the limited vision incident to pure democracies, made the ideas and policies of the westerners a tangle of contradictions. If they interpreted "the people" to mean themselves gathered in their local election or militia districts rather than the people of Pennsylvania or of the United States, the mistake was natural. When had the state or the nation done anything decisive to help them solve their problems, to exterminate the Indians, to open the navigation of the Mississippi, or to build good highways? When Hugh Henry Brackenridge, the Pittsburgh lawyer, complained that they seemed to think they could remain a part of the government and yet wage war against it, and that they thought it was theirs to forgive the government rather than to be forgiven, the answer came readily. Were not those the selfsame ideas that had actuated the Continental Congress before the Declaration of Independence? Brackenridge, at the time that federal laws were being defied in western Pennsylvania, was approached by John Gaston, a client who had a case due to appear before a state court. Gaston asked when it would come up.

"Not at all," said Brackenridge.

"How so?" asked Gaston in surprise.

"Why," returned the lawyer, "the government is gone to the devil; the courts are overthrown; all law is at an end; there can be no justice now. The strong hand must manage all things. Is this M'Clure a stout fellow? Has he any sons? Cannot you and your sons beat him?"

"Ah," said Gaston, "that will not do."

"That may be," retorted Brackenridge, "but there is no help for it; that is all that can be done now; at least until some other government, and other courts of law, are set up."[4]

The Monongahela Pioneers

Brackenridge was trying to show his client that the state and federal governments were interdependent and that one could not exist without the other. Gaston refused to take him seriously, however, and the lawyer gave up in discouragement. John Gaston, in his ignorance of political science, can scarcely be blamed for taking the matter as a joke and for failing to perceive the connection. A great civil war has since arisen out of the issue, and there are still those, even among men learned in the law, who act on the assumption that they can ignore whichever laws they choose.

Enough has been said to show that the elements dominant in the East entertained very low opinions of the civic righteousness of the back countrymen. Beyond doubt, aside from the superiority inherent in the attitude of the people of any older settlement, this was wishful thinking, for the East desired to retain its social, economic, and political ascendancy. The doctrines preached by the pioneers were aimed at a destruction of this ascendancy, and the East consequently took steps so to cloud the issues that the opinions it engendered have not been effectively blasted to this day. Of course the pioneers were lawless when judged by the standards of the older settlements, but when judged in the light of western conditions, as well as by what are now considered inherent human rights, this was far from being universally true. Westerners insisted upon the right of the white man to earn a living at least and to safeguard this right by sharing in the government. They put into wider effect the doctrines of the Declaration of Independence, which were regarded by the ruling easterners merely as platitudes except as applied to the chosen few.

View the hackneyed examples of western lawlessness in this light, and a great deal becomes clearly revealed as consistent and logical. The Gnadenhütten massacre, often cited as the foulest blot on the frontier escutcheon, was applauded by some borderers as a courageous seizing of the nettle. The Moravian Indian settlement had undoubtedly been a convenient way station for Indian raiding parties and, moreover, some of its inhabitants were positively known to have joined themselves to the hostiles.[5] Even if a few innocents perished in the slaughter, frontier sentiment easily excused that with a shrug of the shoulders. Why all the pother about a few Indians? The argument is refreshingly reminiscent of the white man's methods of uplifting the African savages or the heathen Chinese. As for the pleasant western habit of refusing to obey law officers, well, the same condition had existed east of the mountains twenty years before and had received the approbation of the very men who now waxed wroth when given a dose of their own medicine. True, the militia was not subordinate to its officers, but why should it be? The men elected the officers and proposed to govern their actions. Everybody knew that water could not rise higher than its source, so why should a militia officer put on high and mighty airs? The westerner wagged his head appreciatively at the story of the captain of militia who presented a large order upon the paymaster.

"How many men do you command?" demanded that official.

"None."

"What's this? You command no one, yet you have the effrontery to present a bill like this?"

"Yes, you see, I command no one, but I am commanded by ninety."

The pioneer defended himself ably against the East's thrusts in the back. Who would know better than himself what measures were necessary? Courts were few in number and the expenses of "lawing" were outrageous. The force of public opinion was as powerful an agent for preserving order in the West as in the East. The coward, the bully, and the thief were summarily "hated out" of the community—the latter after having the law of Moses, that is, thirty-nine stripes, applied to his back. It was true that there was some brutality among the riff-raff, notably the horrible practice of "gouging," but this group included only the drifters, the Indian traders, and the boatmen. Anyhow, why lay this charge particularly against the West when it was common among the vulgar anywhere? It was true that there were numerous persons who were ignorant, filthy, and lazy, but they were a part of any community on either side of the mountains and were despised by the intelligent and thrifty citizens who made up most of the population.

If the effete easterner complained that the westerner did not bear his share of the expense of government, let him but look to the tax records and there he would see writ large that the western counties were nearly always the first to return their full quotas, except for the hated excise on liquor. Even during the late war the Monongahela country had more than done its share. In addition to various independent companies the Seventh and Thirteenth Virginia regiments had been raised mainly within the later borders of southwestern Pennsylvania, the former for service in the East. The Eighth Pennsylvania from the same region had been raised for service against the Indians in the West, but over the protest of the inhabitants it had been ordered east and had made a heroic and little known march over the mountains amidst the rigors of the winter of 1776-77. It is a fact that many of Morgan's famous riflemen were recruited from the country just north of Mason and Dixon's Line. General Irvine, who commanded in the West during the last years of the Revolution, was better able than his predecessors to comprehend western problems and to sympathize with the westerner's point of view. "I have no reason as yet," he wrote to President Moore of Pennsylvania in 1781, "to complain of the people for the refractory, ungovernable, loose manners generally ascribed to them. I assure

you, sir, my pity for their situation is rather excited than wrath
or indignation kindled."[6]

With their ideals and environment so different from those
of the East, it was no wonder that the men of the trans-Alle-
gheny region were recurrently agitating for a severance of the
political ties and for the erection of a new state. The last years
of the Revolution saw the most serious phase of this movement
up to the time of the Whiskey Insurrection, and one resident
was moved to write that he did not believe there were ten men
west of the mountains who would not take up arms against
Pennsylvania. Much of this agitation, of course, was stirred up
by the Virginians west of the Monongahela after that region had
been assigned to Pennsylvania, but there were sympathizers in
Westmoreland County who in 1782 went so far as to fire upon
Pennsylvania assessors.[7] The establishment of an adequate
civil government and the slowing down of the Indian raids at
the close of the war probably helped to avert a crisis, and the
guess may be hazarded that many of the influential conservatives preferred to retain the support of the conservative East
rather than to cut loose and trust their fortunes to a new government that would almost certainly have been dominated by
frontier democrats.

The western Pennsylvanian, had he so chosen, could have
truthfully boasted that he was more religious than many of
his eastern brethern. Of course, amidst some of the more
remote settlements and certainly among the frontier traders
and boatmen this was not true, but, relatively speaking, religion
was better supported in the West than in the East, and that
voluntarily. There was a Calvinist severity in the judgment
of pleasures and recreations. Some of the more strict would
listen to the singing of nothing but the Psalms of David and
would stalk out of church when the pastors dared to introduce
the new Watts hymnal. A few years before the passage of the

federal excise had withered Washington's laurels in the estimation of the Monongahela country, Brackenridge wrote a word of advice to the young publishers of the *Pittsburgh Gazette,* concluding in a semi-serious vein: "If you print an almanac I would advise you to leave out all profane songs, except in the praise of general Washington, and put in a psalm or hymn tune in their place."[8]

Western Pennsylvania had already attained the front rank as a center of Presbyterianism, a position it has never lost. Revivals had begun as early as 1778 in the closely crowded forts in which the settlers took refuge from the Indians. The Redstone Presbytery was set up in 1781 at a time when it could not hold presbytery meetings because of the Indian raids, but by 1793 it had grown so in membership that it was split in two, a procedure that was to occur again and again. The German sects were also strong, particularly in the sections toward the mountains, and the Methodists and Episcopalians existed in respectable numbers. Ministerial diarists recorded that the people flocked eagerly to hear them, and even in many remote valleys, inhabited by no more than a dozen families, the settlers were trying to find some way of erecting churches and supporting pastors.

Where there were no churches, rough sentry-box pulpits were provided in the open air, and the congregations sat upon the ground or on log benches. Nor was the use of these open air meeting places confined to the mild weather. There were times when the people had to brush the snow from the benches before they sat down to listen to the sermon. The pioneer churches were usually of rough logs, sometimes built in one day, but Pittsburgh had erected one of squared logs in 1786. Church attendance was not without its perils. Charles Beatty recorded that while he was preaching in a crowded cabin on a rainy day the sermon was twice interrupted by the necessity of killing reptilian intruders.[9] The diary of Robert Ayres for Sunday, June 8, 1794, contains this entry concerning an incident that happened at the Episcopalian church at Woodville: "I administer'd yᵉ Sacrament in doing of which while on our knees at the Table, the house (wᶜ was raised upon blocks) fell off and caused a great alarm; a Dog being caught under the house, we were inform'd to cease till the dog got out, in the attempt he bit 2 or 3 persons, but all was well ended and we Rec'd & I then preach'd . . . to about 4 or 5 hundred persons."

Congregations were so poor that it was a real problem to provide for the support of the ministers, and the latter often had to work in the fields during the week to add a little to their scanty income. The Presbyterian church of Upper Buffalo, confronted by a financial crisis, was said to have received donations of wheat, ground it into flour in the mill of a member of the congregation, loaded it on a flatboat, and sent it to New Orleans under the care of a volunteer crew. Nine months later, after the venture had been given up as lost, the crew returned with money sufficient to pay off all obligations. The flour had been sold in New Orleans at the top market price of twenty-seven dollars a barrel.[10]

The pastors of these western churches were fit leaders of the dour, hard-working, frugal members of their congregations, especially in the Presbyterian sects. Calvinists as they were, these pastors believed in the dignity and importance of the ministry, and their education, piety, and ability made them well able to live up to the ideal. They were also men of courage who were not afraid to stand up and be counted, as was thoroughly proven in the hottest days of the Revolution. In fact, so prominent were the Presbyterian ministers in the opposition to the British that the entire movement was sometimes half seriously known as the Presbyterian Rebellion. Their religion also included the more practical kind sometimes dubbed "muscular Christianity." Parson Elder of Paxtang (near Harrisburg) was the hero of a story that may be apocryphal but that perfectly illustrates the point. It was during the British conquest of New Jersey, when the local patriots were raising a company for the American army, that the good parson was asked to open a recruiting meeting with prayer, and he obliged with one that ended as follows: "We beseech Thee, through our Lord and Saviour Christ, mercifully to give us triumph, yet not ours but Thy blessed will be done. And, oh, Lord God of the Universe, if Thou are unwilling by Divine grace to assist us, *do stand aside and let us fight it out!*"[11]

Education, contrary to a fairly common conception, was no handicap on the frontier. Indeed, it was quite the opposite. Graduates of Princeton were numerous in western Pennsylvania and, at least among Presbyterians and Episcopalians, candidates for the ministry were required to be well schooled. Ministers usually made it their business to give instruction to the young men of their neighborhood, and in this way a number of important colleges received their start. The common people were not well educated but they were anxious for their children to have every advantage, as is seen by the number of academies that sprang up, one in almost every considerable community.

The diversity of nationalities in western Pennsylvania is one of the most striking characteristics of the region all through its history. James B. Finley, a pioneer preacher born in 1781, boasted that his grandparents were of four different nationalities—Scotch, German, English, and Welsh. John Pope, of Virginia, made a voyage from Pittsburgh down river in 1791 and listed the crew of his boat as composed of an Irishman, a German, a Kentuckian, a Welshman, a Virginian, and a man born at sea.[12] This mixture of origins on the Monongahela was simply a mirror of the "Old West" immediately east of the mountains. There was a more or less general pattern followed in the peopling of the successive Pennsylvania frontiers. The English and Welsh, having come first to Pennsylvania, settled the choicest lands of the southeastern section close to Philadelphia. The German immigrants who followed after 1717 had to push on to the frontier, so that within the succeeding century they expanded over central Pennsylvania and turned that region into the domain of the "Pennsylvania Dutch." The Irish, Scotch, and Scotch-Irish who began to come in great numbers about 1740 settled in the pockets of poorer soil unoccupied by the Germans and on the new frontier closest to the mountains. It must be admitted that with all their virtues the Scotch and Scotch-Irish were not as industrious and thrifty as the Germans. They were, moreover, a frontier people by nature, individualists, restless, impatient of restraint, proud, and often captious. They therefore drifted to the frontier, sometimes even when it entailed a sacrifice of material comforts, selling out their half-improved land to the expanding Germans, who stolidly settled down to wrest a living from the soil.

It would be a mistake, however, to say that the Scotch and Scotch-Irish element always moved out before the German advance. Central Pennsylvania today is occupied by the descendants of all immigrant stocks. By the time the Monongahela country was filled English, Irish, Scotch, Scotch-Irish, and Germans were living there side by side. It is also to be borne in mind that the Monongahela country of 1794, at least west of the river, was probably peopled by Virginians as much as by Pennsylvanians. Among those who came in from Virginia were numbers of Scotch and Scotch-Irish whose parents had streamed southward from Pennsylvania through the Shenandoah Valley, and there were also many Germans whose migrations had paralleled those of the Scotch and Scotch-Irish and who by now had lost their German language and culture and were indistinguishable from their neighbors. Virginians of English descent from the yeomen of the Piedmont and the Shenandoah were present in even greater numbers, and there were also some of the Virginia aristocratic elements. Maryland was represented by a smaller number of settlers of similar origins.

National strains had become mingled in the "Old West" even before the beginning of the settlement of the Mononga-hela country, so that it is impossible to make precise statements as to the proportions of the various elements. It may be said with some confidence, however, that the census of 1790 lists more surnames of English (including Cambrian or Welsh) origin in the settlements of southwestern Pennsylvania than of any other racial group. This was probably because of the heavy immigration from Virginia and Maryland, in both of which the English stock was dominant.

The next most numerous element was of Scotch origin, in-cluding Scotch from Ulster in northern Ireland as well as direct-ly from Scotland. Just how wide the distinction was between the Scotch-Irish, as the first group is called in the United States, and the Scotch is a controversial matter, but they certainly did have more similar than dissimilar characteristics. There is no conclusive reason for believing that the Scotch groups, even taken collectively, outnumbered the English stock in south-western Pennsylvania, or for that matter in any large western area; but they unquestionably played a very prominent part in the early history of the West. The independence and con-tentiousness bred into the people of the Scotch border by their conditions of life and by their adherence to the Scotch kirk's form of Calvinistic dissent had been characteristic of the Scotchmen and Ulstermen even before their migration, so that in western Pennsylvania they naturally assumed the leadership in a society that was being molded to their taste by local conditions. The Presbyterian Church, the Scotch-Irishman's legislative assembly as well as his social and moral mentor, was the first to come upon the frontier. So true was it that this church afforded almost the sole refuge of the religiously inclined in the early years that it actually swallowed up whole congregations of other denominations. With the Scotch-Irish apparently giving the tone to frontier life (it was not yet evident that they were merely falling in with the natural course of evolution) it was easy for contemporary travelers to assume that the Monongahelans were overwhelmingly "Irish."

The two chief stocks in the Monongahela country were English and Scotch, but the Germans were appearing in solid communities in Westmoreland and Fayette counties. Irish Catholics were by no means rare, and families of Dutch, Huguenot, and Swedish descent were sprinkled here and there. These various national elements, with their diversity of experiences since they had left the old country, were meeting at the forks of the Ohio and were being fused into one people. Already in the seventeen-nineties the younger generation was having some difficulty in understanding the speech of the elders who had been born or reared in the old country. The latter, for their part, never quite recovered from homesickness for their native lands. The rigors of the wilderness bore hard on them and left them something less of the amenities of life than they might have enjoyed at home. The lawyer Hugh Henry Brackenridge, one of this number, sadly wrote:

> There's neither Highland man, nor Lallan',
> That's here the same;
> But finds him scrimpit o' the talen'
> He had at hame.[13]

The German-speaking Germans migrating to the West directly from the Pennsylvania-Dutch region found themselves strangers in this developing comity of nationalities. Their ignorance of English made them both suspicious and objects of suspicion and fostered the libel that they were not as capable as other peoples. Apparently no one had discovered how to manipulate the German vote, for in the earlier years of the West, at least, the politicians strove to freeze them out of a place in the political sun. In consequence they were for the most part reticent and uncoöperative, devoting themselves strictly to improving their economic situation, until the passing of the language barrier gradually introduced them to the political arena and then merged them with the rest of the people.[14]

There was one attitude, however, on which the pioneers of all origins agreed—that was on hatred of the excise. This hatred was not of New World origin but was rooted deep in the European past. The taxes laid by the petty lords of the continent had been gathered by the year 1600 into the hands of the kings or other authorities, but were not being lightened. At one time in Amsterdam "a dish of Fish with its sauce, before it be served up to the table, pays Excise thirty several times." The abuses current in Spain, France, Germany, and the Netherlands finally made their re-entry into England despite the stubborn resistance of the people. When in 1626 a commission attempted to introduce the excise on liquor, Parliament declared it unconstitutional, and the secretary of state when he mentioned it in the House of Commons "was interrupted, called to the bar, and nearly sent to the Tower." In 1641, when a temporary excise was laid, the inhabitants of London rose in a riot, burned the excise house, and were quelled only by the use of troops. The next year, when it was rumored that the excise was to be renewed, the Commons declared that "these rumours were false and scandalous, and that their authors should be apprehended and brought to condign punishment."

Viewers with alarm not only saw that liquor would be more expensive but also professed to fear that it would necessitate the enrollment of a standing army, which would be expensive as well as dangerous to liberty. In 1734, when agitation arose for an excise, a wit likened it to the Trojan horse and asserted that "it hath an *Army* in its belly." Sir Robert Walpole won popular approval by declaring that "he would not be the minister who should carry out any measure of this sort." The defeat of the excise was celebrated by a wave of public rejoicing punctuated by bonfires and the burning of effigies. Cockades bearing the words "Liberty, Property, and no Excise" appeared in the hats of the citizens, and the University of Oxford celebrated for three days, doubtless featuring the plentiful consumption of the liberated tipple. Even Blackstone in 1766 wrote for the eyes of law students that the excise laws were "hardly compatible with the temper of a free nation" and warned against the dangers to liberty entailed by a strict enforcement, as well as the opportunities opened for corruption. The forthright Samuel Johnson capped the sheaf by writing in his dictionary this definition of excise: "A hateful tax levied upon commodities, and adjudged not by the common judges of property, but wretches hired by those to whom excise is paid."[15]

With such sentiments as these current, it is no wonder that excise collectors were looked upon as social pariahs. The poet Burns, forced by penury to accept a place as an exciseman at fifty pounds a year, excused himself with pathetic wit: "I would much rather have it said that my profession borrowed credit from me, than that I borrowed credit from my profession." The poetical exciseman's bitter verses on the devil and the exciseman must have found an appreciative audience among the "axcise" hating frontiersmen of the western Pennsylvania wilds.

The Monongahela Pioneers

The Deil cam fiddlin thro' the town,
    And danc'd awa wi' th' Exciseman,
And ilka wife cries:—'Auld Mahoun,
    I wish you luck o' the prize, man!

We'll mak our maut, and we'll brew our drink,
    We'll laugh, sing, and rejoice, man,
And monie braw thanks to the meikle black Deil
    That danc'd awa wi' th' Exciseman.

Brackenridge, in his satire *Modern Chivalry*, took occasion to have his comic character, Teague O'Regan, appointed to the excise service. This was shortly after the insurrection, when the westerners' mode of amusing themselves by tarring and feathering the excise officers was still fresh in the public mind. O'Regan, therefore, received his tar and feathers and was set adrift in the wilderness. A few days later he was captured by some hunters and palmed off as a natural curiosity upon the learned members of the "Philosophical Society," who solemnly gave it the epithet of *Anthroposornis*, or manbird.[16]

The Monongahela countryman's attitude toward an excise was partially the result of economic causes. The region's lumber, grain, and meat were too heavy to be transported at a reasonable cost across the mountains under prevailing conditions, and there was no certain market down the river. Rye was in little demand except for making whiskey, which at times sold in the West for as little as twenty-five cents a gallon. There could not have been much profit in distilling for cash sale in the West, even when, as in 1784, the army paid fifty cents a gallon for whiskey and forty cents a bushel for rye.[17]

The real profit came in selling whiskey in the East, where "Monongahela rye" was not long in creating a demand that enabled it to bring double what it did in the West, though of course much of this advance in price was absorbed by the expense of transportation. Stills, therefore, were imported in ever increasing numbers. Since a one-hundred-gallon still was worth a two-hundred-acre farm within ten miles of Pittsburgh, not many farmers could afford to own one. The result was that neighbors either clubbed together to buy a still for the common use or took their grain to a prosperous neighbor who could afford the initial outlay. Soon every settlement came to have its still, anywhere from six to thirty families taking a certain amount of grain to the common distiller and receiving a stipulated quantity of whiskey. "In this manner," read a Westmoreland petition of 1790, "we are supplied with this necessary article, much upon the same conditions that our mills furnish us with flour; and why we should be made subject to a duty for drinking our grain more than eating it, seems a matter of astonishment to every reflecting mind."[18]*

The high ideals of liberty and of the inviolability of property when produced as arguments against the excise were strongly seconded by the fact that whiskey held a well-nigh impregnable social position in the back country. George Dallas Albert thus summarizes it: "The use of whiskey was universal. The quality was good, the taste pleasant, its effect agreeable. Storekeepers kept liquor on their counters and sold it in their stores, and the women customers used it as well as the men. Farmers kept barrels of it in their cellars. It was sometimes drank with tansy, mint, or maple-sugar, but mostly taken

* Circumstances and techniques varied so greatly that it is not easy to know how much whiskey—or what proof—the Monongahela distiller could make from a bushel of rye. Mr. J. B. Thome of Joseph E. Seagram and Sons has kindly cited Harrison Hall, *The Distiller* (Philadelphia, 1818), as referring in one place to a yield of 2.75 gallons per bushel of rye, and in another referring to 3.5 to 4 gallons per bushel. Mr. Thome is of the opinion that Hall referred to British proof spirits, which could be 114.2 U.S. proof. If we speculate that 3 gallons to a bushel was reasonable, then a horse carrying two 8-gallon kegs was carrying the equivalent of slightly over five bushels of rye; a horse could carry four bushels of rye in grain. The sixteen gallons probably brought a dollar each in the East.

straight. It was good for fevers, it was good for a decline, it was good for ague, it was good for snake-bites. There was nothing named in the materia medica but old whiskey possessed some of its curative properties. On the testimony of Col. Crockett, it made one warm in winter and cool in summer. It was used at all gatherings. Bottles of it were set out on the table at christenings and at wakes. At funerals in the winter season huge coffee-boilers and buckets of warm whiskey-punch were passed around and the people invited to drink, and tin-cups were filled and carried from time to time to the bearers. Ministers drank it.... On an occasion when Bishop Onderdonk came to Greensburg to administer confirmation, before going to church he went into the bar-room of Rhorer's hotel in full canonicals and called for and drank off a tumbler of strong brandy without giving offense to the faithful. Rev. Father McGirr's drink was whiskey-punch, of which it is said he could drink with any of his day without giving scandal."[19]

Whiskey was regularly issued to the army as a part of the rations, and during the insurrection the government increased the whiskey ration to encourage distillers to pay the excise tax. Whiskey was as commonly used on the frontier as beer and wine were in Europe. The farmer's wife set it on the table as a beverage at mealtimes and it was taken as a strengthener between meals. It was supposed that its use was necessitated by the exposure incident to farming and other outdoor work during the long severe winters and scripture was quoted to convince those who doubted this. Whiskey was the most freely accepted article of barter, and cases were known where the minister's salary was paid in "old Monongahela rye." Men of the greatest respectability and of considerable property were engaged in its manufacture, and they were the chief opponents of the excise during the first three years after it was laid by the United States.

Whiskey Rebels

The western Pennsylvanian's attitude toward whiskey was thus the result of social as well as economic circumstances and was developed long before there was a federal excise law. It was unfortunate that the frontiersman's many grievances against the new federal government had added to them this overt campaign to tax an article that lay at the bottom of their social and economic life and was regarded as an indispensable necessity to life, health, and happiness. The Whiskey Insurrection, asserted the clerical author of *Old Redstone,* "arose from no special fondness for the intemperate use of the article. It was simply the result of a delusion respecting their rights, and an impression that they were wrongfully and oppressively taxed in the very article which alone they could turn to account in trade and commerce, and thereby secure to themselves and families the *very necessaries of life.*"[20] Nevertheless, it must be admitted that the important part that whiskey played in the social and personal life of the pioneers was a factor in their opposition to the excise.

Chapter II: *"Gentlemen of Respectability"* *— and Others*

THE metropolis of the Monongahela country in 1794 was the little tree-shaded village of Pittsburgh, situated in the triangular flood plain between the forks of the Ohio. Just across the Allegheny River lay the edge of the wild and mysterious "Indian country," from which occasionally there still emerged bands of savages to harry outlying settlements and to give Pittsburgh itself more than one night of terror. Across the Monongahela River rose the high bluff known as Coal Hill because of its outcropping veins of coal, which were mined to furnish the village and the country down river with fuel. In the narrow strip between the river and the bluff nestled several small dwellings shaded by graceful white-barked sycamores. Back of the town rose the green slope of Grant's Hill, so called because it was there that the troops under Major Grant were cut to pieces by the French and Indians in 1758. Here a Frenchman named Jean Marie kept a tavern, and its grassy environs with their beautiful shade trees, well kept gardens, and graveled walks made it the local show place and the chief resort of the townsmen on pleasant afternoons and evenings.

Since its foundation as an English settlement in November, 1758, Pittsburgh had grown from scratch to a population of approximately a thousand, with about one hundred and fifty log houses and fifty others of frame or brick. In accordance with the surveyor's plan, the principal streets were laid parallel to the rivers and the cross streets, leading away from the rivers, met at obtuse angles in the interior of the town. The houses were faced to suit the conveniences or whims of the owners, and the taverns were distinguished by painted signs bearing pictographs with such names as "The Green Tree," "The Black Bear," "The Whale and Monkey," and the "Sign of General Washington." The streets, of course, were unpaved and so in season were deserts of dust or seas of mud. Unlighted at night, and with few sidewalks, they furnished precarious footing to the unsteady gait of the home-bent wassailer, and by both night and day they were the happy hunting grounds of dogs and hogs and children. The Whiskey Boys had a disturbing habit of galloping along the streets at full speed, yelling and firing their rifles, and so much of a menace did this become that the burgesses laid a penalty of five shillings upon offenders, probably much to the amusement of the buckskinned lads from the country. At about the same time notice was given the inhabitants that they should not suffer their hogs to run at large. As to whether either measure was effective the record saith not.[1]

In 1790 John Pope characterized the town as "inhabited with only some few Exceptions, by Mortals who act as if possessed of a Charter of Exclusive Privilege to filch from, annoy and harrass her [sic] Fellow Creatures ... Goods of every Description are dearer in *Pittsburg* than in *Kentuckey,* which I attribute to a Combination of pensioned Scoundrels who infest the Place."[2] Already the town had become a resort of hard-headed bargain drivers. Its strategic position at the head of navigation and the terminus of the wagon and pack-horse trails across Pennsylvania indicated, to quote Hugh Henry

Brackenridge, that it "would one day be a town of note."[3]

The business of the town centered on Market Street, which led away from the Monongahela, and on Water Street, which ran along the Monongahela. A steep bank lay between Water Street and the river, but deep serrations pierced by flood and rain encroached upon the street so closely as to block the way for wagons at some points. The uneven surface of the ground made it possible for parts of the town to be flooded at times of moderately high water.[4] These, however, were the times when business was most brisk. The bank would be lined with flatboats, somewhat resembling the modern river houseboats, destined to carry slow freight. Lighter and more valuable goods were carried on keelboats, which were rowed downstream and were walked upstream by poles set to the shoulders of brawny boatmen.

Pittsburgh was even then a polyglot town. The nasal twang of the Yankee, the burr of the Scot, the clipped enunciation of the English, the brogue of Ireland, the gutturals of Germany, and the buzz of busy French tongues were all familiar to the inhabitants. Political animosities were rife between Germans and those who claimed English as their native language, and these animosities were expressed in the columns of the *Pittsburgh Gazette,* which, founded in 1786 by a young man named John Scull, held the proud claim of being the young West's first newspaper. Germans and English also worshipped in different churches, where they listened to sermons in their respective languages. The editor of the *Gazette* served as the postmaster as well, nobly fulfilling the biblical injunction not to let his right hand know what his left hand did by using the columns of his paper to complain of the poor mail service between Pittsburgh and Philadelphia. A "Mechanical Society" met at the tavern of Andrew Watson, and the Pittsburgh Fire Company proudly sported a hand engine, probably the only one on the American continent west of the mountains. In spite of the roughness and even sordidness of life in the village, a start toward higher education had been made by the foundation of the Pittsburgh Academy (now the University of Pittsburgh) in 1787, largely through the efforts of the town's most enlightened citizen, the lawyer Brackenridge.

Old Fort Pitt, near the point where the rivers met, lay in a state of partial ruin; the walls supporting the ramparts had fallen away and greenery had taken possession of the mounds. Even the bricks, burned at the king's expense were being hauled away to the town for building material. North of the fort lay a deep pond that sometimes afforded duck shooting. Farther up the Allegheny lay what had once been called the King's Artillery Gardens in which, because of the forethought of a former British commandant, there now grew an orchard of apple and pear trees that bore excellent fruit. Beyond the gardens was situated Pittsburgh's latest defense, Fort Fayette, though why it had been placed up the Allegheny River in the middle of a swamp was a puzzle to military men. The stockaded fort was reënforced by four blockhouses and enclosed an acre or so of ground. It contained a brick arsenal and a barracks with thirty rooms. The shallow ditch that surrounded it was of little value, and Victor Collot, a French military engineer, asserted that on a dark night four grenadiers could burn the entire works without allowing a single member of the garrison to escape.[5]

On the plain between Fort Fayette and the town was the fairground with its race track. Twice a year, in June and October, this spot became the rendezvous of the inhabitants from far and near. Within the racecourse and outside it were scores of booths, built frontier-fashion as lean-tos—that is, a ridgepole supported in two forked sticks, with long boughs laid slanting against it. In these booths were sold every frontier necessity and many eastern luxuries, not to speak of the whole gamut of eatables and drinkables. Through this rude mart surged the crowd—uniformed soldiers from the garrison in search of amusement, buckskinned "long hunters" and Indian fighters in town on a spree, horny-handed boatbuilders and mechanics, sunburned rustics in jeans with their linsey-woolsied sweethearts, and a few "gentlemen" and men of "respectability" from the town. The dogs and children abandoned the duller joys of the streets and the rivers to witness the kaleidoscope of the fair, perhaps dodging between the legs of the frontier stalwarts to get a glimpse of two famous gougers in action or to gaze in open-eyed wonder at some visiting Indian chieftain.

At the cry "To horse" the crowd surged about the confines of the racecourse, while the judges on their scaffolding importantly watched the proceedings to see that the races were run in accordance with the none-too-strict frontier code. The races over, the crowd split up again to seek further diversions. "Dogs barked and bit, and horses trod on men's toes, and booths fell down on people's heads! There was Crowder with his fiddle and his votaries, making the dust fly with a four-handed or rather four-footed reel; and a little farther on was Dennis Loughy, the blind poet, like Homer, casting his pearls before swine, chanting his master-piece in a tone part nasal and part guttural,—

> Come, gentlemen, gentlemen all,
>   Ginral Sincleer shall remem-ber-ed be,
> For he lost thirteen hundred men all,
>   In the Western Tari-to-ree![6]

Colorful as may have been the dusty and riotous fair, the Princeton-bred Hugh Henry Brackenridge preferred to write of the social charm of Pittsburgh: "In the fall of the year and during the winter season, there is usually a great concourse of strangers at this place . . . about to descend the river to the westward, or to make excursions into the uninhabited and adjoining country. These, with the inhabitants of the town spend the evening in parties at the different houses, or at public balls, where they are surprised to find an elegant assembly of ladies, not to be surpassed in beauty and accomplishments perhaps by any on the continent. It must appear like enchantment to a stranger . . . to see, all at once, and almost on the verge of the inhabited globe, a town with smoking chimneys, halls lighted up with splendor, ladies and gentlemen assembled, various music, and the mazes of the dance. He may suppose it to be the effect of magic, or that he is come into a new world where there is all the refinement of the former, and more benevolence of heart."[7]

The author of this bare-faced propaganda was for twenty of the most tumultuous years of western Pennsylvania history its most prominent citizen, though scarcely its most influential one. Born in 1748 in Scotland, his parents brought him to York County, Pennsylvania, at the age of five years, and there in the sterile Barrens he grew to young manhood. The stern realities of frontier life did not stifle the growth of ambition, and he finally landed in Princeton as a student of theology. There he was an associate of Freneau and Madison, a roommate of William Bradford, and a tutor of Henry Lee. The last two especially were to play vital parts in Brackenridge's future. There, also, the recognition by others of his facility in literary exercises doubtless first definitely formed his life's most cherished desire to become a literary man.[8]

After his graduation in 1771 Brackenridge taught in an academy on Maryland's eastern shore. By 1777 he was with Washington's army as a chaplain, striving by his sermons to heighten the patriotic zeal of the soldiery during the Pennsylvania campaign. It soon became apparent to him, however, that he could not subscribe wholeheartedly to Presbyterian dogma, so, resolving to have a fling at the fulfillment of his literary ambitions, upon the British evacuation of Philadelphia he scraped together his scanty capital and journeyed to the metropolis to become an editor.

In this year of our Lord, 1778, Philadelphia was a welter of political strife, not merely between Tories and Whigs, but also between factions of patriots, national, state, and local. At the opening of the Revolution, Pennsylvania was governed by an assembly chosen by a strictly limited Quaker oligarchy and its allies, which distinctly leaned toward the loyalist side. The eastern aristocrats, notably Robert Morris, John Dickinson, and Thomas Mifflin, who were heading the revolutionary movement in the state, had been so hindered by the loyalist assembly that they finally made allies of the democratic elements, which had seized the governments of the back counties. As a result the new constitution promulgated in 1776 so broadened the suffrage as to place the power of the one chamber assembly in the hands of the "patriots," most of whom were in the interior. No sooner had the constitution gone into effect than the easterners saw their mistake and began an agitation for reform, but the westerners did not propose to give up their advantage. The revolutionists were now split into the "Constitutionalist" West and the "Anti-Constitutionalist" East, and this division was to mark the fundamental issue until 1790. The East proposed the addition of an upper house as a check upon the democratic assembly, and the West bitterly fought against it.[9]

Brackenridge, as yet without any fixed principles of political science and willing to be objective, was humorously bewildered. "For my own part," said he, "I must confess that the arguments for and against, seem so perfectly to balance one another, that I can hardly tell to which I shall submit myself. When a single-legislature man takes me by the sleeve, and tells me of a house of Lords, and a King upon the back of them, I am greatly startled and in doubt what to say: When, on the other hand, a double legislature man asks me to dine with him and begins to push about the bottle pretty freely, I am almost brought to be of his opinion, that the multitude in all ages have been devils and that no man, nor even they themselves can be safe in a commonwealth that is not checked by a variety of councils in the legislative body. If both of these meet me in the street, as is sometimes the case, I am held between them, and alternately shaken by their arguments. First, I nod to one and then to another, like a man that is half asleep, and recovers in the angle of a chimney."[10]

Brackenridge descended into the political arena with all the zeal of an Irishman entering the melee at a county fair, and with the same lack of discrimination. Wherever he saw a head he hit it. The *United States Magazine,* which he founded, thus had a colorful even though brief career, as Brackenridge exhibited to the full his genius for treading on other people's toes. Unfortunately for himself he selected for his most ambitious promenade the august toes of General Charles Lee, who had recently written a half facetious, half flirtatious protest to the Tory belle, Rebecca Franks, who had ridiculed him for wearing green breeches patched with leather. To divert her anger Lee tried to cast the blame upon the *ci-devant* chaplain who had published the letter. Brackenridge issued a scorching reply, calling his opponent "an insignificant, capricious, and fluctuating weazel," and probing dangerously close to Lee's secret treason. The result was that Lee, horsewhip in hand, thundered upon the young editor's door. Brackenridge, cautiously looking out of an upper window, was spied by the angry general.

"Come down," cried Lee, "and I'll give you as good a horse-whipping as any rascal ever received."

"Excuse me, General," replied the imperturbable Bracken-ridge, " I would not go down for two such favors."[11]

There may be a touch of the apocryphal in the anecdote, but it perfectly illustrates Brackenridge's love of the humorous even on the most solemn occasion. One would like to imagine Lee bursting into laughter at the repartee and forgetting his mission, but unfortunately, as with most humorous yarns, what came next is not known. The *United States Magazine,* at any rate, was a failure, and Brackenridge, who had been employing his leisure in the study of law, now turned his back upon the East and in 1781 started for Pittsburgh to take up the life of a frontier lawyer.

One night on his westward journey he lodged in the squalid cabin of Harmon Husband, a settler in a glade of the Allegheny Ridge. Husband, an honest but ignorant, uncouth, and eccentric individual, had been a preacher in the backwoods of North Carolina during the Regulator troubles. In spite of the fact that he had worked zealously and openly for peace, he had been proscribed by the victorious government party and had taken refuge in the wilds of Pennsylvania.[12] Here this simple-minded champion of peace and justice was fated to become a sacrifice to another government testing the strength of its young arm upon a disorganized rabble of backwoodsmen.

Meanwhile, however, Harmon Husband was finding solace in the composition of a commentary upon certain passages in Ezekiel. Says Brackenridge: "It was the vision of the temple; the walls, the gates, the sea of glass, &c. Logger-head divines, heretofore, had interpreted it of the New Jerusalem; but he conceived it to apply to the western country; and the walls were the mountains, the gates, the gaps in them, by which the roads came, and the sea of glass, the lake on the west of us. I had no hesitation in saying, that the commentary was analagous to the vision. He was pleased; and said, I was the only person, except his wife, that he ever got to believe it. Thought I, your church is composed, like many others, of the ignorant and the dissembling."[13]

Brackenridge entered zealously into the work of developing the western country. He sympathized heartily with most of the pioneers' viewpoints, especially their hatred of the Indians and their hunger for land. With his customary forthrightness, however, he pointed out to the legislature of Pennsylvania that the current secession movement in the western part of the state would curtail the public receipts from the sale of western lands and make it difficult to pay the large sum promised to the Penns for their surrender of proprietary rights. Whether or not the result was attributable directly to Brackenridge, the legislature soon passed a law declaring treasonable all agitation in favor of a new state. Brackenridge later awoke to the realization that the preservation of the West to the state had merely cleared the way for a swarm of land jobbers.[14]

A boyhood on the frontier and a young manhood in the East enabled Brackenridge to see clearly both sides of subjects of sectional controversy, but his blunt nature scarcely fitted him, in early life at least, to play the politician by running with the hare and hunting with the hounds. His first venture into office-holding ended in a glorious fiasco. By 1786 it had become apparent that the region around Pittsburgh was ready to be separated from Westmoreland and Washington counties, and it was resolved to elect a Pittsburgher to the assembly to accomplish the task. Brackenridge had become prominent as a lawyer, orator, and writer for the *Pittsburgh Gazette,* and he was elected over the opposition of much of Westmoreland. Upon his arrival in Philadelphia Brackenridge began to take a prominent part in legislative matters concerning the West. Before long, however, his hasty temper plunged him into a situation that was to halt temporarily his political progress.

The problems most interesting to the West were those of legalizing simpler methods of taking up land and of clearing the titles, the opening of the Mississippi, and the introduction of greater quantities of money. The western solution to the first and last was in part to allow settlers to pay for lands with the old certificates of indebtedness issued by the state. The East, on the other hand, led by Robert Morris, wished to erect a bank, the notes of which would serve as additional currency. Now one of Brackenridge's campaign promises had been that he would oppose the bank, but under the influence of Robert Morris he aligned himself with that financier on this issue.

Bound by mutual policies and interests, several of the western legislators met one evening at the home of Chief Justice McKean, among them William Findley, of Westmoreland, the political Nestor of the West, who was the acknowledged leader of the group. Emigrating to Pennsylvania from Ireland in young manhood, Findley had played a locally prominent part in the Revolution and had served for a time as a captain. With the close of the war he entered the political arena as a Constitutionalist. Though a weaver by trade and without formal education, he had read omnivorously, absorbing enormous quantities of information as sand absorbs water—and, according to his critics, profiting as little by it. With a keen sense for the practicable, he managed to satisfy his radical constituency with his cautious progressivism and served in the state assembly or in Congress most of the rest of his life, which lasted until 1821.[15]

Now, however, Findley, David Redick of Washington County, John Smilie of Fayette County, and Brackenridge were discussing the proposed bank, and Redick observed that it looked as though Robert Morris and his friends intended to make the bank an advantage to themselves rather than to the people. At this the fiery Pittsburgh lawyer blazed forth: "The people are fools; if they would let Mr. Morris alone, he would make Pennsylvania a great people, but they will not suffer him to do it." When Smilie objected that no man had the right to make such an observation, Brackenridge "dropped his brows" and refused to say more. Finally, however, in answer to Redick's questioning, he announced that he would reconcile the people to his change of front by explaining the situation in the *Pittsburgh Gazette*—thus giving color to his hearers' later charges that he thought the people such fools as to be persuaded by anything he chose to tell them.[16]

During the rest of his legislative service Brackenridge worked untiringly for the West. He had Allegheny County erected by the assembly and succeeded in having five thousand acres set aside for the Pittsburgh Academy. He strove manfully for better roads, for a land-title bill, and to force some sort of action on the Mississippi question, but all in vain. The fact that he was able to prove Findley's apathy toward these measures did him no good, "for the people thought it impossible that plain simple men could be wrong, and a profane lawyer right."[17] The wily Findley checkmated his every move and effectually destroyed every chance of reëlection.

Brackenridge, however, was to have his revenge. When the question of calling a state convention to decide upon the acceptance of the federal constitution came up in the assembly the two men took opposite sides. In a desperate endeavor to block the calling of the convention, Findley and his followers absented themselves in order to prevent the formation of a quorum. Two of the absconders were located and forcibly brought to the assembly hall by a group of citizens, and the bill to call a convention was passed. The assembly thereupon broke up and Brackenridge returned to Pittsburgh. As the only Federalist assemblyman from the western part of the state he took an active part in the campaign that followed, pilloried Findley as "Traddle the Weaver" in a series of Hudi-brastic satires, and accused him of having hidden in a strange garret to avoid being carried into the assembly hall. Though he was defeated as a candidate for the convention, Bracken-ridge had the pleasure of celebrating the adoption of the new constitution by giving an oration before an assembly of fifteen hundred people gathered on the slope of Grant's Hill.[18]

This brief flight in politics had caused Brackenridge to lose his popularity with the people. The younger lawyers and politi-cians, such as James Ross and David Bradford, who had started several years after him, now caught up with and passed him. With his practice almost gone, he was still too proud to leave the country, nor in fact would good policy have dictated such a course. Patient for once, he set himself to regain lost ground during the following years, and, perhaps because of what ex-perience had taught him, it presently became apparent that he was forging ahead.

Meanwhile he began to occupy his leisure in the composi-tion of the first volume of *Modern Chivalry*. The hero of the book was Captain Farrago, a sort of Pennsylvania Don Quixote, who, followed by the Irishman Teague O'Regan, set out to have a tilt at the political and social sins and foibles of the day. Findley, again as "Traddle the Weaver," along with others of his ilk, came in for a lambasting. In the course of this half-savage, half-humorous tale Brackenridge outlined quite clearly his political philosophy. Wealth and social prestige were not enough to fit a man for public life, nor was education alone. What was needed was native talent and common sense together with education—and by education he meant principally a training in the classics and the law. The people, for the most part, were fools, easily led by demagogues who were free with honeyed words and barreled whiskey. It was evident that his own bitter experiences as a legislator were foremost in his mind as he lamented the hopeless state of popular government.

> What profits it to have knock'd down
> The great Cornwallis and Burgoyne
> If in the meantime money-less
> Your agriculture languishes?
> It is the fault of those at helm
> That these distresses overwhelm,
> For if just measures were pursued
> Our government would do us good:
> And mischiefs that are come to pass
> Be remedied by proper laws.
> But those you send are loggerheads
> And might as well be in their beds;
> Or if they have a little share
> Of sense and industry to spare,
> They lay it out for their own use
> And personal interest introduce.[19]

The outcome of experience and reflection on the part of Brackenridge was the formation of a political philosophy that had much in common with that of Jefferson but diverged from it at some points. The people were ignorant and emotional and easily led astray by demagogues, therefore it was the duty of the men of sense and "respectability" to enact the rôle of sympathetic guardians and to furnish capable leadership by the exercise of tact and moderation and, when necessary, procrastination and mild deceit. This guardianship, moreover, was to be for the welfare of the people, not for the benefit of any certain class, least of all those ambitious members of the aristocracy who had nothing to recommend them but wealth and superficial education.

Vice and dishonesty Brackenridge regarded as follies in the eye of reason, and he believed that the rightly trained mind avoided them naturally. Rigidly honest himself, he was not inclined to give more than a negative merit to the quality. Avarice and speculation he abhorred, and until late in life he even despised the accumulation of more than enough for mere comfort. Theoretically, and probably sincerely, tolerant of the poor and ignorant, he was so earnest and whole-souled in his pursuit of any object that he often appeared harsh and of a hasty temper. For example, lawyer though he was, he thoroughly disapproved of going to court, and when prospective clients approached him he would exclaim, "Go away, sir; no man of sense goes to law—did you ever hear of my going to law?" These mannerisms gave him a reputation for eccentricity, which he humorously denied by asserting "that he was the only one of his acquaintance that was like everybody else."[20]

The way in which Brackenridge met and married his second wife is one of the classics of western Pennsylvania. It was said that one day as the corps of lawyers were riding together, as was their custom, from one court to another, they saw a barefooted country girl named Sabina Wolfe leap a rail fence without touching it, to head off the cows she was driving.

"If she does that again," said Brackenridge, "I'll marry her."

Sure enough, she did it. Sometime later a convenient rainstorm drove the lawyer to the girl's home for shelter. When it came time to go he asked that his horse be brought, but when the father ordered his daughter to perform that office Brackenridge insisted on doing it himself. He had ridden only a few miles when he turned around and went back to the Wolfe homestead and asked the old gentleman for the hand of the fair Sabina. Finally convinced of the lawyer's sincerity, Wolfe objected that he needed her in shrubbing his meadow, not being able to bear the expense of hiring it done. Upon this Brackenridge offered him ten dollars for the purpose, then, obtaining the girl's consent, married her and sent her to Philadelphia to spend a year "under the Governance of a reputable female Character, whose Business . . . [it was] to polish the Manners, and wipe off the Rusticities which Mrs.

Brackenridge had acquired whilst a *Wolfe*."[21]

Within five years after leaving the assembly Brackenridge had not only earned a national reputation as a political satirist but had also regained so much of his squandered popularity that he was again considered an available candidate, this time for Congress. Meanwhile, however, he had antagonized the most powerful members of the clique that had originally backed him for the legislature—that is, the "Neville connection." Events were thus already bringing into opposition the future leaders of the moderate and conservative forces that were to clash over the proper method of dealing with the insurrection. Since many of the occurrences of the movement against the excise were to center about the persons and personalities of the Nevilles it is necessary to introduce them upon the stage on which the Whiskey Insurrection was to be enacted.

The head of this clan was John Neville, an aristocratic Virginian, born in 1731, the son of George Neville, who had been kidnapped from England as a lad, and of Ann Burroughs, a cousin of Lord Fairfax. John Neville became acquainted with the West as a soldier in Braddock's expedition and in Dunmore's War and moved to the Chartiers Valley seven miles from Pittsburgh probably in 1775. The same year with one hundred Virginia militiamen he occupied Fort Pitt, and he commanded there until 1777. Later he commanded Virginia troops in the East and the South. In 1780 he was taken prisoner at Charleston, but he was exchanged in time to be present at the siege of Yorktown. At the close of the war he was brevetted brigadier general.

Upon his return home Neville was elected to the assembly and became the Washington County member of the supreme executive council. In fact in 1784 he was prominent enough to run for president and vice president of the council. In state politics he was identified with the conservative Anti-Constitutionalists, but such was his popularity in his district that he was elected to the convention called to vote upon the new federal constitution, and he voted for the acceptance of that document. By this time he had amassed a considerable fortune, having held or sold close to ten thousand acres of land. Bower Hill, his home in the Chartiers Valley, across the hills southwest of Pittsburgh, was one of the finest establishments at that time in the western country.[22]

Up to the time of his appointment as inspector of the excise, John Neville was one of the most popular men in the Monongahela country, in spite of his Federalist principles. A lavish entertainer both at Bower Hill and at his town house on Pittsburgh's Water Street, he bore as well a reputation for generosity to the poor. There is, it is true, a story of his having fired bird shot at a many-petticoated negro woman who had disobeyed some orders, but then the woman was at a considerable distance and the general was trying to teach her a lesson as well as to amuse his friends. Personally he seems to have been able and affable and to have deserved the respect of the community, in spite of a certain arrogance toward social inferiors and those who disagreed with him. At least when he died his tombstone witnessed "The sincere regret of his friends and the tears of the neighboring poor."[23]

John Neville's son, Presley, was also a Revolutionary veteran. Born in 1756, he was educated at the University of Pennsylvania. His country home, which he called Woodville, was situated on a slope across Chartiers Creek from Bower Hill, and his Pittsburgh home was on Water Street. His wife was a daughter of General Daniel Morgan. A typical gentleman in the then current sense of the word, generous to a fault when his own interests were not negatived, good-natured, tolerant, and easy going, Presley Neville yielded easily to the opinions of the other members of the clan, though Brackenridge credited him with being the most intelligent of them all. An expensive, though by no means a vicious, liver, he was inclined to be indolent. He once undertook to study law under Brackenridge, but after six months abandoned it, giving as his excuse "that the profession of the law was not an occupation *fit for a gentleman.*"[24]

John Neville's wife was a daughter of the Oldhams, a prominent Virginia family. Her sister was the wife of Abraham Kirkpatrick of Maryland, a Revolutionary major who had settled in Pittsburgh and had built up a fortune by speculation and money lending. Though Kirkpatrick was "as brave a man as drew his sword" even his grandnephew, Neville Craig, admitted that he was kind and chivalric "by fits and starts" and loved argument so well that he would change sides rather than let discussion cease.[25]

Major Isaac Craig came into the connection by his marriage to Amelia, John Neville's daughter. Born in Ireland about 1742, he came to Philadelphia at twenty-five years of age or thereabouts and worked at his trade of carpenter. At the outbreak of the Revolution he became the American navy's first lieutenant of marines, serving aboard the "Andrew Doria" during Commodore Hopkins' descent upon the island of New Providence. Later as a member of the land forces Craig was in the Christmas campaign of 1776 and in the Pennsylvania campaign of the next year. After a period of service in the arsenal at Carlisle he took part in Sullivan's Indian campaign. In 1780 he was ordered to Fort Pitt, and from then until his death in 1826 he was a resident of Pittsburgh or its vicinity. At the close of the war he formed a mercantile partnership with Stephen Bayard. This partnership, as the agent of Turnbull, Holker, and Marmie of Philadelphia, engaged in salt manufacturing, sawmilling, and distilling, and in 1784 it purchased for the Philadelphia firm the land on which Fort

Pitt stood. In 1791 Craig became deputy quartermaster general in the West, a position that was by no means a sinecure. The forwarding of Wayne's supplies was in his care, and he was busily engaged in this work during the worst of the insurrection. IIis son lauded him as "a sincere Christian, an honest man, a faithful and diligent officer, a good citizen, enterprising and public spirited, a kind neighbor, an affectionate husband, and a most indulgent parent." Brackenridge, not quite so partial in his favor, likened him to a muskrat—from which vivid simile the observant student of nature may deduce what he pleases.[26]

These were the members of the "Neville connection," and among them they mustered a formidable array of offices. John Neville, until recently a member of the legislature, was federal inspector of the revenue; Presley Neville was a member of the assembly, surveyor of Allegheny County, which then extended to Lake Erie, and brigade inspector of the militia; Isaac Craig was deputy quartermaster general of the United States army, deputy commissary, and a notary public. With their wealth and their offices the members of the family must have wielded a tremendous influence in the village of little more than a thousand inhabitants by their employment of workmen and patronage of shopkeepers. As Brackenridge pointed out, "they must conduct themselves, with more delicacy, than is usual with men, if they do not form at least a damnable, if not, 'a damned Junto.'"[27]

It is no wonder that the Neville influence with the leading men of the vicinity was predominant. John Woods, the son of the man intrusted by the Penns with the laying out of the plan of Pittsburgh, was the Neville attorney and was linked to them by other business ties as well. With his usual facility for getting into trouble Brackenridge earned the "Junto's" enmity by several times appearing as a lawyer against members of the family. This enmity was heightened by certain circumstances concerning which the only evidence available is that of Henry Marie Brackenridge, the son of the lawyer, though Neville Craig, the family apologist of the Nevilles, could not or would not deny their essentials. According to the story Brackenridge, about 1792, instituted "proceedings against Kirkpatrick, to compel him to bring back a free colored woman, named Eve, whom he had sent off to Kentucky, and either sold into slavery or intended to sell. The cause was prosecuted with energy, and the defendant held so firmly in the grip of the law, that he was compelled to bring the woman back and restore her to freedom. Kirkpatrick was furious . . . Armed with a bludgeon, [he] came suddenly on Mr. Brackenridge, while sitting carelessly under the shade of some trees, on the bank of the river. The blow missed his head, but fell on his left shoulder, from which he never entirely recovered. They seized each other, and rolled down the bank, but were almost immediately separated. A prosecution was pending for this, during the insurrection."[28]

Leaving Pittsburgh for a circuit of whiskey rebeldom, one finds that Chartiers Creek, which empties into the Ohio a short distance below Pittsburgh, flows through the heart of Washington County on a course roughly parallel to the Monongahela and west of that river. A few miles above the mouth of Chartiers were the country estates of the Nevilles. Farther up, at a point seventeen miles from Pittsburgh, was Canonsburg, settled by and named for John Canon. Like most other Washington County communities Canonsburg was strongly Presbyterian.

The leader of Presbyterianism in those parts was Dr. John McMillan, born in 1752 and educated at Princeton, attending during some of the same years in which Brackenridge was there. As pastor of the Chartiers and Pigeon Creek congregations he established about 1780 a "log college," which was superseded by Canonsburg Academy by 1794. McMillan's influence among the Presbyterians of the West was so great that Brackenridge humorously dubbed him the "Cardinal." When the lawyer was challenged to a duel by an irresponsible hothead he made public answer:

> MacMillan the ecclesiastic,
> Will burn me with religious caustic;
> Tell all the people that the devil,
> Has bound me hand and foot to evil.
> Can I avoid the horrid fury
> Of Presbyterian judge and jury?
> No. No. 'Tis best t' avoid the sin,
> And sleep as usual in a whole skin.[29]

McMillan knew no fear or favor and was said to have censured publicly the wife and daughters of the wealthy and aristocratic General George Morgan for coming to church in a carriage. The excise troubles found him boldly championing the cause of the federal government and refusing to allow the disaffected to partake of the communion. This was not from any scruple against the use of whiskey, for the good doctor, in common with other contemporary divines, received part of his salary in liquor and used it. It is said that once when he and the devout Joseph Patterson were traveling together they stopped to water their horses at an inn and by way of making some compensation for the service called for a glass of whiskey. Patterson proposed that he ask grace and upon his companion's assent began a long blessing, during which Dr. McMillan drank the whiskey. When Patterson had finished his prayer and saw that the glass was empty, McMillan greeted his blank stare with the admonition, "Brother, you must watch as well as pray."[30]

About seven miles farther up Chartiers Creek and a little to the east was the town of Washington. Perched on a rugged plateau, the citizens of the village could look out on a beautiful rolling terrain, good for general farming and even better for grazing. In 1794 Washington boasted that it had about one hundred families. Two years earlier twenty-three manufacturing trades had been carried on there, this being seven more than Pittsburgh could show. A spacious public square held a jail and a new brick courthouse, the cupola and gilded vane of the latter being the pride of the town.[31] In spite of these indications of progress, Washington, like the remainder of the West, still stuck in the mud, with only the difference that it realized the situation. The *bête noire* of increased taxes was a fruitful cause of opposition to proposed improvements and illustrated perfectly the growing cleavage between the classes. "Tom Stick in the Mud," for example, wrote with his tongue in his cheek: "For my part I've lived all my born days . . . up to the eyes in mud and never a bit the worse for it, and I can't see why other people should think themselves better stuff than we. I loves fun, and, at our end of the town, it would sometimes make you die with laughing to see your calico-carcassed, spindle-shanked folks sticking fast in a crossing-place and leaving their shoes behind them."[32]

Though founded only in 1780 Washington could muster a coterie of able men scarcely second to those of Pittsburgh. David Redick, who surveyed and planned the town, was an Irishman and like most other prominent westerners was a Revolutionary veteran. Admitted to the bar in 1782, he had served as vice president of the supreme executive council and as a member of the constitutional convention of 1790. During the whiskey troubles he was prothonotary and clerk of the courts of Washington County.

Doubtless the most important political figure in Washington County was the young lawyer, James Ross. Born of Scotch-Irish ancestry in 1762 in what is now York County, he, like so many other western Pennsylvanians, was educated at Princeton. The year 1782 found him teaching in McMillan's school of the prophets and studying law books borrowed from Brackenridge. Ross was said to have served in Crawford's ill-fated Sandusky campaign. Admitted to the bar at the age of twenty-two, his rise was phenomenally rapid. Possessed of a fine personality and presence coupled with a brilliant intellect and extraordinary balance, he was retained by George Washington as one of his western business managers. At twenty-seven Ross took part in the Pennsylvania constitutional convention. His career was further advanced by marriage to a daughter of the prominent and wealthy Woods family of Pittsburgh and Somerset in 1791. Three years later he was elected United States senator to fill the vacancy caused by the Senate's rejection of Gallatin. In politics Ross was an ardent Federalist and for twenty years the party's acknowledged leader in Pennsylvania. He was twice defeated in races for gubernatorial honors while serving in the Senate and once after his retirement to private practice before the Allegheny County bar. Until his death in 1847 he was the leading civic and legal light of Pittsburgh—"old man eloquent" in a day when the western Pennsylvania bar was a constellation of famous orators.[33]

Rarely has an immigrant made as rapid a success as did Alexander Addison, another of Washington Town's legal celebrities. Born in Scotland in 1759 and educated for the Presbyterian ministry at Aberdeen University, he emigrated to Washington County in 1785. For some reason his ministerial qualifications failed to impress the western Pennsylvania Presbyterian hierarchy, so he took up the study of law under David Redick. In 1791, six years after he entered the country, he was appointed president judge of the fifth judicial district of Pennsylvania, which included the counties of Westmoreland, Fayette, Allegheny, and Washington. Addison was a man of dignity, judgment, and erudition, with the gift of eloquence often keenly sarcastic, but his broad Scotch dialect was a handicap he never overcame and it detracted from his popularity. An advocate of states' rights during his earlier American career, he soon developed into a Federalist, and he was a tower of strength in the cause of law enforcement during the insurrection. This course might have been forgiven by western Pennsylvania Democratic-Republicans had he not afterward continued to adhere unbendingly to the opposite faction. His insistence upon rebuking a fellow judge for giving to a jury what he, Addison, regarded as unwarranted charges, finally led to his downfall. A Democratic-Republican intrigue—guided, it was said, by Brackenridge—led to his impeachment, conviction, and removal from the bench. Like Ross he took up private practice in Pittsburgh, but he died four years later in 1807.[34]

The most popular lawyer in Washington was David Bradford. A recent emigrant from Maryland, where he had been born about 1760, he was admitted to the bar in 1782 and was appointed deputy attorney-general for the county the next year, an office that he held until he fled from the region in 1794; in addition he was elected to the state legislature in 1792. Bradford's success was such that he was soon living in the finest house in town, the stairway of which was reputed to have cost a guinea a step. In spite of this affectation he was able to retain the good will of the people, though by many of the more solid citizens, particularly his fellow lawyers, he was later considered to have been lacking in stability and judgment.[35]

East of Washington Town on the Monongahela and centering around Mingo Creek was the region that was to become the heart as well as the hand of the insurrection. A region of small farmers, it could boast no citizen comparable to Neville, Brackenridge, Ross, or Addison, yet its Democratic Society, made up of average men, was to show itself almost a match for the combined wealth and learning of the Monongahela country.

Across the river in Fayette County the low hills rolled away to the foot of Chestnut Ridge. Here, in the northern part of the county, had been established the first English settlements west of the mountains. A few miles farther south and almost in the shadow of the ridge lay the county seat of Fayette, the village of Uniontown, sometimes known as Beeson's Town from its founder.

At the time of the excise troubles Fayette County had one citizen of transcendant ability. This was the famous Genevan, Albert Gallatin.[36] Born in 1761 in the city of John Calvin, and educated in the tradition of aristocracy, Gallatin early came in contact with followers of Rousseau and the Physiocrats, and this contact set his feet upon the path of liberalism. He broke away from home in 1780 and, landing in Massachusetts, served for a while in the American army, then traveled south to Richmond. Becoming possessed of some western lands, he resolved to make his home on the frontier, and in 1785 he settled in Fayette County. A glass factory that he set up in his town of New Geneva was one of the first in the West. A citizen of western Pennsylvania for forty years, his connection with its local history and politics was closest in the years during and preceding the Whiskey Insurrection. The dignified hospitality of his home, "Friendship Hill," made it the resort of the leaders of the western wing of the nascent Jeffersonian party.

The federal constitution found in Gallatin a vigorous opponent because of its "awful squinting toward monarchy." He even attended a protesting conference and was the author of its declaration of opposition to the constitution. When the party opposed to the radical constitution of Pennsylvania gained the ascendancy in the legislature and called a convention to draft a new constitution for the state, Gallatin was again in opposition and attempted to line up the western counties to block the move. Upon the defeat of his design he was elected to the convention and he was active in the formation of the state constitution of 1790. The next year he entered the legislature as a member of the minority party and speedily became one of the leaders. This was largely due to his willingness to undertake the drudgery of committee work. In the session of 1791-92 he was a member of thirty-five committees and drew up all their reports and bills. Especially did he shine in financial matters, his report of the committee of ways and means being hailed as a masterpiece. The result of his diligence and thoroughness was that the Federalist legislature sent this aristocrat by birth and breeding and democrat by choice and election to the United States Senate.

During his few weeks in the Senate Gallatin was a thorn in the side of the secretary of the treasury, for he sponsored and had adopted a resolution calling upon that official for a detailed report on financial affairs. Hamilton, surprised and grieved at this evidence of distrust, assumed the air of injured innocence that he wore so well and answered that "the Consciousness of devoting myself to the public service to the utmost extent of my faculties, and to the injury of my health, is a tranquillizing consolation of which I cannot be deprived by any supposition to the contrary."[37] This astounding statement was the only reply to the Senate's demand. Gallatin was punished for his temerity by the strict party vote that in February, 1794, ruled him out of the Senate on the technical ground that he had not been a citizen the nine years stipulated by the Constitution as a qualification for the senatorial office. His political ability had been proven, however, and it was only a matter of time until he would be called back to the national arena. Already he was recognized as the foremost Republican financial expert, and his courage, industry, and honesty, as well as his absolute control of his temper, added to his value. True, he was inclined to adopt an unpartisan point of view on party matters, but this was balanced by his willingness to give up his own opinions when overruled and to go along with the majority of the party. It was this very ability to compromise that carried Gallatin to the verge of rebellion and led to the commission of what he latter called his "only political sin."

Chapter III: *Mr. Hamilton's Excise*

AN excise on spirituous liquors was by no means a new thing to Pennsylvanians. As early as 1684 such a tax had been imposed, and from that time on to 1791 Pennsylvania probably was never without an excise. During the colonial wars it was resorted to with the specific purpose of providing money to aid in fighting the French, and at other times bills of credit were issued against it and gradually retired as the money came in. The excise of 1756 was the occasion of a bitter quarrel between Governor Morris and the assembly because the former insisted, in accordance with his instructions, that the disposal of the money from the excise must remain with the proprietary representatives. From the foundation of the colony to the repeal of the last excise law in 1791, Pennsylvania had at least nineteen laws laying taxes upon spirituous liquors, not to mention numerous acts regulating the sale of liquors or supplementing the main acts.[1] Prior to the Revolution, however, there appears to have been little taxation of liquors distilled from domestic products, although the laws applied to such liquors if sold at retail. Rum, in spite of the tax, was so cheap in Philadelphia that the farmers stopped distilling their grain and exchanged it for rum.

During the Revolution, because of the difficulty of import-

ing rum, whiskey distilling became very profitable, in spite
of the continuance of the excise. Distilleries sprang up everywhere. "In many parts of the country," wrote Findley, "you
could scarcely get out of sight of the smoke of a still-house."
So extensive was the demand that wheat as well as rye came
to be used and a scarcity of bread and forage threatened. "The
clergy from the pulpits," Findley went on, "and in some instances by judicial warnings of presbyteries, inveighed against
this alarming destruction of bread from the army and the poor,
and against the still-houses, as the general nurseries of intoxi-
cation and licentiousness." The earlier laws regulating the
sale of liquor in small quantities had been repealed, so those
disposed to get drunk could be satisfied at the stills at very
small expense.

The effect of this state of affairs was the passage in November, 1778, of a law that prohibited the distillation of all
kinds of grain during a part of the year. This was eased later
to allow the use of rye and barley, and finally the entire law,
since it was practically a dead letter, was repealed.[3] There
seems to have been no regular collection of the excise on domestic liquor in the West before the end of the Revolution,
and it is significant that from 1771 to 1775, though there were
collectors appointed for Westmoreland, Bedford, and Northumberland counties, which then included the least thickly
settled parts of the state, the accounts of these collectors, with
one trifling exception of less than sixteen pounds, remained
unsettled. As a matter of fact there could not have been very
many stills in the extreme West, because the first one in Pittsburgh was set up in 1770.[4]

The excise law of 1780 was intended to furnish money to
pay Pennsylvania's share of Congress' allowance to the army
to make up the depreciation in its pay. The collections were
falling even in the East by this time, but the general assembly

persisted in its efforts, passing an excise law in 1781 that was to run for ten years and another supplementary law in 1783. The collectors of Bedford, Northumberland, Washington, and Westmoreland counties were to receive twelve and one-half per cent of their collections, and those in Philadelphia only one-sixth as much. Robert Morris offered in 1786 to farm the excise, paying the state seventy thousand pounds annually for the privilege, but, though at best the state could collect only fifteen thousand pounds a year, the proposal was rejected as smacking of despotism.[5]

The year 1784 was signalized by an attack upon Philip Jenkins, an exciseman of Fayette County, by three men who forced him to relinquish his office and at the same time helped themselves to about twenty-two pounds of public money.[6] Robbery may have been the motive of this attack and opposition to the excise the excuse, but the victim probably received scant sympathy from his neighbors. The attitude toward excisemen in the western counties was so bad that there was considerable difficulty in obtaining respectable men to fill the collectorships.

In April, 1783, a broken-down taverner of Philadelphia, named William Graham, was appointed collector for Washington, Fayette, and Westmoreland counties. He was far from being successful in the office, and it was only by accepting small bribes from distillers, willing to pay something to be rid of him, that he was able to live. At first, more despised than feared, he was the butt of country jokesmiths; among other pranks his wig was singed, hot coals were put in his boots, and the tail of his horse was bobbed. It was well known that he was corrupt, and the people complained that he had acted contrary to law at various times. He not only admitted the last charge but also asserted to Edward Cook, one of the Fayette County judges, that the magistrates should protect him in this, as he was doing a public service. Cook thereupon replied that, if Graham did not feel himself bound by the law in performing his office, he should not complain if the people did not observe the laws in dealing with him.

A year or so after Graham's arrival the persecution became more serious. During a court meeting at Greensburg he was called to the door of his room in a lodginghouse and upon responding was seized by a person who announced himself as Beelzebub and attempted to pull Graham out, saying that he should be delivered to the other devils who waited without. Graham wrenched himself away and drawing his pistols managed, with the assistance of some friends, to bar the assailants from the room. Graham kept watch at the door all night and would not suffer anyone to leave. Some of those whom he had forcibly detained brought suit against him for false imprisonment and damages, alleging that the rioters had stolen their saddlebags and money. Graham's attempt to prosecute the marauders was unsuccessful, as all those he named were able to prove alibis.[7]

Following this incident advertisements were posted offering a reward for the collector's scalp, whereupon he fled to Washington County. There, near Cross Creek, a mob of about one hundred persons attacked him in open day. A contemporary described the ensuing scene a few days later: "His Pistols which he carried before him taken and broke to pieces in his Presence, his Commission and all his papers relaiting to his Office tore and thrown in the mud, and he forced, or made to stamp on them, and Imprecate curses on himself, the Commission and the Authority that gave it to him, they then cut off one half of his hair, cued the other half on one side of his Head, cut off the Cock of his Hat, and made him wear it in a form to render his Cue the most Conspicuous, this with many other marks of Ignominy they impos'd on him & to which he was obliged to submit, and in the above plight they marched him amidst a Crowd from the frontiers of this County to West-moreland County, calling at all the Still Houses in their way where they were *Treated Gratis,* and expos'd him to every Insult, and mockery that their Invention could contrive. They set him at Liberty at the entrance of Westmoreland but with Threats of utter Desolution should he dare to return to our County." Brackenridge expressed the opinion concerning the guilt of the attackers "that an honest fellow ought not to be severely treated, who had done nothing more, than to shave the under hairs from the head of an excise man, who wore a wig at any rate." At this time the lawyer was at the height of his popularity, and he was retained by the leaders of the rioters to combat the suit that Graham brought against them. The collector was so afraid to enter Washington County that he came in the company of the judges to give his testimony. Twelve of the rioters were found guilty and forced to pay heavy damages. Soon afterward Graham resigned and left the region.[8]

Graham's successor in Washington County was a local man, John Craig, who really tried to enforce the law and in consequence became so unpopular that political pressure was brought to bear to force his removal. In the other western counties little was done, outside of seizing liquor brought across the mountains without permits. Even this did not meet with public approval, but the informers doubtless felt fully recompensed with the half of the liquor legally forfeited to them. The collector of Allegheny County, Hunter, backed by James Brison, the prothonotary, attempted in 1790 to enforce the law and seized a quantity of unlicensed whiskey. Brackenridge, however, appearing for the defendants, took advantage of the popular hatred of the act to have the action quashed. Another attempt of Hunter's to bring seventy distillers to trial was foiled by Brackenridge on a technicality. Thereafter the state excise was a dead letter in the West, though in the East an increasing revenue was being obtained from it.[9]

The federal excise upon distilled liquors of domestic manufacture had its origin in the winter of 1790-91, when the Hamiltonian political machine was putting through its far-sighted nationalistic program against the ineffectual, but none the less bitter, opposition of a disorganized minority. The Federalists had for some time looked with longing upon an excise as a means of income, and as early as June, 1790, had attempted to push through Congress a bill providing for one, but had failed. Now with a party disciplined by the hope of profits another bill was introduced with every prospect of success. "Mr. Hamilton," wrote William Maclay, the biliously democratic senator from the "sticks" of Pennsylvania, "is all-powerful, and fails in nothing he attempts."[10] So true was this estimate that even Jefferson and Madison, the leading opponents of the Federalists, were maneuvered into situations in which they were forced to stand aside while the Hamiltonian steam roller flattened out their cherished principles.

The story of the linking of the excise with Hamilton's program is involved and at times obscure. The northern political leaders, eager to attach the moneyed class to the federal government, wanted the latter to assume the obligation of meeting the unpaid state debts. The southern leaders, since their states had paid most of their debts, opposed the move, but they wanted the permanent capital of the nation located in the South. There were the elements of a bargain. Briefly, the facts seem to be that Jefferson and Hamilton, meeting a group of their respective supporters at dinner, agreed over the wine that the federal government should assume the debts of the states and that the capital of the new government should be located on the Potomac. The next step was to raise enough money to pay the debts thus assumed, and Hamilton proposed that about eight hundred thousand dollars should be raised by a duty upon imported liquors and upon those distilled within the country.

The excise bill as introduced into the House of Representatives aroused a storm of protest. Much of the opposition arose from hatred of an excise on liquor, but perhaps even more opposition came from those who would have fought any method of raising money to pay the assumed debts. The money, they asserted, was going to a group of wealthy speculators who had not borne the burden during the heat of the day, but who had bought the obligations for a song and then corruptly influenced the government to pay them at face value. Newspapers, taprooms, and streets teemed with slanderous gossip. The *Maryland Journal* of February 11, 1791, attempted to blast the popular opposition by printing an imaginary dialogue in which a Federalist told of his conversations with various democratic acquaintances.

"What's the matter? said I to Balbus, whom I found in a violent passion. Don't you know, said he, that Congress have passed an Excise-Law? And what then?—Why, said he, we shall immediately have excise-men. Did you ever hear, said I, of a tax that collected itself?"

Crambulo, whom the Federalist met next, inveighed against the folly of fighting a war to free the country from an excise only to have one laid by the new government. "True, said I, we fought *Great-Britain,* for insisting that she had a right to make laws in LONDON, to bind us in AMERICA." Next the Federalist fell in with Ignarus. "Fine doings! said Ignarus; but I'll never submit, you may depend upon it, to an Excise-Officer's entering my house, or breaking open my doors, at his pleasure! And you may depend upon it, said I, that the case can never happen. Why not? said Ignarus. Because, said I, the Excise-Law which has terrified you so, gives to the officers who are to collect it no such power. I turned a corner and met Rumor. So, friend! said he, in a kind of whisper, the Excise is come among us, and we shall be ate up with Excise-Officers. Have you calculated their number? said I. No, said Rumor, I have not read the scheme, and you know I never study such things."

The next acquaintance met was Candidus, and the Federalist complained of the passion exhibited against the excise by Balbus, Crambulo, and the others. Cried Candidus: "You gave them pepper fifteen years ago, in the *Canada Address,* and now they show some of its effects. What! said I, do you favour the Excise? Do I favour the Excise, he replied in his usual manner. I hate it, and the government which framed it! I thought so, said I; but you can give a reason for your hatred. Let me assign what reason I may, said Candidus, you will believe but one, that I hate the Excise, because it strengthens government by effectually providing for its necessities; and the government which lays it, because it is a Government of Vigour."

The Canada Address mentioned by Candidus was an appeal by the Continental Congress in 1774 to Quebec for support on the ground that the British have "subjected you to the impositions of *Excise,* the horror of all free states; thus wresting your property from you by the most odious of taxes, and laying open to insolent tax-gatherers, houses, the scenes of domestic peace and comfort, and called the castles of English subjects in the books of their law."[11] The Federalists explained that the law now under consideration was not an excise. An excise, they said, was a duty levied on small quantities of liquor, which the wealthy, by storing away liquor by the cask, escaped paying. This bill, on the contrary, laid a duty upon all distilled liquors upon importation or at the stillhead.[12] This surely was not discrimination against the poor man, speciously argued the bill's sponsor, the unctuous Sedgwick of Massachusetts. After all, said he, opening the bag and letting the cat out, capital, property, and income were not proper gauges for the laying of taxes. The true criterion was the amount that was left, after a man had paid the cost of living expected of him in his station in his community. And what could tap this excess more neatly than—he carefully avoided the term excise—a duty upon spirituous liquors?[13]

Jefferson and Madison, having agreed to assumption, felt that they could not consistently oppose any reasonable scheme for raising the money to meet the debts. The former, taking advantage of his executive position, quietly withdrew into his shell to await the passing of the storm. Madison, forced by his position in the House to make some kind of pronouncement, said that he saw no other way of raising the requisite money.[14] The College of Physicians of the City of Philadelphia, on the other hand, proclaimed the excise a positive benefit, and petitioned Congress to impose such heavy duties upon distilled spirits as to restrain their intemperate use.[15]

The brunt of opposition in the House was borne by the fiery James Jackson of Georgia. Though often outvoted by "silent majorities" his "monitor within" prompted him to rise "in opposition to a system unfriendly to the liberties of the people." He denounced the excise as "odious, unequal, unpopular, and oppressive." The South, where there were no breweries or orchards, found spirituous liquors necessary and salutary. This interference with the liberties of the people was going entirely too far. If the College of Physicians proceeded as it had begun it might soon petition for the passage of a "law interdicting the use of catsup, because some ignorant persons had been poisoned by eating mushrooms." Here he diverged to expose the root of the controversy. The United States should not sacrifice its liberties by wantonly contracting debts that would entail the laying of burdens too heavy to be borne. "I plainly perceive," he shouted, assuming the prophetic mantle, "that the time will come when a shirt shall not be washed without an excise."[16]

Less scintillating but equally earnest viewers with alarm spoke from time to time. Parker of Virginia prophesied that the excise would "convulse the Government; it will let loose a swarm of harpies, who, under the denomination of revenue officers, will range through the country, prying into every man's house and affairs, and like a Macedonian phalanx bear down all before them." Even the mercantile element should oppose the bill, he said, for the unreasonable import duties would promote smuggling to the detriment of legitimate business. The estimate of money needed was too high, urged sundry representatives, each bringing in differing sets of figures to prove the point. Why not substitute some other tax, such as one on salaries, or—happy thought of the irrepressible Jackson—one on lawyers? A Federalist rose to oppose the suggestion of a direct tax and quoted the secretary of the treasury as saying that such a tax should be left for future emergency. "In that case," fired back the ebullient Jackson, "why not leave two for emergency?" George Clymer of Pennsylvania, speaking in favor of the bill, admitted that the Pennsylvania excise had met with some resistance, but asserted that the offenders had been caught and severely fined. Jackson, whose quips seemed never to have been missed by the reporter, thereupon retorted that if the offenders had been severely fined "he had been well informed that the fine had been as severely remitted."[17]

Thus the battle raged, the gadfly opposition losing no opportunity to propose an amendment or to hamper progress by quibbling. It tried to limit the duration of the act, to limit the compensation and number of excise officers, and to forbid them from doing election work. A particularly heated argument was staged on the question of what constituted a village, and Jackson, in his usual irreverent manner, suggested that the problem be referred to the College of Physicians, who, "since they had tried to squirt morality and instruction into the minds of the members, might also be able to squirt understanding."[18]

The opposition outside Congress was meanwhile swelling in volume and would have given pause to anyone less self-confident than the Federalists. The North Carolina representatives laid their state's lukewarmness toward a federal government to dread of just such eventualities as this. The Pennsylvania House of Representatives, after a long debate on the propriety of interfering in the business of Congress, passed, forty to sixteen, a set of resolutions, said to have been written by Gallatin, decrying the excise, and the members spread on the journal their reasons for voting as they did. Strange as it may seem, John Neville, the man who was shortly to become an excise inspector, voted for the resolutions. Maclay observed with his usual acidity that Findley, Gallatin, and the other leaders of the opposition had "nothing further in view than the securing themselves niches in the six-dollar temple of Congress," referring to the six-dollar-a-day pay of Congressmen. The Pennsylvania resolution found an echo in distant North Carolina, the legislature of that state a year later praying for a modification of the act.[19]

Every effort to block the passage of the bill failed, however, and it passed on January 27 by a vote of thirty-five to twenty-one. New England, New Jersey, and Delaware were solidly for the bill and the far South was against it, with the exception of one lone vote from South Carolina; New York favored it four to two, Pennsylvania and Virginia split their votes evenly, and Maryland cast three against and one in favor.[20]

The day after the House disposed of the bill, it was received in the Senate and was given the first reading. The Senate did not keep a record of the debates, so the progress of the bill cannot be followed closely, but the journal of William Maclay gives occasional glimpses from the author's prejudiced and pessimistic viewpoint. "Were Eloquence personified," said he, "and reason flowed from her tongue, her talents would be in vain in our Assembly; or, in other words, when all the business is done in dark cabals, on the principle of interested management."

The phase of the bill to which Maclay objected most loudly was the attempt to organize excise districts without regard to state lines, which he interpreted as a step toward destroying the liberties of the states. He even quoted King of New York as declaring that they "had no right to pay any more attention to the State boundaries than to the boundaries of the Cham of Tartary." Maclay drew a dark picture of the future: "Annihilation of State government is undoubtedly the object of these people. The late conduct of our State Legislature has provoked them beyond all bounds. They have created an Indian war, that an army may spring out of it; and the trifling affair of our having eleven captives at Algiers (who ought long ago to have been ransomed) is made the pretext for going to war with them and fitting out a fleet. With these two engines, and the collateral aid derived from a host of revenue officers, farewell freedom in America."[21]

It would be hazardous, perhaps, to go too far in the direction of accusing Hamilton of having projected the excise for use in whipping the recalcitrant localistic elements of the country into submission to the dominant Federalist machine. It is hard to escape the conclusion, however, that the excise was the device used by speculators in state securities and by the great property holders in general to shift the burden of "assumption" to the shoulders of the consumers. At the same time the new nationalistic element, scenting immense profits to be gained by the manipulation of the federal government, and recognizing the states as their chief opponents, took advantage of the opportunity to try to weaken the latter. These two actions, at least, were deliberate policies and were pushed in spite of very patent public opposition. As Hamilton tersely remarked, he had "long since learned to hold popular opinion of no value."[22]

The act of 1791 divided the United States into fourteen districts of one state each, with the provision that the president could alter the boundaries of the districts by adding portions of the greater districts to the smaller. Each district, administered by a supervisor, was divided into surveys, each in charge of an inspector. The surveys, in turn, were divided into collectorships, each with a collector, who was to gather the tax. Virginia had seven surveys, Maryland two, and Pennsylvania four. George Clymer, a signer of the Declaration of Independence, was supervisor of the Pennsylvania district and also inspector of the first survey, in the vicinity of Philadelphia. His salary was one thousand dollars a year and one half of one per cent of the money he collected. The fourth survey was composed of Allegheny, Washington, Fayette, Westmoreland, and Bedford counties, which comprised in general the western part of the state, and was in charge of General John Neville. His salary was four hundred and fifty dollars a year and one per cent of what he collected. The collectors were entitled to four per cent of the money they collected. Two schedules were provided for domestic distilleries: one for those in city, town, or village, and the other for country distillers. For the first class, payments ranged from nine to twenty-five cents per gallon, according to proof, and provisions were made for abatements for cash and for quarterly payments. For the second class, the distillers could pay at the annual rate of sixty cents per gallon for the capacity of their stills or at nine cents for each gallon of production. Illegal liquor was to be forfeited, one half going to the person lodging the information.

The amending act of May 8, 1792, reduced the rates to seven to eighteen cents for the first class of distillers. Country stills of capacity under four hundred gallons could pay fifty-four cents per gallon capacity annually, ten cents per gallon capacity for each month they were in use, or seven cents for each gallon produced. Each county was to have an office of inspection, and entry was to be made in June. The third act, of June 5, 1794, provided that, if there was no office of inspection in the distiller's county, he should enter his still at some office within the district. Owners of stills of one hundred gallons capacity or less could enter them for a term of a month to a year, paying at the monthly rate.[23]

As has been seen, the heredity, the pyschology, and the situation of the Monongahela farmer all conspired to make him an enemy of the excise. The expense of transportation to distant markets reduced the profit on the product of his still to a scant margin, and, as Hamilton pointed out in his able report of March 6, 1792, the distiller thought that he would have to pay the excise from this margin, not realizing that the consumer always pays the tax. Hamilton further pointed out that since it was the consumer who paid the tax, each section of the country would yield only its fair proportion, and if the West had to pay more it was only because it used more whiskey. This was exactly the case, but the fact was far more vital to the westerner than Hamilton would admit. Heredity, convenience, and habit made whiskey his characteristic tipple as well as the most acceptable article for barter. When, cash or barter, a gallon of whiskey could bring in the West no more than half what it brought in the East, John Buckskin was bound to complain if he had to pay the same tax. When the average farmer did not see twenty dollars cash in a year, the payment in cash of the excise on his still immediately became a major problem, especially if the whiskey was used only for barter.

Perhaps it was true, as Hamilton suggested, that the commissary spent in the West as much in one year as the taxes amounted to in four or five, but this did not help the back country farmer much. He bartered his whiskey and other products at a reduced valuation to the store-keeper; the latter sold them to the army or to the Spanish in Louisiana and then sent the cash East to purchase the goods he bartered to the farmer. Sometimes the farmer bettered his situation by sending his wares to the East by pack train or by loading them on a flatboat destined for New Orleans; but, if he did obtain a little cash, he almost invariably had to deposit it with an agent or the store-keeper for transmission to the eastern speculator from whom he had bought his farm. In this way the West was perennially drained of its cash, and even the wealthy often found themselves hard pushed to meet their obligations to eastern creditors.

It can readily be seen that when business was conducted in this manner the large distiller was at an advantage, especially if he was located in a town. He could sell his whiskey directly to the commissary for its full value in cash, but the small distiller in the back country received only a part of its value in barter. There were ways, moreover, of greasing the palms of the Spanish officials on the Mississippi so that a flatboat loaded with whiskey could slip through the prohibitive customs barrier and be sold for a round profit in Spanish dollars, and it was estimated in 1794 that one hundred thousand gallons had been sent down the Ohio from the vicinity of Pittsburgh.[24] It was true, as some distillers complained, that the excise act allowed for no drawback on whiskey thus shipped out of the country by the back door, but even so the man with capital could make his profit. In fact, there soon arose among the larger distillers the feeling that perhaps, after all, the excise was a good thing, as it would act to put the smaller ones out of business. In some parts of the country a further factor worked for the elimination of the small fry. It was a peculiar fact that the law, which to the common suppliant seemed incomprehensible, had a surprising way of clearing up before the well paid efforts of superior legal talent. John Buckskin, watching in open-mouthed wonder the evolutions of the lawyers, became more than ever convinced that the excise was one more move, and probably the decisive one, in the government's campaign to reduce him to the economic, political, and legal status of a European peasant.

For years the West had urged a land tax as the most equitable method of taxation. The purpose in this was twofold: first, the East would bear the greatest burden, since land there was more valuable on account of superior improvements and proximity to markets; and second, it was hoped that the taxing of the western land held by speculators would force them to sell it at reasonable rates and thus hasten the development of the West. Now it was perfectly apparent to the westerner (his legislative representatives had seen to that) that the laying of the excise was a clever move on the part of the eastern plutocracy to escape a land tax, and the latter's acceptance of a tax on fine imported wines and spirits did not convince the backwoodsman of their disinterestedness. The eastern retort that westerners were natural born grumblers and would have fought a land tax as bitterly as an excise did nothing to improve the relations between the sections.

Another factor in the opposition, and one with which government officials had scant patience, was the fact that the Monongahela countryman's pride made him resent, almost hysterically, the inquisitorialness of excise officers with their searches and seizures, their markings with paint and branding irons. "What was it caused the Revolution, if it was not this?" the westerner asked, and refused to be convinced that such actions from a government seated in Philadelphia were any less dangerous to liberty than from one seated in London. Some of the more radical Presbyterians also found an additional fault in the fact that the law required them to make oath, for this was a violation of their conscientious scruples.

It is possible that the westerner would have submitted to these conditions, galling as they were, had not one other circumstance added to insult and injury what he regarded as certain ruin. This was the provision for trial of excise cases arising in Pennsylvania in the federal court in Philadelphia. The small distiller felt sure that the law had been cunningly contrived to catch him no matter how honestly he tried to abide by it, and with a farm and still worth five hundred dollars at the most, he was driven almost frantic by the prospect of attendance at a court three hundred miles from home, with the absence for an unpredictable number of weeks during the farmer's busy season, and with the burden of payment of lawyers and witnesses. It looked to him like deliberate and premeditated confiscation. This view was further supported by the fact that though Congress in March, 1793, had authorized the holding of special sessions of federal courts near the scenes of alleged offenses, no such sessions were ever called in the Monongahela country in connection with the enforcement of the excise law.

The excise was hated not only for its direct results but also for what was expected to follow. Salaried officers, always distrusted on the frontier, were a part of the excise system, and the western Pennsylvanian, meeting his cronies at church or at the store, prophesied the extension of the tax to other articles and the building up of a numerous corps of salaried officers who would fasten tyranny in the saddle more firmly that it had ever been under the royal Georges.

The excise was by no means the only cause of western discontent. The drainage of specie to the East had been a problem long before the passage of the federal excise law and resulted, as has been said, from the obligations due to the East for land and necessities. The difficulty of transportation made it impossible to export western lumber, meat, and grain in exchange, and this state of affairs was to continue until the Louisiana Purchase and the development of the steamboat made intersectional trade possible. Meanwhile, the Monongahela countryman, whose comprehension of the situation was sharpened by his sufferings, complained that the government was not interested in opening the Mississippi to American commerce and that it favored the Indians above its own citizens. The westerner, unable to find specie to buy from the speculators who had engrossed most of the desirable land, clamored for admission to the Northwest Territory. Pennsylvania's plan to establish a settlement at Presque Isle was certain to arouse the resentment of the Iroquois, so had been vetoed by the federal government amidst the West's clamorous accusations of pusillanimity. The fact that the British remained in the western posts, which they had agreed to surrender at the close of the Revolution, did nothing to popularize Washington's administration in the West.

Another complaint had to do with arduous and ill-paid militia service. Each man, under penalty of a heavy fine, had to equip himself with provisions and a rifle, the last no small item in the average farmer's budget, and had to answer instantly any call for service. Let a band of Indians but make a raid in the county and the militia would be called out and kept under arms, perhaps for weeks, with nothing to do but curse a government so selfish and stupid that it had not long ago erased such varmints as Indians from the face of the earth.[25]

The foregoing is a presentation of the case from the limited point of view of the small farmer and distiller. Without attempting to minimize the validity of his objections when applied to his circumstances, it is apparent, when one takes a sweeping view of "progress"—if one approves of that much discussed movement—that John Buckskin was fighting against the larger eventual welfare of humanity. Hamilton and his proponents with their new political and economic philosophy were easily able to explode the backwoodsman's arguments.

One by one official apologists or newspaper contributors set up the westerner's arguments and knocked them over—some of them quite effectively. They pointed out the absurdity of trying to enforce a law without officials and demonstrated that inquisitorialness was, under the law, confined to an irreducible minimum. As for distance from markets and its accompanying handicaps, the settlers had accepted this knowingly when they moved to the West. As for scarcity of cash, surely a tax estimated at one dollar and a half a family was not excessive. It was absurd to fear a growth of bureaucracy and tyranny when the people of the West had a voice in the Congress, in fact when western Pennsylvania had three members although its population would scarcely entitle it to two. If the Monongahela farmers were dissatisfied, let them appeal to Congress, and if their grievances were valid, the law would be changed. This view was sound theoretically, but not practically, as the South later found to its cost. It was admitted that there were imperfections in the excise law, notably the matter of trial over the mountains, but they would soon be remedied. Indian policy, the western posts, and the navigation of the Mississippi, it was said, were by no means being neglected, and chapter and verse were cited to prove it.[26] After all, the United States was young, and there were other sections to be satisfied besides the noisy young West. Let patience have her perfect work.

These arguments, logical and reasonable as they were, failed to satisfy John Buckskin, and as the months went by he became increasingly clamorous in his demands that state and federal governments do something to reduce his burdens and to provide an outlet for his products. And the East, as is the habit of privileged sections in every age, was quite unmindful of the hardship being imposed upon the hinterland, but went on molding the national economy to suit the ideas of the young men who headed the Federalist Party and who represented the manufacturing and mercantile elements of the nation.

Chapter IV: *The Beginning of Direct Action*

A CRESCENDO of popular agitation in the Monongahela country occupied the three years from the passage of the federal excise act to the outbreak of the "insurrection" in the summer of 1794. Whose were the hands that fed the flame it is at this late date difficult to discover, as those responsible, if there were such, were clever enough to cover their tracks. Neville and the others who stood for the excise insisted that the prominent men in the opposite faction deliberately fomented the trouble to advance their own political fortunes. The accused, in turn, naturally denied the charges. The "insurrection," they asserted, was the spontaneous movement of a desperate and none too farsighted populace, a movement that flared up and gained its momentum without leadership. Indeed, said they, such apparent leaders as the movement boasted were pushed ahead by irresistible public opinion, most of them protesting and going along only through fear and in the hope of mitigating the dangers of the outbreak.

The choice of General Neville as inspector of the excise for the fourth survey was nicely calculated to wean away from the opposition the wealth and "respectability" of the region. Neville had openly opposed the state excise; he had voted against it in the legislature, and had gone so far as to say, when

Graham had been maltreated at Cross Creek, that "they did not use the rascal half as bad as he deserved" and that he should have had his ears cut off. He had voted for the resolutions of protest against the federal excise only a few days before his appointment as inspector. It was said that when Neville was reminded that he would, by accepting the office, forfeit the good will of his neighbors, he answered that "he did not regard their good will, he had got an independent salary of 600 a year." Neville may not have made that answer, but the report that he had, coming after his years of seeking the suffrage of the people for election to public office, diminished the prospect of popular coöperation, and ingrained further the western distrust of salaried officers.[1]

The passage of the excise bill posed a pretty problem in political procedure for the politicians who had opposed it. William Findley, who had voted for the Pennsylvania resolutions against the bill, made no public pronouncement but waited cannily to see which way the cat would jump. Meanwhile, to the disgust of Maclay, who fell into conversation with him one day on the street, he discreetly scratched the administration's back, saying that the excise law must be obeyed and that it was "very honorable management to raise the debts to their full value."[2] Upon their return home Findley and the other western members of the state legislature who had supported the opposing resolutions, seeing the temper of their constituents, threw themselves zealously into the battle against the excise. Those who had favored the excise found themselves confronted at the polls by strong opposing candidates as well as by aroused public sentiment. The resolutions and the reasons in their favor were published and were dissected and discussed at every fireside and tavern. Certain inconsiderate citizens at this point called attention to the embarrassing fact that Pennsylvania still had an excise law on her statute books. Hasty promises to remedy this oversight were made, and in fact the law was repealed at the next session of the legislature, in September, 1791.[3]

The opposition to the federal excise in the Monongahela country found its chief expression at first in numerous petitions and resolutions of protest. Militia musters were particularly fruitful in these documents,[4] but the most important and far-reaching were those drawn up at popular meetings at Brownsville, Washington, and Pittsburgh. The Brownsville meeting took place on July 27, 1791. The attendance was wholly of volunteers, and since it was harvest time few were from a distance. William Findley and a few others came from Westmoreland County. Findley made a lengthy discourse, counseling moderation and pointing out the matters with which a petition might deal. He was heard with great attention and those present seemed to agree with him. Since no petition was ready for adoption it was decided to call another meeting in Pittsburgh on September 7. Election districts in the four western counties were asked to send delegates to the county seats on a certain day in August, and there, having sounded the public sentiment of their county, the delegates were to choose three representatives to go to Pittsburgh.[5]

The only county delegation that met was that of Washington on August 23. The radicals were in complete control and proceeded to draw up and adopt a violent resolution that classed excise officers as public enemies and called upon the citizens to treat them "with contempt, and absolutely to refuse all kind of communication or intercourse with the officers, and to withhold from them all aid, support, or comfort."[6]

The meeting called for Pittsburgh was held on September 7 at the Green Tree Tavern on the Monongahela water front. It was attended by eleven delegates. Edward Cook, associate judge of Fayette County, was elected chairman. David Bradford, James Marshall, and John Woods were, together with Cook, the leaders of the meeting. Sometime before the meeting Marshall had asked Brackenridge to prepare an address and some resolutions for adoption by the meeting, and these were now brought forth. After some debate, at which Brackenridge was present as a spectator, the documents were referred to a committee composed of Cook, Bradford, and Woods. Woods, perhaps influenced by enmity to Brackenridge, insisted that there were treasonable expressions in the resolutions and address, notably one that read: "Until our remonstrances shall roll like a tempest to the head of the government." Brackenridge later asserted that Woods probably "mistook a figure for a threat, and had not literary taste sufficient to distinguish."

At any rate the text was so changed that Brackenridge immediately disclaimed all responsibility for authorship, but this was not to save him in later years from accusations of treason. The resolutions as finally adopted were about what might have been expected—protests against the financial policy of the government and assertions that the excise was subversive of liberty and discouraging to agriculture and manufacture. The address to the people was to the same effect as the Washington resolution and urged the "cultivating the idea amongst ourselves, that excise offices ought not to be accepted. If there can be found virtue enough in the people, to refuse such commissions, the law cannot be carried into effect, and it will be the same as if it did not exist."[7]

It is possible that resolutions were the safety valves that prevented explosion of western resentment against the East. It is worth noting that so long as the government did not try to interfere with the right of assembly and petition, the western tail of the federal kite was content to trail along the ground, but as soon as this right was challenged it caught in the bushes and threatened to bring down the kite. Some of the Federalist leaders in the Monongahela country did not hestitate to declare their sympathy with the malcontents. Neville, however, who now had an ax to grind, bemoaned to Clymer the dangers inherent in the situation and retailed disapprovingly that the opponents of the excise "frequently mentioned that we are the people and that Congress are only our servants."[8]

The intolerance of public opinion in the Monongahela country on the one hand and the high-handedness of Federalist officials in the East on the other put men of moderate sentiments in a difficult situation. Anything they might say or do was bound to be misinterpreted by one side or the other, each faction saying in effect, "Ye that are not for me are against me." Judge Addison, as honest and incorruptible a conservative as one could find in the West, seems to have approved the excise law in theory, but he held the conviction that the powers given to the federal courts would inevitably lead to the swallowing up of the state courts and with this the essence of state rights. To meet this danger, he advocated "constitutional resistance" to the law. His meaning, it would seem, should be clear to any reasonable being, but the advocates of the law were no more reasonable than the opponents, and they immediately raised a hue and cry that no resistance to a law could be constitutional. This unfortunate phrase was the main count in Hamilton's campaign to discredit Addison and was pointed to as illustrative of the treasonable thinking of the West.[9]

Brackenridge in his *Incidents of the Western Insurrection* characterized the popular resentment against the federal excise in vivid, though perhaps exaggerated, style. Said he: "A breath in favour of the law, was sufficient to ruin any man. It was considered as a badge of toryism. A clergyman was not thought orthodox in the pulpit, unless against the law: a physician was not capable of administering medicine, unless his principles were right in this respect: a lawyer could have got no practice, without at least concealing his sentiments, if for the law: a merchant, at a country store, could not get custom. On the contrary, to talk against the law, was the way to office and emolument. In order to be recommended to the government, as a justice of the peace, you must be against the law. To go to the Assembly, you must make a noise against it; and in order to go to Congress, or to keep in it, you must contrive, by some means, to be thought staunch in this respect.—It was the *shibboleth* of safety, and the ladder of ambition."[10]

Findley thought in later years that Brackenridge overestimated the unpopularity of those who favored the excise, at least in Westmoreland, but toward the close of 1792 he was writing Governor Mifflin that the Federalists were taking the lead in disapproving of the excise and that, even if the most influential citizens of the western country were to advocate the law, it would only set the people against it the more.[11]

There was considerable misunderstanding of the law among the more ignorant of the common people. It was bruited about and believed in some quarters that there would soon be a tax upon the common necessities of life. One simple-hearted woman was under great concern because of a report that a tax was to be laid on spinning wheels. The joke-loving Brackenridge, to whom she expressed her fear, noting that she wore a nightcap, hastened to assure her that that was by no means the worst—there was talk of placing one on nightcaps. Another wag convinced some people that there was soon to be a tax upon newly-born male children. The inhabitants of remote sections in some cases refused to give information to strangers lest it prove that they were aiding excisemen.[12]

Through all the period of controversy over the excise, the Presbyterian Church, which was by far the strongest denomination in western Pennsylvania, was a tower of strength on the side of enforcement. When one recalls that the thunders of the Presbyterian clergy against the royalist cause a few years earlier had helped to dub the revolt of the colonies "the Presbyterian Revolution," it may appear logical that the Calvinists should have stood by their own handiwork. The common man, however, having learned that lesson of revolution, was not so attached to the new government that he could gag at treason, and the chief men among the radicals were Presbyterians. The time was to come when the warfare between the clergy and the recalcitrant laymen was to become open, and it is difficult to avoid the conclusion that the official position of the church was the decisive factor in the outcome of the insurrection.

As was to be expected, the first violent actions were more or less desultory, though Neville was soon going about in fear of his life.[13] Robert Johnson, collector for Washington and Allegheny counties, was the recipient of the first attentions when on September 6, 1791, he was waylaid near Pigeon Creek in Washington County by a gang of sixteen men. According to his story they were dressed in women's clothes, but he recognized several of them, including John, Daniel, and David Hamilton. They cut off his hair, tarred and feathered him, seized his horse, and left him to find his way to friends as best he could "in that mortifying and painful situation." The federal district court of Pennsylvania issued several warrants as a result of this affair, one of them against John Hamilton, who two years later was sheriff of Washington County and a colonel in the militia.

Joseph Fox, a deputy marshal, was assigned to serve the warrants. He reached Allegheny County in October, carefully concealing his errand, but he was so intimidated by the popular opposition to the excise that he feared he would not return alive if he tried to carry out his duty. The result was that he adopted the expedient of serving the processes by messenger; he sent a simple-minded old cattle drover named John Connor, who had no idea of the true nature of his mission. As a consequence, the messenger was whipped, tarred and feathered, robbed of his horse and money, and left tied in the woods for five hours. The case dragged on and on, and two years later when the processes were finally served a notice appeared warning those served that the processes had been forged by Johnson as a ruse to get them to Philadelphia and put them under the power of the federal court.[14]

Fox had scarcely left the West before other outrages occurred. There were two cases of assault, and Daniel Hamilton of Washington County was accused of both. In addition a certain Robert Wilson was attacked and treated even worse than Johnson had been. Wilson was a young man, cultured and well educated, but probably mentally unbalanced, who had been looking for a position as a schoolmaster. As he journeyed about he inquired of the distillers he met whether they had entered their stills and he seemed to imply, and perhaps believed, that he was a collector. The result was that he was taken from his bed one night in October, 1791, by a disguised mob and carried five miles to a blacksmith shop. There he was stripped and his clothes were burned; he was seared in several places with a hot iron, then tarred and feathered. Even under torture his delusion persisted. He did not beg for mercy, refused to stop his spying, and put up such a vigorous struggle that his persecutors were daubed with their own tar and feathers. The court of Allegheny County, where the outrage occurred, began proceedings, but before the processes were served Wilson left the region. The proceedings were then dropped and the accused were released on writs of habeas corpus. Two witnesses were seized by armed men and carried away. Seventeen of those concerned in the abduction of the witnesses were tried before Judge Addison and most of them were fined. Addison himself admitted that those punished were "the least guilty or miserably poor."[15]

A month or two after the attack on Wilson a certain Roseberry was tarred and feathered for saying that if they did not obey the law the people of the West could hardly expect protection from Congress.[16] After this there seem to have been no overt acts in opposition to the excise until July of the next year, though associations against it were being organized.[17] Neville had established his headquarters for Washington County at Washington in the house of William Faulkner, a captain in Wayne's army, and attended there two days a week. Faulkner was advised by several gentlemen that he was making a mistake in allowing a revenue office to be opened in his house and was urged to discontinue it. According to his own story Faulkner was alarmed by this and went into the country to sound out public opinion. At Benjamin Parkinson's place a Robert Morrison confronted him with a copy of the *Pittsburgh Gazette* in which Neville advertised the location of the excise office in Washington, and Faulkner was forced to admit its accuracy. Thereupon he was roundly damned for a rascal and public enemy and it was threatened that the "Association," which now comprised five hundred members, would make an example of him. Later in the day at David Hamilton's he met a group of malcontents. Said the captain in his deposition: "Daniel Hamilton then came forward and after giving a Whoop or two caught hold of some of the hair of this deponent, on the top of his head and asked him if he understood that, meaning if he understood being scalped." Faulkner understood perfectly and promised to withdraw his permission for the use of his house.

About the middle of August the neighborhood of Washington was alarmed by the report that a band of armed men painted as Indians was lurking in the bushes along the road from Pittsburgh. Neville was warned by John Canon and Craig Ritchie of Canonsburg that their purpose was to waylay him. Neville, accordingly, did not go to Washington. There was probably some delay in the execution of Faulkner's promise, for on August 24 a band of thirty men with blackened faces, apparently from the Mingo Creek settlements, rode into town, surrounded Faulkner's house and forced their way in. Faulkner was away but they proceeded to search the house, while they breathed out threats of slaughter against him. The excise notice was torn down and the sign of the president's head—Faulkner evidently kept a tavern—was filled with bullet holes, the rioters saying that that was the man who had signed the excise act. The local magistrates and other men of "respectability" were interested and probably approving witnesses of these transactions, and afterwards at least one of them, David Bradford, entertained some of the rioters in his home.[18]

Rumor, as usual, had its share in shaping the public mind. Neville, as early as December, 1791, was writing Clymer that the people were threatening to close the Pittsburgh excise office as soon as Wayne's army, then encamped near the town, moved down the river. The author of the *Review of the Revenue System* recounted the current opinion that Alexander Hamilton proposed to use the army to silence the objections of the Monongahela country to the excise, calling out troops under the color of deputizing "citizens" to assist the law officers. Wayne, it was said, refused to support the scheme, maintaining "that the army was raised to protect the people and not to oppress them." Whether or not the report was true, it got about and helped to raise Wayne in the public estimation.[19]

The increasing bitterness of the opposition to the excise led to the calling of a second conference at Pittsburgh on

August 21, 1792. In addition to Bradford, Marshall, and Cook, a number of other prominent men appeared, among them John Canon, Benjamin Parkinson, and John Hamilton, all of Washington County, and Albert Gallatin and John Smilie of Fayette. The townspeople of Pittsburgh, it was said, would have nothing to do with the meeting. Canon was elected chairman and Gallatin secretary. Committees of correspondence were appointed, a remonstrance to Congress was ordered to be drawn up, and a strong resolution against excise officers was adopted. "Resolved, therefore," it read, "that in future we will consider such persons as unworthy of our friendship; have no intercourse or dealings with them; withdraw from them every assistance . . . and upon all occasions treat them with that contempt they deserve; and that it be, and it is hereby most earnestly recommended to the people at large to follow the same line of conduct towards them."[20]

The actions of the conference and particularly the resolution quoted raised a storm of protest in the East, even among the very men who twenty years before had been signing very similar resolves. On September 15 Washington felt constrained to issue a counterblast (which, incidentally, also bore the signature of Jefferson) warning the malcontents to "desist from all unlawful combinations and proceedings whatsoever, having for object or tending to obstruct the operation of the laws." Brackenridge, who had declined a seat as a delegate in the meeting, was of the opinion that the resolutions were not treasonable but were "the last step short of using actual force." Even the cautious Gallatin was to see the day when he would refer to his signing of the resolves as his "only political sin" and declare with relief that he had not been their author. Gallatin also pointed out that the members of the conference were not in reality delegates, but had attended of their own volition, so their sins could not be laid to the people. In this he was right, but the very respectability of the assembly was indicative of popular opinion in the region. The undercurrent of feeling must have been running strong if the cautious and solid leaders of the community, with property and reputations to lose, were willing to come out so boldly. Such men as Neville blamed them for blowing upon the embers of revolt; Brackenridge asserted that already it would have been "difficult to add to the heat or flame of it."[21]

An immediate result of the second Pittsburgh meeting and of the Faulkner riot was the sending of George Clymer to western Pennsylvania by the secretary of the treasury. Clymer, who was supervisor of the Pennsylvania district, was to accomplish several objects; notably, to make a report on the general state of the fourth survey, to encourage the excise officials and guarantee them indemnification for any property destroyed, to use his influence with the leaders of opinion in Allegheny County to win their support for the law, and to collect evidence concerning the second Pittsburgh meeting and the Faulkner riot in Washington County.

The journey was undertaken with great caution, not to say secrecy, and the anti-Federalists found much amusement in spreading the details, and no doubt manufacturing many of them to suit the occasion. The *Pittsburgh Gazette* printed a humorous version of Clymer's adventures in the West, which was reprinted in the *National Gazette* and other Philadelphia papers. The story was that Clymer had traveled to Pittsburgh under an assumed name and put up for the first night there at the Indian Queen. He spent the next day with General Wayne, who was then quartered on the edge of the town, and returned late at night with the general for escort. It so happened that the taproom of the tavern was occupied by several officers outside the camp against orders. When the word came that Wayne was approaching, they left in such haste that chairs and tables were overturned in their flight. Clymer, hearing the uproar, feared that "a banditti" had come for him, and he and the general retreated precipitately.

Clymer's official report stated that soon after he reached Pittsburgh he called together the influential men of the town and disclosed his business. They, said Clymer, asserted that Pittsburgh had not been represented in the recent meeting convened to protest against the excise and that they were not in sympathy with its program. Clymer replied that it looked otherwise to the world and suggested a public disavowal, but the Pittsburghers demurred. He then sent for John Canon, the chairman of the conference, and painted the situation so dark that Canon was almost frightened into a disavowal. Canon was "not a man of the strongest mind," according to Clymer, but the latter expected his disaffection would weaken the opposition. Clymer decided that going to Washington to collect evidence on the Faulkner case was too dangerous, so he wrote to Addison and asked him to take the depositions of certain persons regarding the case. Addison, who was a stickler for judicial dignity and moreover was in a delicate situation because of his approval of the excise, was unwilling to be made a cat's-paw for the performance of duties not a part of the judicial office. In reply to Clymer's letter he refused to fulfill the request, reiterated his belief that the federal judicial system was a menace to the independence of the state courts, and suggested that if Clymer was afraid to come to Washington alone some Washington members of the Pittsburgh conference would soon be making the journey and he (Clymer) could come with them. These blunt declarations only made Addison's situation worse by adding Clymer to the roster of his enemies.

The supervisor's departure under a cavalry escort furnished by Wayne was the finishing touch to what the Monongahela country was disposed to regard as a comedy of errors. Even the staid Addision polished off some verses ridiculing Clymer and gave them to John Scull for anonymous insertion in the *Pittsburgh Gazette,* but Brackenridge, who usually received the blame for anonymous verses, persuaded Scull to withhold them. When the humorous account of Clymer's travels already referred to appeared, Clymer answered with some intemperate aspersions against the Monongahela country. These were rebutted by "Monongahela," possibly William Findley. The net result after the laughter had died down, probably was, as "Monongahela" claimed, that Clymer had done "more to defeat the execution of the excise law, and irritate the people against it than the Pittsburgh committee with all their resolves."[22]

Clymer's report to his superiors had very little good to say of the fourth survey. Neville probably furnished most of the information contained in it, for Clymer certainly did not wander very far afield in prosecuting his inquiries. Washington was characterized as the worst county with relation to the excise law, Bradford and Marshall were named as the ring-leaders in the opposition, and it was asserted that the clergy and the justices of the peace were coöperating with them. Fayette County was more moderate, more because of lack of occasion for violence than from any good will. Gallatin and Smilie were the leaders there. Westmoreland County had not joined generally in the association against the excise because of the canniness of Findley, "the father of all the disturbances of the Western Country," who wished to save his own character. Petitions had been circulated, instead, and signed individually. Excise officers, however, were subject to violence there as elsewhere. Allegheny, "afraid to run counter to the general spirit," had taken no decisive part. Bedford was better disposed to the law than any of the rest, though poorer and more thinly settled.

Nearly the whole survey, Clymer reported, was disaffected

toward the federal government, because of the machinations of Findley and Smilie. "Individuals there are, undoubtedly, who think rightly, but all their men of distinction who think rightly are either sordid shopkeepers, crafty lawyers or candidates for office, not inclined to make personal sacrifices to truth or honour.—There is besides no small reason to suspect an infusion of state jealousy. It may be said, too, in general, that the duties of citizenship are but poorly understood, or regarded when the moral sense is so greatly depraved as it is in this country, by the intemperate use of the favourite drink—He must be inattentive indeed who does not make this observation."[23]

Presley Neville stated that the second Pittsburgh conference resulted immediately in the growth and expression of a disrespectful attitude toward the excise officers, particularly toward his father. June, 1793, was enlivened with an illustration of the truth of this statement when Presley, attending as inspector-general a militia muster at the mouth of the Youghiogheny, witnessed the burning of his father in effigy.[24]

Fayette County did not keep its spotless record very long. The official who most frequently suffered from the ill will of the mob was Benjamin Wells, collector for Fayette and Westmoreland counties. He either had an offensive personality or was guilty of venality, for even those in his district who were inclined to accede to the law objected to having dealings with him. So marked was this antipathy that upon the first day appointed for assessing at Uniontown he did not dare to appear, and those who came to enter their stills went away without accomplishing their object—doubtless very much disappointed.

The number of riots in which Wells figured as the center of attention is not certain. Fortunately for him, he was absent during an attack on his home in Fayette County in April, 1793, but his house was broken into and his family was threatened.

The Beginning of Direct Action

On the twenty-second of the next November Wells's house was again attacked; six men, their faces blackened and partly covered by handkerchiefs, were the assailants. This time Wells was at home and was forced to surrender his commission and account books and to agree to publish his resignation within two weeks or have his house burned. Wells claimed that he recognized John Smilie's son as one of the group. Efforts to identify and arrest the rioters were fruitless, and President Washington three months later tried to enliven the hunt by offering a reward of two hundred dollars for each capture of an assailant. The collector, meanwhile, held on to his office.[25]

In spite of Fayette's intransigence, 1793 was quieter than the preceding year. Even in that county several processes were served against distillers who had failed to enter their stills, and they appeared at Philadelphia. Hamilton, himself, stated that the spirit of obedience to the laws appeared to be gaining ground during the latter part of the year, and he attributed the setback of 1794 to a deliberate plot on the part of the opponents of the excise.[26]

This accusation points directly to the Democratic societies and necessarily brings in the progress of events in the East. Already in January, 1793, the reader of the gazettes could hear the premonitory rumbles of the coming frenzy for ideas and things French, but it was nothing to the storm that broke over the country with the landing of Genêt in Charleston. His slow, well calculated journey northward through the stronghold of democracy sent before him one of those waves of popular sentiment to which the cold Anglo-Saxon is fallaciously supposed to be immune. Almost overnight the country broke into a pox of pro-French fervor. Banquets, parades, bonfires, the thunder of cannon, floods of rum, and torrents of oratory filled the hours of day and night. There was a fanfaronade against kings and monocrats and many toasts were drunk to hands across the sea. Patriots from Atticus to Zeno rose from the dead and filled the papers with stilted iambics and lurid diatribes. The argus of liberty warned of chambered wantonness, the eagle of freedom struck down the vulture of corruption, and the sons of republicanism banded themselves together to prepare for the fatal hour of strife. French phrases became the rage and even the southern planter was quoted as addressing his slave, "Citizen Pompey, clean my boots."

This was not all sound and fury. Privateers were being armed at American ports and were bringing in British prizes. Bodies of troops were being raised to attack Canada, Louisiana, and Florida. The very children of Philadelphia ran riot in a spasm of Francophile enthusiasm, while their elders ranged the streets in mobs seeking for emblems of royalty they could destroy. The staid John Adams was to write years later that "ten thousand people in the streets of Philadelphia, day after day, threatened to drag Washington out of his house, and effect a revolution in the government, or compel it to declare war in favor of the French revolution and against England. The coolest and the firmest minds, even among the Quakers in Philadelphia, have given their opinions to me, that nothing but the yellow fever, which removed Dr. Hutchinson and Jonathan Dickenson Sergeant from this world, could have saved the United States from a fatal revolution of government."[27]

It was at the beginning of these events that Democratic clubs had their rise. The German "Republicans" of Philadelphia organized even before the coming of Genêt to the city, and that person upon his arrival a few weeks later baptized the "Democratic Society of Pennsylvania." This body provided for the organization of county "meetings" within the state and called upon like minded citizens all over the country to "erect the temple of LIBERTY on the ruins of *palaces and thrones*."[28]

The Beginning of Direct Action

"Demoniacal clubs," as the Federalists loved to call them, sprang up from Maine to Georgia, and the government and the public were bombarded with a barrage of articles, resolutions, and addresses against titles, levees, high salaries, the keeping of birthdays, unduly large governmental debts, political corruption, and most of all the hated doctrine that government administration was the business only of government officials. Without minimizing the absurdity of their Francophile maunderings and the intemperance of much that was said and written, it may yet be claimed that these democratic societies were important as the promoters of the new philosophy of the right and duty of the citizen to take an unceasing share in his government and provided a wholesome check to monarchic tendencies in the United States.[29]

There has always existed among the advocates of things as they are a curious impression—undoubtedly sincere—that those who wish to change conditions are possessed by the desire because they are lazy and shiftless, or envious of those who sit in high places, or because they take a psychopathic delight in hurling monkey wrenches into civilization's machinery— or, as the King James version would express it, because they are "possessed of the devil." The British had not yet given over their pious fulminations against the Americans' vicious upsetting of the divine scheme of creation, before the rebels in turn found their new authority challenged. The humorless indignation with which the erstwhile rebels viewed this development is not without its amusing side. It is hard to understand how Hamilton and his henchmen could escape feeling a little ridiculous as, frothing at the mouth, they called down the vengeance of heaven upon the archrebels who, in outrageous defiance of every law of God and man, persisted in opposition to the most glorious constitution ever struck off by the hand of man and to the all-wise administration set up as the result of the adoption of that immortal document.

The "Father of his Country" was a confirmed opponent of the societies and a comment of his will serve as an example of the manner in which the Federalists denounced them: "That these societies were instituted by the *artful and designing* members . . . primarily to sow the seeds of jealousy and distrust among the people of the government, by destroying all confidence in the administration of it . . . is not new to any one who . . . has been attentive to their manœuvres. I early gave it as my opinion to the confidential characters around me, that, if these societies were not counteracted . . . they would shake the government to its foundation."[30]

The modern belief that an opposition party has a useful function to perform was certainly not popular with the Federalists of 1794. Contributors to the newspapers often lacked the temperateness of Washington and it was probably to ridicule them that "the gentle Xantippe" wrote a letter purporting to remonstrate with the citizens of Kentucky for harboring a Democratic society:—"that horrible sink of treason—that hateful synagogue of anarchy—that odious conclave of tumult —that frightful cathedral of discord—that poisonous garden of conspiracy—and that hellish school of rebellion and opposition to all regular and well balanced authority. Here then is the source from whence all your sedition flows, and until those crotalophorus and ostentiferous institutions are disconcatinated—and the individuals who compose them experience a decollation, their querulous bombilations and debulitions will never cease to obnubilate the prospects of their superiors."[31]

The program of the Democratic societies was by no means new to the West. Hardly an item of their social and political program not the product of the situation but had been popular in that region since the first pioneers had followed the setting sun beyond the limits of the tidewater settlements. It is no wonder that the westerners, well nigh disheartened by the indifference of the East to their plight, took courage at these indications of a revival of political consciousness across the mountains. The rage for things and phrases French spread over the Alleghenies. Brackenridge blossomed forth in the *National Gazette* of April 20, 1793, with an article beginning "Louis Capet has lost his caput. From my use of a pun, it may seem that I think lightly of his fate. I certainly do. It affects me no more than the execution of another malefactor." In spite of this seeming savagery, the moderation of the West in following the lead of the eastern *sans-cullottes* in 1793 should have filled Alexander Hamilton with gratitude as he wrestled with the knotty problem of nipping the revolution budding in his own front yard.

The strongest of the Monongahela country's societies was the one in the Mingo Creek settlement established February 28, 1794, probably on the foundations of the association that had dealt with Faulkner. Brackenridge has left the only surviving account of this society's organization, and he says flatly that it was the cradle of the insurrection in as much as it fostered the contempt for law and the exaggerated ideas of liberty that brought on the trouble. The founders of the society were actuated by several motives. Some had been disappointed in their search for public office, others wished to use it as a means of influencing elections, and some merely desired to make themselves conspicuous. Some members saw in it an escape from the expensive processes of civil courts, and it actually took upon itself jurisdiction in cases between members. The secretary of the society, John McDonald, explained that since the people were so "outrageous to do something" about the excise laws and the costs of government and had talked of attacking Neville and burning Pittsburgh, the institution of a society was conceived by the more moderate as a means of confining their activities to discussion. The place where the sessions were held was usually the Mingo meetinghouse, south of the present village of Finleyville, and it was said that the attendance was sometimes as much as three hundred.

Brackenridge thus describes the constitution of the society: "It was . . . to be governed by a president and council. The council to consist of members chosen every six months, by the people of the several captain's districts . . . The society to meet the first day of every month; to keep a journal of its proceedings; the secretary and deputies to be rewarded at the discretion of the society; the *president, council, and deputies, for any speech or debate in the society, not to be questioned in any other place.* No person holding an office of trust or profit under the state, or United States, to be a president, &c. The societies . . . *to hear and determine all matters in variance, and disputes between party and party;* encourage teachers of schools; *introduce the Bible and religious books into schools;* to encourage the industrious, and the man of merit. . . . no district citizen to sue, or cause to be sued before a single justice of the peace, or any court of justice, a citizen of the district, before applying to the society for redress, *unless the business will not admit of delay;* the president not to be under 25 years, and to be elected by ballot . . . *Nothing in this constitution to be so construed, as to prejudice any claims of the state, or United States.* The constitution to be amendable by a convention called for that purpose."[82]

Only one other Democratic society seems to have functioned in the fourth survey. This was the one at Washington, formed probably in March, 1794, with James Marshall as president, David Bradford as vice president, and other prominent and respectable citizens among its officers and on its corresponding committee. Probably it was a chapter or "meeting" of the Democratic Society of Pennsylvania, as its complete name was given as the "Democratic Society of the County of Washington in Pennsylvania." It was said to have been in correspondence with the Democratic societies in Philadelphia and New York, and surviving fragments of correspondence show that it was in touch with the Democratic Society of Kentucky. The address of the latter, *To the inhabitants of the United States, west of the Allegany and Apalachian mountains,* which was devoted to the demand for the opening of navigation of the Mississippi and which brought in the "odious and oppressive excise" only incidentally, was nevertheless approved by the Democratic Society of Washington "so earnest were a Majority to remonstrate before the present session of Congress would rise, and others in order to convince the people of Kentuckey that we feel ourselves the same people with them in many of the most important political considerations." Copies of the approving resolution were sent to President Washington and to William Irvine, a Pennsylvania member of the House of Representatives. A correspondence was begun between the two societies, but there is no indication as to how extensive it became.[33]

The only surviving resolves of the Washington Democratic Society are to be found in current newspapers. Those of June 23, 1794, began, "Resolved, that on reviewing the conduct of the executive of the United States we are under the painful necessity of censuring in sundry particulars." The bill of particulars that followed had nothing to do with the excise, but showed a keen interest in the country's diplomatic affairs. The administration was censured for remaining neutral in the war between France and England, for not pressing the spoliation claims against England to a successful conclusion, for carrying on secret negotiations, and last—a little nearer home—for preventing the laying out of a town at Presque Isle. The Democratic Society of Kentucky concurred in these resolutions.[34]

The *Pittsburgh Gazette* of April 26, 1794, gives a brief notice of an attempt to widen the Democratic society organization in the fourth survey: "At a meeting of a society from the four counties at the house of Samuel Sinclair, at the mouth of Yough, April 15, 1794. . . . Resolved, That the following be proposed as a constitution for forming a Republican Society, in each colonel's district throughout the four counties." This may have meant that there were "meetings" of the Democratic Society of Pennsylvania in each of the four western counties, but it is scarcely likely that such organizations could have existed in three of the counties without leaving any trace. A movement that may have been allied with the Democratic societies resulted in the holding in Pittsburgh on April 19 of a convention of delegates of the election districts of Allegheny County. A long report was adopted censuring the federal administration for its handling of national affairs, and closing on a distinctly threatening note: "We have observed with great pain that our councils want the integrity of spirit of republicans. This we attribute to the pernicious influence of stockholders or their subordinates; and our minds feel this with so much indignity, that we are almost ready to wish for a state of revolution and the guillotine of France for a short space in order to inflict punishment on the miscreants that enervate and disgrace our government."[35]

It was sometimes difficult to obtain revenue officers of ability and good reputation. General Neville possessed both, but Robert Johnson, the collector for Allegheny and Washington counties, though honest, was possessed of little force of character, and Benjamin Wells, collector for Fayette and Westmoreland, was judged by some to be despicable and untrustworthy. Neville evidently felt that he came in for a share of contumely. It was the custom for the presiding judge of a court to invite persons of "respectability" within the bar, but the inspector complained, unmindful of Addison's delicate position, that he, pointedly, was not invited within the bar, but that three others, including his son Presley, were.[36] According to Findley, Bedford County had valid grounds for complaint against its collector, John Webster. He had been in the habit of seizing liquor on the road from poor people who were taking it to barter for their necessities. Occasionally he merely collected the tax, but usually he kept all the liquor and in addition he sometimes detained the horses, returning them after some delay, ostensibly as a matter of favor. On the other hand, he avoided troubling the distillers who had influence or money and even pointedly ignored their breach of the law when they called at his tavern with illegal freight. He was also accused of withholding his receipts from the government. Complaint was made to the proper authority but nothing came of it, and Webster continued with his oppression.[37]

There were a number of seizures of whiskey in the four western counties, some of them leading to bad blood amongst neighbors. The air was thick with recriminations and the newspapers were studded with affidavits as men sought to pin on one another the blame for supporting the unpopular cause. Andrew Boggs of Washington County appealed to Neville to exculpate him of ever having sought a revenue office. Neville complied, printing his statement in the *Pittsburgh Gazette* and ending it with these words: "Nor can I conceive how his neighbors could charge him with a thing never thought of by me, unless they judged from his honesty and integrity, that he was a proper person to fill such an office; besides, there is officers already sufficient for that county, unless the people would get better tempered, which I hope will soon be the case."[38]

Neville had reason to complain of the temper of the people. In Allegheny County January had been signalized by several outrages. William Richmond, who had been one of the witnesses kidnapped to prevent the prosecution of the Wilson case, and Robert Shawhan had their barns burned, together with their hay and grain.[39] These seem to have been the first examples of direct action against those complying with the law as distinguished from revenue officers and those who had rented their houses for revenue service. The result was an intensification of the fear felt by distillers who had a mind to submit to the law.

The movement for compliance was strongest among the more important distillers, or, as it was commonly expressed, among those who were "influential" and "respectable." They saw that success in resisting the excise might result in similar treatment of other laws, and as men of property the stand their interest demanded was clear. There was also to be considered the fact that the law was squeezing the small distillers out of business, another reason for compliance on the part of the large distillers. The army contractor, moreover, was buying only legal liquor, and the distillers wanted the cash he would pay. Possibly as a sop to the smaller fry and possibly as a move toward saving their faces, it was agreed by the large distillers that efforts should be made to place good men in office in exchange for a general submission to the law. In March, 1794, during the Fayette County court, the chief opponents of the excise in that county, meeting at dinner in a tavern, proposed that they would submit to the law if Wells were displaced and an honest and reputable collector put in his stead. Wells, himself, quoted Addison as strongly condemning the law as unjust, inequitable, unnecessary and useless and as threatening to leave the tavern if he (Wells) were allowed to stay there. Findley, on the authority of James Ross, who was present, stated that the meeting aimed at the removal of all the excise officers of the survey and the substitution of reputable men.

Findley, when approached by Ross and asked to name acceptable men who would take offices, made excuses for refusing. He had had experience under the state excise and did not propose to get his fingers burned again. He probably foresaw a wave of resentment on the part of the small distillers, though instead of saying "small distillers" he actually set down "obstinate and undiscerning" distillers. The Fayette meeting, at any rate, was a turning point in the development of resistance to the excise in the Monongahela country. Thereafter the "influential" and "respectable" elements were at least secretly for the law, while the small fry, seeing themselves abandoned to the tender mercies of the federal government, began to rely more openly upon violence.[40]

General Neville, during the first part of March, had a foretaste of what was to come later. One Saturday evening as he and his wife with their granddaughter, Harriet Craig, were returning home from Pittsburgh, the girth on Mrs. Neville's horse became loosened and Neville dismounted on the side of a hill to tighten it. While he was engaged in this two men overtook them and went on up the hill, then a man and a woman came up. The man stopped and asked if he were General Neville. Receiving an affirmative answer, he said "I must give you a whipping" and sprang down from his horse and seized Neville by the hair and throat. The inspector succeeded in breaking the grip of his assailant and knocked him down; then, fearing that his cries would recall the two men who had passed, Neville seized the prostrate man by the throat. At this the man begged that he be spared, and the woman pleaded so piteously that finally Neville released him. By this time he had recognized his assailant as a certain Jacob Long.

About the time of this attack Neville heard that there were threats being made of tarring and feathering William Coughran, a distiller who lived near the boundary of Allegheny and Washington counties, and that some were asserting that within three weeks no complier with the excise law in Allegheny

County would have his home left standing. Neville and Johnson rode out to investigate these rumors and to call upon certain "obstinate" distillers. On their return they were pursued by a party of sixty, who, failing to come up with their intended victims, stopped at the home of a distiller named James Kiddoe, who had recently complied with the law, riddled his still with bullets, and tried to set fire to his stillhouse. There was a persistent rumor that the militia were planning an attack on Neville, and he wrote to Clymer that he was keeping candles burning all night and his negroes always armed to repel attack.[41]

Opposition ran so high that some of the Westmoreland distillers, fearing attacks from the radicals, appealed to Findley for advice as to whether or not the government intended to enforce the law and protect those who obeyed it. It was probably as a result of this application, though Findley does not say so in his *History of the Insurrection,* that thirty of the people of Westmoreland, with William Findley at their head, petitioned General Jack of that county's militia to embody "associations" among them for self-defense as well as to enlist a corps of volunteers from the militia to "assist in Suppressing Riots and traitorous designs."[42]

In May or June the same James Kiddoe who had had his stillhouse fired had parts of his gristmill carried away, and at about the same time William Coughran's still was shot full of holes, his gristmill badly damaged, and the saw from his sawmill stolen.[43] It was at the last named outrage that John Holcroft, a leader of the rioters, humorously referred to the process of shooting holes into the still as "mending" the still. From this he coined the expression of "Tom the Tinker's men," which he applied to the rioters, and the term within a few days became the popular name for opponents of the excise who resorted to violent action against their neighbors' stills.

Papers signed "Tom the Tinker" presently began to appear, posted in conspicuous places here and there. Some of them warned individuals to be more circumspect in supporting the law and others sought to recommend general measures for the guidance of those opposed to the law. Holcroft was reputed to be their author, and, though, after the coming of the army, he vigorously denied the truth of the allegation, the tradition sticks to this day.[44]

At about the time that Tom the Tinker became prominent the radicals began to revive the Revolutionary custom of erecting liberty poles. It is difficult to say now what was the origin of the custom, whether in the maypoles of England, the war standards of the European continent, or the totems of the American Indians. At any rate, it was well understood in the United States that the raising of a liberty pole was a call for popular rising against tyranny. The poles often bore streamers with inscriptions or devices, such as a snake divided and the words "United we stand, divided we fall."[45]

The month of June was specified by the law as the time when all stills were to be entered, and it was provided that each county should have at least one office of inspection. Neville advertised in good time the names of the collectors and the places for entry. John Webster, on Stony Creek, acted for Bedford County; Philip Reagan, for Westmoreland; Robert Johnson at the house of John Lynn in Canonsburg, for Washington; and Benjamin Wells at Stewart's Crossings, for Fayette. Neville himself acted for Allegheny County "in my house on Charties Creek, and on every Friday, at the Brick Redoubt in Pittsburgh." The object of Tom the Tinker was to force the closure of these offices, thus making it impossible for the distillers to comply with the law.[46]

John Lynn, deputy collector for Washington County, was marked off the list when a party of men broke into his house, seized him, and took him to the woods, where they cut off his hair and gave him a coat of tar and feathers. He was forced to swear never to reveal the names of his assailants nor to permit an excise office in his house. He was left tied to a tree until morning, when he succeeded in extricating himself and returned home. After scrubbing himself with grease, soap, and sand he "exhibited himself to the boys in the Academy and others, and laughed and made sport of the whole matter." A few days later his house was attacked again and partly pulled down, and Lynn was forced "to find an asylum elsewhere." Robert Johnson, who had been initiated into the same mysteries three years earlier, was forced to admit that there was no office of inspection in Washington County, but he advertised that stills could be entered in the other counties. Neville wrote Clymer that Abraham Singhorse and Craig Ritchie, prominent men of Canonsburg, were movers of the attack on Lynn. Several attacks were made upon Reagan during the month, but were successfully withstood by Reagan and John Wells, son of Benjamin Wells, a deputy collector. In Allegheny County Neville admitted on June 20 that not a still had as yet been entered.[47]

Pennsylvania's opposition to the federal excise was not confined to the western section, though resistance never took so violent a form elsewhere. Much of the back country of the state was Antifederalist, accepting the government as it was because it had to. At a barbecue in Cumberland County in the summer of 1793 Oliver Pollock neatly expressed this attitude in a toast: "The Officers of the Executive and Judiciary departments of the United States, may they never be worse than they are."[48] Evasions of excise payments were common; the evaders salved their consciences with the argument that if they paid the tax they could not afford to remain in business. The *Oracle of Dauphin* of Harrisburg and the *Carlisle Gazette*, the leading papers of mid-Pennsylvania, found space for diatribes on both sides of the excise issue, and in fact, if one could judge by the newspapers alone, the issue was more alive there than in the Monongahela country. The period of greatest popular activity in the Susquehanna country, however, did not dawn until after the violent opposition in the West had given the example.[49]

Fisher Ames, high Federalist of Massachusetts, stated that the views of the whiskey rebels "had tainted a vast extent of the country beside Pennsylvania." A contributor to the *Oracle of Dauphin* wrote that "if any person travels from north to south on this continent" through the back country "every individual . . . will tell him, (a few expectants excepted), that the excise law is disagreeable." In Ohio County, Virginia, now the northern panhandle of West Virginia, the opposition followed the lead of the rioters of adjacent Washington County, Pennsylvania, and forced distillers to ignore the law.[50] Kentucky was opposed to the excise along with the remainder of the West, but offered no violent opposition.

The backwoods of Georgia and the Carolinas, on the other hand, could not look to the opening up of navigation as a solution to their problems even as much as could the Monongahela country. As James Jackson had pointed out in Congress, liquor was considered a necessity in the southern hinterland, and the absence of orchards and of a knowledge of the art of brewing made whiskey the only resort. Hamilton reported to Washington in September, 1792, that, not only in the four western counties of Pennsylvania but also in a great part of North Carolina, the excise had "never been in any degree submitted to." In May, 1794, Tench Coxe reported that, as a result of opposition to the law in Kentucky and in the two western surveys of South Carolina, revenue reports from these sections were fragmentary. In Pennsylvania the law had been so effectively evaded that the supervisor had been unable to make a report for two years.[51]

Why was it that the most serious outbreaks of violence against the excise occurred in the Monongahela country of Pennsylvania when the law was almost if not fully as oppressive to several other sections of the hinterland of the United States? The answer to this question must be advanced with diffidence in the face of what is admittedly an imperfect knowledge of the political, social, and economic crosscurrents of the West of the 1790's. Even if this question is answered there remains the problem of why Washington County led the remainder of the fourth survey in the violence of its opposition.

Southwestern Pennsylvania was at this time the oldest of the western settlements and the most populous; it contained in 1790 almost seventy-seven thousand people. The population was, for those days, fairly compact and permanent and for the most part agricultural, and the insurrection was essentially an agrarian movement. Nevertheless there was a rising commercial and industrial class, which was opposed to the uprising. Alexander Addison, reasoning from the viewpoint that the welfare of that class promoted the welfare of all, argued that the increasing wealth of the region made vigorous protest untimely. The small farmers could not see the logic of his argument. Perhaps wealth was on the increase, they admitted, but they felt themselves shut out from partaking of its benefits. It looked to them as though the rising commercial and industrial class was allied with the federal government to crush out the small entrepreneur and to cut off the farmers' only source of income. Confronted by this and other injustices, the farmer was moved to revolt and naturally struck at the most tangible evidence of what he regarded as oppression.

The economic factor, however, cannot be regarded as an irresistible urge to revolt. The Germans did not revolt, though there is no reason why they should have felt oppressive conditions less than their neighbors, or why, in spite of their reputedly superior thrift and industry, their produce could have found its way to market any more easily and so guaranteed them a larger income. It is worthy of note that Washington County, where the controversy was most acute, had the fewest Germans, while as one advanced eastward to Bedford and Westmoreland the stolid and conservative German element became increasingly prominent. The political control of the region was vested largely in the English-speaking people, and the Germans, who were not yet being educated in English, could take little share in political life as it was then carried on. As a consequence the Germans distrusted their Scotch-Irish and English neighbors, and this resulted in a tendency on their part to hold back from any activity in which these neighbors might be engaged, particularly any perilous opposition to government. It is a remarkable fact that out of a list of over one hundred names of men comprising all who are known to have been connected with the opposition to the excise or reputed to have been active against it, the recognizably German names do not amount to a half dozen.

The distillation of domestic materials was comparatively more important in the Monongahela country than in any other region. Probably twelve or thirteen hundred, or about twenty-five per cent of the stills engaged in this business in the United States about 1794, were located in Pennsylvania's fourth survey. If later averages held true at this period ten per cent of the total must have been within the confines of Washington County alone. Even allowing for the fact that the number of stills is not a certain indication of volume of production, these figures still have their significance. The more stills there were in a community, even though they were small, the greater would be the opposition to the excise, if other conditions contributed to accentuate this opposition, as they did in the Monongahela country.[52]

The existence of Democratic societies in Washington County is undoubtedly connected with the virulence of the resistance there, not as an original cause, but as the result of a prior state of mind and then as a contributing cause. The fact that the overt acts of the insurrection were planned and carried out by members of the Mingo Creek or Washington societies is significant. Why, then, was there no revolt in Kentucky, where the Democratic societies were strong? It was, perhaps, because in that state the excise issue was sublimated to the overwhelming demand for the opening of the Mississippi. Kentuckians saw in the prospective attainment of that goal a panacea for all their ills, a speedy and certain means of obtaining a flood of cash that would make the payment of the excise a picayunish matter.

But there were Democratic societies in western Virginia, and where these did not exist there were certainly Antifederalist principles that would make the excise obnoxious whether or not it was oppressive. True enough, but population there was sparsely scattered through a mountainous region and moreover was probably transitory to a large extent. The people could make their whiskey free from interference from revenue officers, or could easily pack up and journey westward. Where these conditions did not obtain, as in the Shenandoah Valley, there were in August and September, 1794, sporadic outbreaks against the excise, but these were easily subdued. No doubt there, as in western Pennsylvania, the small distiller either went out of business or retreated to the mountain fastnesses and became the forerunner of the moonshiner.

Why did not the optimism that manifested itself in Kentucky find a place in western Pennsylvania? As a matter of fact it did, and this is probably one of the factors that prevented the outbreak from becoming more serious. Although Pittsburgh was six hundred miles above Louisville, it had visions of an important trade with New Orleans and vigorously supported the movement for the opening of the Mississippi. The Federalists and most of the other leading men of the Monongahela country had faith that this dream would come true and were unwilling to go beyond the holding of conferences and the emission of petitions and addresses in their support of the interests of the West, especially as drastic action was likely to take them out of the frying pan only to land them in the fire. The common people, on the other hand, confronted by what seemed certain ruin if the excise were enforced, were not willing to wait. The accident of a shot fired from a wheat field at a revenue officer and a marshall and of a militia muster being held on the same day led to the taking of a last desperate step. It is questionable, however, if this should be regarded as more than an attempt to bluff the federal government. The hesitant pauses between the overt acts, the long-winded conferences, and the weakness of the measures adopted should be evidence of this, and it cannot be doubted by anyone familiar with the circumstances that the movement if left to itself would finally have died away for lack of driving power. The leaders, if they can be called such, were popularity seekers like David Bradford, or hotheaded and irresponsible men of the people like Daniel Hamilton and Benjamin Parkinson. It was unfortunate that the Democratic societies existed to coördinate in some measure this unreasoning movement, else what is now known as the "Whiskey Insurrection" would probably never have occurred.

Chapter v: *Bower Hill*

THE opposition of the western Pennsylvanians to trial in Philadelphia for breach of the federal excise law appeared so reasonable that finally on April 4, 1794, upon the recommendation of Alexander Hamilton, a bill was introduced into the House of Representatives making such cases cognizable by state courts when they arose in places more than fifty miles from the seat of a United States district court. The bill passed both houses in final form on June 3 and was signed by the president on June 5. The progress of the bill must have been followed with interest in the West, as Hamilton himself suggested, and no doubt there were hopes on the part of law-abiding citizens that it would, by removing one of the chief objections to the excise, make it easier for the discontented elements to submit.[1]

Hamilton's report on August 5 expressed his conviction that the imminent passage of the easing measure had prompted the western recalcitrants to "bring matters to a violent crisis." He studiously avoided, however, mentioning in his report one essential fact—that the processes, the serving of which brought on the acute phase of the insurrection, were issued, not under the amended law, but under the old one, and were returnable to Philadelphia. It was this fact that formed the nub of the western argument that Hamilton "contemplated and planned to promote the violent crisis which took place." The evidence is purely circumstantial, but it deserves a hearing. The United States district court at Philadelphia issued on May 31, while the easing law was in Congress, seventy-five processes against distillers who had not registered in June, 1793, and at least sixty-one of these processes were against distillers in the fourth survey. These writs were entered in the docket on May 31, but were *not served until July,* several weeks after the new law had been approved.[2]

Tom the Tinker's argument now becomes clear. If Hamilton was desirous of promoting the peace and easing the burden on the West, surely he could have waited for the new law before making out processes for offenses nearly a year old, especially since they were not to be served until July. The imprint of the cloven hoof of the secretary of the treasury seemed to Tom to appear quite clearly in the whole business. Even today, though there is no conclusive evidence that Hamilton inspired the issuance of the processes under the old law, his ability to keep an ubiquitous finger in all governmental pies lends an air of suspicion to the circumstances. Why, moreover, did he allow the false impression to exist that the resistance in the West was to processes served under the new law, if he did not intend to promote the opinion that the western intransigents must be put down by an army? This view is given color by Hamilton's admission to Washington, September 1, 1792, that it might be necessary "if the processes of the courts are resisted, as is rather to be expected, to employ those means which in the last resort are put in the power of the Executive."

Washington, himself, even as early as 1792, was not ignorant of the possible consequences of the enforcement of the excise law. "I have no doubt," he wrote to Hamilton, "but that the proclamation will undergo many strictures; and, as the effect proposed may not be answered by it, it will be necessary to look forward in time to ulterior arrangements. And here not only the constitution and laws must strictly govern, but the employing of the regular troops avoided, if it be possible to effect order without their aid; otherwise there would be a cry at once, 'The cat is let out; we now see for what purpose an army was raised.' Yet, if no other means will effectually answer, and the constitution and the laws will authorize these, they must be used as the dernier resort."

William Findley, who as a leader of the stubborn opposition party gained Hamilton's hatred for himself and the West, was the foremost advocate of the view that the administration was deliberately trying to create a situation that would excuse the use of an army. Findley asserted that Hamilton had held that "a government could never be considered as established, till its power was put to the test by a trial of its military force." Hamilton's actions in the enforcement of the excise law, moreover, according to Findley, were such as to foster trouble rather than to allay it. Although Findley's charges cannot be said to be proved, it must be admitted that Hamilton's worship of military force and his highhanded and arbitrary, yet at times skillful and effective, methods of dealing with opposition lend presumptive evidence to support the Pennsylvanian's case. Madison is authority for the statement that in October the "fashionable language" in Philadelphia was that the insurrection would "establish the principle that a standing army was necessary for *enforcing the laws*." It is difficult to escape the suspicion that the headstrong leader of the Federalists saw a heaven-sent opportunity to strengthen his régime by proving the necessity of a standing army and at the same time bring into disrepute the windy Democratic societies of the East by attacking their weaker western brethren who had been incautious enough to commit overt acts against the laws.[8]

Bower Hill

United States Marshal David Lenox left Philadelphia June 22 to serve the processes mentioned above. Lenox experienced no difficulty in Cumberland, Bedford, and Fayette counties and served his writs without molestation. On the evening of July 14 in Pittsburgh Lenox was introduced to Brackenridge at the latter's house and expressed his satisfaction that he had met with no insult or injury in the execution of his mission.

The next day Lenox and Neville rode out to serve the four or five remaining writs, all of them apparently in that part of Allegheny that had once belonged to Washington and that was exposed to the influence of the Mingo Creek Democratic Society. Four processes were served within a few hours, and all the recipients, according to Lenox, showed their contempt for the law. At least one of the processes distributed during the morning was served in a harvest field in the midst of a group of reapers. As soon as the officers had left, the news was bruited about the countryside. Since this was in the time of harvest and neighbors were engaged in helping in one another's fields and perhaps were overheated by liberal potations of whiskey, it did not take long for a band of thirty or forty men to get together and decide upon pursuit.

Between eleven and twelve o'clock in the forenoon the marshal and the inspector stopped at William Miller's farm in the Peter's Creek region to serve a process against him. Miller and Kirkpatrick, Neville's brother-in-law, were cousins, and Miller had in the past given his political support to the family. It was a severe shock now to see the general ride up the lane with a strange man and to have the latter unfold a paper and begin to read a summons to set "aside all manner of business and excuses" and appear in his proper person before the judge of the district court of the United States at Philadelphia upon August 12. "I felt myself mad with passion," said Miller afterward. "I thought 250 dollars would ruin me; and to have to go [to] the federal court, at Philadelphia, would keep me from going to Kentucky this fall, after I had sold my plantation, and was getting ready. I felt my blood boil, at seeing general Neville along, to pilot the sheriff to my very door."

Miller refused to receive the writ and Lenox remonstrated with him and pointed out the folly of opposing the law. Just then Neville, who was sitting on his horse in the lane, called to Lenox to hurry, and Miller, looking up, saw a party of men running across the field as though to head off the marshal. Lenox and Neville set off at once, and the pursuers, seeing them in motion, fired a rifle from a distance of forty or fifty yards, Miller thought with the purpose of hitting them. Upon this Lenox reined in and upbraided the men and Neville seconded him, but the rioters "answered in a language peculiar to themselves." Discretion then prevailed over valor and the two men rode on, followed for some distance by the countrymen. Neville turned off to Bower Hill and Lenox went on to Pittsburgh. The latter had served all his processes save one on John Shaw, who lived on the way "down country."[4]

It so happened that on this very day Dr. Absalom Baird of Washington, the brigade inspector of the county militia, was at the Mingo Church to hear appeals from some of the members of the Mingo Creek regiment for exemption from service among the eighty thousand militiamen lately requisitioned by the governor. Suddenly a man appeared, running from the encounter at Miller's, and cried that "the Federal Sheriff was taking away people to Philadelphia." Notice was immediately sent around to the people to assemble, and a considerable number gathered, some of them armed. After some discussion a council was chosen and various proposals were made as to the line of action. Finally it was decided to capture the marshal and bring him to the meeting place and then pass upon what was to be done with him. At the time it was thought that Lenox was at Bower Hill. John Holcroft was chosen to command the expedition and the men were ordered to meet opposition with opposition and, if they were fired upon, to burn or destroy any obstacle that prevented their success. This party was composed of around forty men, only part of them with guns, and they left on their mission about midnight. Another party of eight men under Captain Pearsol was sent to Coal Hill, overlooking Pittsburgh, to intercept the marshal in case he was missed by the main force.[5]

Bower Hill is about half a mile long at the crest and has the shape of a roughly outlined boot sole, the toe pointing a little north of northwest and coming to an abrupt end high over Chartiers Creek. A deep ravine is on each side of the instep, each ravine running to a head in a shallower depression at the back of the heel. Beyond these ravines and the depression rises a half circle of high hills, their crests about half a mile from the summit of Bower Hill and certainly out of range of the pioneer rifles. The heel contains between one and two acres of reasonably level ground and is forty or fifty feet above the rest of the hill.

The mansion was built on the highest part of the heel, and from its veranda one could obtain a splendid view of the Chartiers Valley three hundred feet below and of the beautiful rolling country beyond. Presley Neville's country home, Woodville, was visible beyond the creek through a lane cut through the forest, and the two households had a system of signals by which they could communicate with each other. A road came in from the east and, crossing the instep, continued on down the side of Bower Hill to Woodville. The Bower Hill mansion was a two-story frame house forty feet long and twenty feet wide, painted and papered in the best manner, and neatly furnished. A list of the goods in the house mentions carpets, four looking glasses, a Franklin stove, pictures and prints, an eight-day clock, and china, glass, and silverware. The census of 1790 had enumerated eighteen slaves and several white servants on the estate. On the southwestern verge of the heel were the negro cabins, and up the ravine from them was the distillery. At right angles from this line of buildings were the barns and stables. The outbuildings, therefore, formed a chevron-shaped line with the apex probably pointing south, and they protected the mansion on the southwest and southeast.[6]

Holcroft and his men arrived at Bower Hill about daybreak, Wednesday, July 16; they dismounted and surrounded the house in irregular fashion. Neville at the time had in the house with him his wife, his little granddaughter, Harriet Craig, and a young woman who was visiting the family. He had just arisen as the attackers marched up and, hearing the commotion, he suspected the reason and challenged them. Holcroft claimed he thought the voice was that of the marshal and answered that they were friends from Washington come with a guard for him. Neville, however, ordered them to "stand off" and emphasized the demand with a shot that struck Oliver Miller, probably the father of William Miller, and wounded him so seriously that he later died. The front door of the house was open, but the attackers, fearing the general might have a swivel gun or cannon waiting for their reception, contented themselves with firing into the windows with their rifles. This was kept up for some twenty-five minutes. Neville within the house continued to fire, while the women lay on the floor to escape injury and loaded the guns. According to Neville's account he succeeded, unsupported, in wounding four more attackers and so discouraged them that they finally withdrew. Holcroft's account was that a signal horn blew in the house and the negro slaves from their quarters fired upon the rioters and wounded several, whereupon they retreated.[7]

Sometime later in the day Neville heard that a large body

of men was assembling at Couch's Fort, an old pioneer defense against the Indians about four miles southeast of Bower Hill, in preparation for an attack in force. He immediately dispatched a servant to Pittsburgh with a request to Major Thomas Butler, commandant at Fort Fayette, for a file of soldiers, and to John Gibson and John Wilkins, respectively major general and brigadier general, to call out the militia to suppress the rioters. Gibson and Wilkins, in their capacities as judges, were also asked to support the sheriff in raising a posse. The soldiers came that evening, seventeen in number, but six of them left early the next morning. Meanwhile Major Kirkpatrick had ridden out to join in the defense.

A few hours after the attack a council of the malcontents was held to determine on further measures. One plan, proposed by John Baldwin, an ignorant and violent countryman, that they hire someone to lie in wait and assassinate General Neville, was voted down by the majority. The group then approved the calling of a greater force to meet the next morning at Couch's Fort and take up the problem. The Mingo Creek militia battalion, which was still gathered in part at the church, agreed enthusiastically to go on to the rendezvous.

The discussion was continued at Couch's Fort the next morning while the militia gathered in. It was apparent that Holcroft and his party would be prosecuted unless they were supported by numbers sufficient to force a compromise. It was finally suggested as a solution that the militia march in force to Bower Hill and demand General Neville's resignation as inspector of the revenue, upon which "he would be received as a good citizen and restored to the confidence of the people." Major James McFarlane of the Mingo settlement, who had been an officer in the Revolution, came in from Pittsburgh with the news that the sheriff was raising a posse to oppose them and that soldiers had gone from the garrison to Bower

Hill, but this seemed only to animate the men and it was determined to put the plan in execution. The only considerable opposition came from an aged clergyman, John Clark, pastor of Bethel Presbyterian Church, which was located within a few rods of Couch's Fort, who endeavored vainly to dissuade them from the enterprise.

By this time a force of around five hundred men had gathered, the bulk of them probably from the Mingo settlements but some from Canonsburg. Bradford and Marshall of Washington had been urged to take part in the projected attack, but they declined, the former excusing himself on the ground that he was the state's attorney. A committee was appointed to make arrangements for the march. When John Hamilton, the regular colonel, refused to serve, the command was offered to Benjamin Parkinson of Mingo, but he declined on the ground that he had not had sufficient military experience. It was then accepted by James McFarlane, though shortly afterward he admitted to a friend that upon reflection he had become aware of the rashness of the project but that they had gone too far to retreat.[8]

The march to Bower Hill was completed by five o'clock in the afternoon and the horses were left in charge of some of the unarmed men. The militiamen then drew up around the manor house "with drums and all military pomp and parade." Just before they closed in Neville left the house and concealed himself in a thicket, from which place he was perhaps a witness of the ensuing conflict. McFarlane and his committee took their place on an eminence near the house to direct the siege, but first they agreed to try peaceable methods. David Hamilton was selected to carry on the committee's negotiations and went to the house with a flag of truce. There he was met by Kirkpatrick, who, according to Neville, had been left "to capitulate for the property." Hamilton demanded that Neville come out and give up his commission and was informed that Neville was not there. He went back to the committee and returned with the demand that six citizens be admitted to search for papers. According to Hamilton, this demand was refused and the refusal precipitated the attack. Kirkpatrick, however, claimed that he agreed to permit the house to be searched but that Hamilton returned a third time with the further demand that the soldiers come out and ground arms. This demand, according to Kirkpatrick, he refused, saying that, if the men were not satisfied with the papers, their object must be to destroy the property. Kirkpatrick's claim that he consented to a search for Neville's papers was a point in Alexander Hamilton's contention that the militia was obstinately bent on rebellion, but David Hamilton's version was later supported by witnesses in court. Meanwhile some of the outhouses were set on fire and some shots were fired by the besiegers. Since no compromise could be reached, the women and children were escorted out of the house and in the direction of Woodville, Presley Neville's home.

Firing now became general on both sides. The militiamen must have posted themselves wherever shelter offered around the skirts of the eminence on which the mansion stood, shielding themselves behind trees or crouching below the verge of the hill out of the line of fire. Certainly they could not have been very far from the group of buildings, both because the terrain would not permit it and still allow their fire to be effective and because the outhouses were set on fire. There is no way of knowing where the commanding officers stood, but the logical place would have been toward the east near the road that crossed the depression at the rear of the heel of Bower Hill. The battle had not advanced very far before the fire from the house suddenly ceased. Some accounts have it that a white flag was waved from a window. McFarlane, at any rate, supposed that a truce was desired and stepped from behind the tree that was sheltering him to order his men to cease firing. No sooner had he appeared than a shot struck him in the groin and he fell to the ground and expired almost immediately.

The battle was now resumed, and it is likely that the militia deliberately set fire to several of the auxiliary buildings, especially the negro cabins, from which, so local tradition says, Neville's slaves were assisting in the defense. It was only a matter of time before the house also would catch fire, so Kirkpatrick decided to come out with the soldiers and surrender. The soldiers were allowed to go where they pleased, and it was said that Kirkpatrick had almost escaped in their midst before he was recognized and detained. Meanwhile in the gathering darkness the work of destruction was accelerated. The men broke up the furniture in the house and set it on fire, articles of value were appropriated, the horses were shot, and the liquor from the cellar was brought out and distributed. Before long the little army that had entered the ground with such parade had become an enraged and drunken mob. Out of the dozen or more buildings on the estate, only one, the smoke-house, was saved, and that, so it was said, because Neville's negroes pleaded that it contained their only food. Even the grain and the fences shared in the general destruction. Neville, himself, in a letter to Tench Coxe, placed the total loss at about three thousand pounds.[9]

About ten o'clock on the morning of the second attack Neville received word that the militia was about to advance from Couch's Fort and he wrote at once to his son in Pittsburgh urgently demanding that the county officials bestir themselves in his defense. Presley Neville immediately set out upon a round of calls. The cautious Brackenridge advised him that his father should give up his commission and thus allay the storm until he was in a stronger position, but Presley contemptuously negatived the suggestion and went on Next he called on Gibson and Wilkins, as militia officers, to order out the militia and march against the rioters, but Brackenridge, upon their appeal to him, gave it as his opinion that they could not do so—that power belonged only to the governor. Neville then asked them, as judges of the court, to raise a posse. Again they consulted Brackenridge, who advised them that they could not legally do this but that Sheriff Samuel Ewalt, then in Pittsburgh could. A short conference followed. The sheriff stoutly asserted that the proposed action was not practicable under the circumstances, and Brackenridge, when pressed for his opinion, agreed with him. "But," continued Brackenridge, "this can be done;—ride out without arms, and address the people. Persuasion will avail more than force. If this is adopted, I will be one to go."

The proposal was readily accepted and within a few minutes the company, composed of Brackenridge, the sheriff, and the judges, was mounted and at the ferry across the Monongahela. Presley Neville, meanwhile, probably disgusted by the quibbling of the law officers, had gathered several friends to go to his father's relief, among them Lenox, Isaac Craig, a Lieutenant Semple, and a young man named Ormsby. The two parties met on the bank of the river, and Brackenridge saw, to his alarm, that Neville and his men were armed. Hesitating to remonstrate with the older men he addressed young Ormsby abruptly:

"What, armed?"

"Yes," replied Ormsby.

"You will not ride with us armed."

"You may ride as you please," said Ormsby. "I am armed."

Presley Neville, "who was mounted on a gay horse, with pistols in his holsters," came to his companion's rescue.

"We are not all born orators," said he to Brackenridge. "We are going to fight, you to speak."

Neville and his friends crossed in one boat and the other party in another. The latter boat stranded on a bar and Brackenridge and one or two of his company leaped their horses out, rode across the bar, and swam the channel on the farther side. It occurred to Brackenridge, while ascending the poplar-bordered road up Coal Hill, that the road was supposed to be guarded by the insurgents and that he and his companions ran the danger of being prevented from reaching the main body they sought. At the suggestion of the sheriff, they took an old and little traveled road to Couch's Fort, which lay at a distance of nine miles. As they rode rapidly along they observed that the harvest fields were deserted by the men and only women and children were to be seen. Once when they stopped at a house to inquire as to the movements of the insurgents the woman whom they addressed recognized the sheriff and appeared alarmed. "Are you of Neville's party?" she inquired, impressing Brackenridge that the popular idea was that the country was on one side and Neville on the other.

It was now agreed, upon Brackenridge's suggestion, that the sight of the sheriff and the judges approaching might put the people in a dangerous state of mind, and he proposed that they should stop at the Hulse homestead about half a mile from the fort while he went on alone. Upon arriving at Hulse's, however, it was learned that the militiamen had marched toward Bower Hill. The company thereupon set out in haste to overtake them; but at the house of a Doctor Adams they learned from some spectators that "all was over, and the house burned; that the people were returning, and in great rage at the loss of their leader." Brackenridge, the sheriff, and the judges thereupon returned to Pittsburgh.[10]

Presley Neville's party meanwhile had gone directly to

Bower Hill and had arrived at the skirts of the besieging force at about the time the firing began. Neville, as Brackenridge commented later, acted a little too much the chevalier. "If there is a gentleman amongst you," he said to the guard, "let him come out and speak to me." The men naturally were offended at his words and tone and raised their pieces threateningly, whereupon he changed his manner and called out that he was not armed (his pistols had not been drawn from the holsters); the guard advanced and arrested him and his companions. They were held during the battle and were witnesses of the action and of the conflagration.

When the insurgents left Bower Hill, the committee decided to take some of the prisoners along to Couch's Fort, in spite of the danger from the intoxicated militiamen. Ormsby, as well as Craig and Semple apparently, were dismissed or escaped, and Lenox and Presley Neville became separated on the journey to the fort. Upon his arrival there Lenox, according to his story, was fired upon in the light of the moon from a distance of five yards but was missed. While the committee was deliberating upon his fate, two men approached with drawn knives and slashed his coat but were driven away; he was then dismounted and taken into a house for safety. There he found Presley Neville. The demand was made of the marshal that he agree not to return the processes he had served west of the mountains, but he insisted that this was not in his power as he was under oath to return them. Presently, however, upon his agreement to serve no more processes west of the mountains and to surrender himself upon demand, he was dismissed. Presley Neville, who had offered himself as the marshal's sponsor, was also allowed to go.

The two men were furnished with a guard at their own request, fortunately for them. A few miles on the road toward Pittsburgh they fell in with a drunken party and would have been shot had not the guards thrown themselves between. The newcomers, however, being the stronger, forced the party to turn back to Couch's Fort, but Lenox succeeded in persuading his guard to let him escape and Neville also got away. Kirkpatrick was equally fortunate; after being marched some distance under guard he was taken up behind David Hamilton and presently was allowed to slip away under cover of the darkness.[11]

The next day, July 18, an ugly tempered crowd met at Mingo Church to attend the funeral of McFarlane. There really seems to have been some danger that the rioters would proceed very shortly to embody themselves again and march on Pittsburgh, there to take vengeance for the death of their leader. The common understanding was that as soon as the writs were returned the government could take out judgments against the lands of those served, and it was offered in support of the proposed march on Pittsburgh that the marshal could be killed and thus the return of the writs be prevented. "It was better that one man should die," it was said, "than so many persons, with their families, lose their plantations."

It was finally agreed after some discussion that David Hamilton should go immediately to Pittsburgh, first to demand the resignation of Neville as inspector, and second to require of Marshal Lenox the surrender of the writs he had served and, naïvely enough, to return his pistols to him. The demand upon Lenox was according to the committee's understanding of his engagement at Couch's Fort, though he himself insisted that he had agreed only to serve no more writs west of the mountains and to surrender himself whenever demanded. The various roads leading away from Pittsburgh were placed under guard to prevent the escape of the marshal in case he decided to take "French leave," and steps were taken to destroy immediately every excise office in the survey.

Hamilton was joined in his mission by John Black, and they arrived at Pittsburgh toward evening. It is probable that they did not consider that their venture into "Sodom" was without risk for they informed those they met that the committee was meeting at Shochan's tavern, about four miles south of Pittsburgh. As a matter of fact they were in no danger. The little city at the "Point" was trembling with fear and the streets were rife with rumors that the insurgents were again on the march, this time bound for Pittsburgh to level the excise office there and to perpetrate no one knew what other enormities. Within half an hour after the arrival of Hamilton and Black, says Brackenridge, it was being told that two hundred had arrived and that a thousand more were encamped upon Coal Hill waiting to descend upon the town. The inhabitants were out in the streets gazing fearfully across the river at the towering height, and some even thought that they saw men in hunting shirts moving about the crest. Here and there ominous whispers arose that it would be better to give up Neville and Lenox to the insurgents than to have the town burned. The ladies, particularly those of the Neville family, were so uneasy that the envoys were finally asked to cross the river and ascertain whether the rumors were true. "Black gravely answered, that there might be six or eight hundred on the hill, or not far off; but that he would cross over, and give orders to disperse: He crossed the river, and came back with an account that there had been none there."

Hamilton, in pursuance of his instructions, called upon General Neville and stated his business. Presley urged his father to comply, and the latter finally wrote out a conditional resignation and gave it to Hamilton to take to the committee. Hamilton read the note and refused to receive it; he said that it would only anger the people and crystallize the sentiment favoring a march on Pittsburgh.

The issue with Lenox was longer drawn out and hardly less serious. Lenox insisted that he must make the returns to the federal court upon the writs already served, but he assured Hamilton and Black that no judgment could be taken on the basis of these writs binding the lands of the men upon whom they had been served. The problem was finally submitted to Brackenridge and, after a night of study, he gave it as his opinion that the marshal was correct. He even offered, in order to satisfy both parties, to appear for the distillers in case the matter came to court, and, if he lost, to pay the penalties himself.[12]

The two commissioners, having done all they could, now made ready to return and report to the committee, and Brackenridge agreed to go with them. Their plan, they said, was to go by Bower Hill to look for the body of one of the men who had been killed, but they feared injury at the hands of Neville's negroes (or possibly from others) and asked several of the Pittsburgh gentlemen to accompany them. Brackenridge consented to go, hoping that he might be able to exercise a moderating effect upon the committee. Robert Johnson, the collector, who was now anxious to resign his office, was told that the committee was sitting at Bower Hill and that if he went there it would accept his resignation and guarantee his future safety. Johnson and Brackenridge, for one reason or another were the only persons to go with the envoys. Brackenridge had been given to understand that he would meet the committee at Shochan's tavern, but in the course of the journey it came out that the committee was neither at Shochan's nor at Bower Hill but was planning to meet soon at a point on Pigeon Creek to receive the commissioners' report. Johnson thereupon refused to go beyond Bower Hill but made out his resignation and sent it on and agreed to publish a copy in the *Pittsburgh Gazette*. Brackenridge also, disgusted at the duplicity of Hamilton and Black, refused to go on, especially since a storm was threatening, and returned with Johnson to Pittsburgh.[13]

Lenox had meanwhile accepted Major Butler's offer of protection and had moved to the fort. Brackenridge had in mind a plan of taking him to Washington and placing him under the protection of the Democratic society of that place, evidently feeling that it was likely to be more conservative than the one in the Mingo Creek region had showed itself to be. The problem was solved, however, without Brackenridge's knowledge or connivance. That night, under cover of a storm, Lenox and Neville set off down river in a boat furnished by Butler and manned by a party of soldiers. They reached Wheeling the next evening, sent the soldiers back to Pittsburgh, and went on to Marietta alone. Thence, accompanied by two guides, they went east by way of Clarksburg, and they arrived in Philadelphia on the eighth of August.[14]

Public excitement and terror continued to rise after the departure of the commissioners from Pittsburgh. That same day John Reed, a complying distiller near Pittsburgh, found posted on a tree near his place a notice signed by Tom the Tinker threatening all who did not join the movement against the excise. The notice, in part, read thus: "And I do declare on my solemn word, that if such delinquents do not come forth on the next alarm, with equipments, and give their assistance as much as in them lies, in opposing the execution and obtaining a repeal of the excise law, he or they will be deemed as enemies, and stand opposed to virtuous principles of republican liberty, and shall receive punishment according to the nature of the offense." Reed was ordered, on pain of having his distillery destroyed, to have the notice published in the *Pittsburgh Gazette*.[15]

Major Craig seems to have been empowered to receive distillers' entries upon the departure of General Neville from

Pittsburgh—at least the major insisted that the office of inspection should not be closed and that the notice advertising it as such should remain upon the door of the old redoubt on Water Street, which Neville had been using as an office. The panicky feeling in the village is illustrated by an incident that Brackenridge claimed actually happened. It seems that the lawyer, aware of the danger of having the notice flaunting before the eyes of any visiting Whiskey Boys and anxious to prevent an invasion in force, went out in the street and asked the first person he met if he had heard that there were five hundred men from Washington County on their way to burn Pittsburgh because the excise office was being kept open. He needed to put the question to only two or three; within a few minutes the town was aflame with the news, now supposed to be true. Major Craig no sooner heard it than he rushed out, ripped the notice from the door, tore it in pieces, and called upon a bystander to witness his action.[16]

Certain certificates and bonds had been lost in the destruction of Bower Hill and an advertisement, signed by General Neville but dated the day after his departure, appeared in the *Pittsburgh Gazette*. The advertisement was a necessary legal step in stopping payment on the notes in case they showed up with forged endorsements; but, according to Brackenridge, the people resented the implication that they might have been concerned in theft or forgery and blamed Presley Neville for the advertisement. This seems to have been one of the counts that led to his proscription a few days later.[17]

Chapter VI: *The Mingo Meeting*

O N Monday afternoon, July 21, a young man from the Mingo Creek settlement led his horse off the Monongahela ferry and then rode down Water Street and out Market to the house of Hugh Henry Brackenridge. Here he dismounted and, entering the front room that served as an office, handed the lawyer a folded note from David Hamilton. It is easy to reconstruct the scene after the young man had gone as the cautious lawyer opened the missive and read an invitation from David Hamilton to attend a meeting of the committee at the Mingo meetinghouse the next Wednesday. He must have glanced cautiously around to see whether he was observed and read the message again with an air almost furtive. After that he folded the paper and tore it into bits, then threw the scraps into a closet along with other waste paper that had collected from time to time in that untidy recess.

What was his perturbation the next day when Presley Neville, of all people, walked into his office and asked if he had not received a note from David Hamilton!

"I have," replied the lawyer, "but how have you come to the knowledge of it?" Neville thereupon answered that the young man who had brought it had disclosed the fact as well as the contents of the note.

"I had never intended to have mentioned it," said Brackenridge, "but here it is." He fished the scraps of the note from the closet and pieced them together anxiously. His legal acumen had warned him that he was in a dangerous position in having received a communication from a man guilty of overt treason, and he saw that his only protection was to convince Neville that the note did not necessarily incriminate him. The younger man read the missive carefully.

"Do you mean to go?" he said finally.

"No," answered Brackenridge, and launched into what was at once a defense of himself and an explanation. "This is high treason that has been committed; and in treason there are no accessories, before or after the fact, all are principals; and I am aware of the delicacy, of having anything to say to people in the predicament in which these are. I have reflected on the subject, and think it not safe to go."

Neville's answer was a surprise. "I would wish you to go," he said, "it might answer a good end." He did not explain his object; in fact it was hardly necessary. The absconding of the marshal after Neville had given surety made it important that he have someone plead for him before the committee—and then Brackenridge, if he went, could seize the opportunity to plead for moderation in opposing the excise. The risk involved was so great, however, that the younger man had considerable difficulty in overcoming the lawyer's reluctance.

"I will go," he yielded finally, "provided you will vouch with what sentiments I go—"

"I will," interjected Neville.

"—and provided some person can be got to go with me, to bear testimony of what I shall say, or do, on the occasion."

With this understanding the two men went out to find others who were willing to go to the Mingo meeting, and in the end they collected a group of prominent and respectable Pittsburghers, including George Robinson, the chief burgess, Josiah Tannehill, the first assistant burgess, and William H. Beaumont, Peter Audrain, and Colonel William Semple. So anxious was Presley Neville that a Pittsburgh delegation attend the meeting that he even furnished a horse for Tannehill.[1]

The Pittsburghers left upon the morning of the meeting, July 23, and stopped near the church at the farmstead of Jacob Friggly to put up their horses. Here they found a tall red-haired man who had much to say in praise of Presley Neville, regretted his distressing circumstances, and took to himself some credit in having protected him on the night of the burning of Bower Hill. Presently it developed that the talkative stranger was Benjamin Parkinson, a leading member of the Mingo Democratic Society committee, and Semple took the opportunity to give him a letter that Presley Neville had handed him privately with the request that he see that it got to the chairman of the committee. The group then left for the meetinghouse.

The Mingo Creek Presbyterian Church was a simple little structure of logs situated slightly up the western slope of the beautiful vale through which ran Mingo Creek. Upon coming in sight of the church Brackenridge was struck by the great number of men gathered there. Not only were the leaders of the attack on Bower Hill present, but also many others, among them David Bradford and James Marshall of Washington, Craig Richie and John Canon of Canonsburg, and even Edward Cook, a sage and respected Presbyterian elder from Fayette County. Why were these staid and comparatively conservative citizens here? Probably because they feared the people, who by now were almost out of hand. Bradford, for example, had been visited and urged to come forward in defense of what had been done at Bower Hill since he had been so conspicuous in the deliberative committees and had encouraged the people to violent measures.

"I encourage," he had cried. "Good God! I never thought of such a thing."

"Yes, you did," was the significant answer, "and if you do not come forward now, and support us, you shall be treated in the same, or a worse manner, with the excise officer." Bradford thereupon agreed to attend, and doubtless the same tactics succeeded elsewhere. Some of these quondam leaders still hoped to stem the tide of popular violence; others, as the sequel shows, hoped to gain personal advantage by riding with the current once they had been forced out beyond their depth.

Every countenance reflected the solemnity of the occasion. Few ventured to converse or even to exchange greetings as they strolled about or reclined on the grass and waited for the meeting to open. Brackenridge, who knew intimately many of those present, wrote later that he did not remember having spoken a single word. From the ground before the church the men now meeting there could see the fresh earth upon the grave of James McFarlane, and if they needed any further reminder of the seriousness of the problems they had met to discuss, they could see McFarlane's brother, Andrew, moving through the throng with a black scarf bound about his arm.

The meeting was opened by the election of Edward Cook as chairman and Craig Ritchie as secretary. Presley Neville's letter was then produced and read by Ritchie. It stated that General Neville and Marshal Lenox had left the country; the latter considered that he was not bound by his engagement to surrender himself because he had been rearrested after his release and had escaped by his own efforts. Presley Neville, for the same reason, felt that he was released from his responsibility as security for the marshal's surrender. The younger Neville was not content to let the matter drop with this exhibition of casuistry, but went on to boast that though the insurgents might burn his house as they had his father's he had enough property beyond their reach. He even spoke a word for Kirkpatrick and asserted that they, as men of honor, should approve his action in defending so intrepidly the house of a friend. No comments were made on the letter at that time, but it is hard to believe that it could have had any but an angering effect upon the men who had been at Bower Hill.

Benjamin Parkinson presently put squarely before the gathering the main problem the group had met to discuss. He rose and addressed the chair, then briefly stated the issue in words that Brackenridge states impressed him as coming from "an agony of mind."

"You know," said Parkinson, "what has been done: we wish to know, whether what has been done is right or wrong; and whether we are to be supported in it, or left to ourselves."

There were a few moments of silence; then Marshall observed very sensibly that it was not necessary to judge of what had been done, but to decide what was now to be done. Bradford then rose and launched into an argument in favor of supporting those who had attacked and destroyed Bower Hill; he spoke at great length and with such violence that his speech was really a harangue. Brackenridge listened in visible agitation, as one of his colleagues reported later. The issue was now clearly drawn, and the Pittsburgh lawyer, perhaps being used to having onerous duties thrust upon him, suspected that he would be called upon for the next address. It was a delicate situation. As he expressed it "there was but a moment between treason on the one hand, and popular odium on the other; popular odium which might produce personal injury before I left the ground." His task was to steer between the horns of the dilemma without becoming impaled on either, and at the same time to point out the dangers of treason and uphold a course of moderation. With this in mind Brackenridge mentally outlined a speech that he hoped would meet the situation.

Bradford had no sooner finished than Marshall rose and solicited Brackenridge to take the floor. The later complied, at first speaking slowly and haltingly, for, as Semple observed, "the current of the people's prejudice seemed to be strongly against him." Brackenridge resorted to one of his common oratorical tricks; that is, diverting the minds of his hearers from the subject at issue by drollery and sarcasm. He recounted with many a humorous flourish the circumstances under which Craig had removed the notice from the door of the excise office. "Sometimes," says Semple, "he would give a sarcastical stroke at the excise, and the inventors of it; and then tell some droll story thereto relating; in order, as I apprehend, to unbend the audience's minds from the serious tone to which they have been wrought up." This treatment also gave him the air of approving the opposition to the excise without being under the necessity of expressing direct approval or disapproval. Presently, when the audience seemed to be in a lighter frame of mind, he explained that the Pittsburghers were not a delegation from the town but had come simply to tell what had been done there with regard to the excise office and to make it unnecessary for any force to come in to close it up. At the same time, disavowing that they held any delegated powers, he avoided the possibility of being drawn into any vote that might force him and his friends to take one side or the other.

He went on to state, however, that he was willing to give advice. "What had been done, might be morally right, but it was legally wrong. In construction of law it was high treason. It was a case within the power of the President to call out the militia." This blunt statement of truth amazed and disturbed the audience; they seem to have thought up until that moment that the offense was cognizable only in the county courts. Having struck this telling blow, Brackenridge went on to suggest a way out of the difficulty. He pointed out that it would be hard to embody the militia from midland Pennsylvania and from the upper parts of Maryland and Virginia because they sympathized with the opposition. This would necessitate drawing the forces from the East and would entail such difficulty, delay, and expense that the president would prefer to offer an amnesty. Because amnesty was the logical object to be sought it behooved those who had been involved in the Bower Hill affrays not to drag in outsiders but to leave them free to act as mediators between themselves and the government.

The anger and confusion with which those involved in the attacks received Brackenridge's statement were clearly evidenced on the faces of Benjamin Parkinson and his friends; those anxious to escape being drawn into the maelstrom of treason were greatly relieved and nodded their heads in assent. Brackenridge saw that there was doubt as to the certainty of an amnesty, so he went on to impress his hearers with the necessity of asking for it and the probability of obtaining it. The first he showed by pointing out the obviously inadequate resources of the region to sustain a successful conflict with the federal government. The second he upheld by citing the tendency of the executive to give way rather than to follow a strong policy—just the accusation that the West was perennially making. On the last argument he "indulged a good deal of pleasantry at the expence of the executive, on the subject of Indian treaties," and went so far as to give an imaginary dialogue between Knox, the secretary of war, and Cornplanter, a recalcitrant Indian chief, whose protests had caused Washington to put a stop to Pennsylvania's plan to open the Erie triangle to settlements, much to the disgust of the westerners. At the end Brackenridge proposed a meeting from all the survey and the sending of delegates to the president in Philadelphia to beg for an amnesty, and he offered to make one of the party.

Brackenridge's revelation of the danger of the situation so

dazed the assemblage that no one seemed capable of standing up to dispute him. Presently the men began to leave their seats, and passing out of the church they went to the spring to drink or stood about in knots discussing their predicament. Daniel Hamilton, the same who had threatened Captain Faulkner with a scalping knife, told Brackenridge that Benjamin Parkinson and Andrew McFarlane were stirring up the people against him, and the other members of the Pittsburgh delegation reported that there was considerable dissatisfaction with his speech. Going within doors again, Brackenridge found a group composed of Cook, Marshall, Bradford, and some others conversing in low tones. He was not invited to join the discussion and when he asked Marshall what were their conclusions the latter answered "I do not know" so shortly that the lawyer, perhaps overinclined to take offense, felt that he was not trusted.

These indications of hostility alarmed the cautious Brackenridge to such an extent that he gathered his companions and started them off; then, making the excuse that he did not want to go alone, he quickly followed them. John Canon urged him to stay but he explained that there was no use, since not being delegated he could not vote on any question. When he had gone a little farther and had caught up with his friends someone called after them but they hurried on, pretending not to have heard. After dining at Friggly's, the Pittsburghers prepared to leave for home, but it was suggested by one of the number that their hasty departure might make it appear as though they were spies. It was thought well for Brackenridge to return to the church to show himself to the people. He accordingly rode back part of the way and, leaving his horse in a hollow, walked into the assembly as though he had not been away. Many of the company had gone and others were leaving. A remnant was listening to a speaker who was trying to explain away an accusation of having appeared to wish to comply with the excise law. Brackenridge returned to the rendezvous but, before he and his friends set out for Pittsburgh, old Jacob Friggly appeared and told them that the conference had called another meeting for Parkinson's Ferry on August 14, to be attended by elected delegates, two to five in number from each township in the fourth survey.[2]

Upon his return to Pittsburgh Brackenridge soon found that, to quote his quaint phrasing, "even on my own shewing, I was not about to be the subject of eulogium." People generally were inclined to wish that decisive measures had been taken in support of the malcontents. "But," said Brackenridge, "what will be the consequences? A war will ensue." The complainants were prepared with a pat answer. "Well," said they, " let those that do not chuse to stand with the country, leave it; there will be enough behind without them: what they leave will help to carry on the war."

Such sentiments as these alarmed the cautious legal man to such an extent that before long he was planning on following the advice. He and General John Wilkins discussed the matter seriously and weighed the safest routes of egress. The latter thought of going up the Allegheny on the pretense of locating lands; the former preferred to go to Philadelphia, but the suddenness with which the Braddock's Field crisis came on frustrated this plan.[3]

The Mingo meeting marked the emergence of David Bradford as an advocate of the policy of sustaining violence by violence. Brackenridge had intended the next conference to be one of pacification; Bradford saw it as an opportunity to stir up further trouble. On August 6 he sent to the inhabitants of Monongalia County, Virginia, an inflammatory letter urging them to send delegates to the Parkinson's Ferry meeting. "We have fully deliberated," he wrote, "and have determined with head, heart, hand, and voice, that we will support the opposition to the excise law."[4]

Once he had cast his lot with the party of resistance Bradford's characteristic rashness led him to favor a program of unreasoning temerity. It would seem that the man must have gone mad with delusions of grandeur, and it is hard to escape the conclusion that he had visions of himself as the Washington of the West, laying the foundation of a new nation. He had seized his opportunity as early as the day of the Mingo meeting. It was on the journey to that place that he proposed to Marshall that they have the mail from Washington to Pittsburgh robbed in order to learn what were the opinions of the people toward the opposition to the excise. John Baldwin and David Hamilton agreed to carry out the plan, but soon backed out.

The plan was then changed to a robbery of the Pittsburgh-Philadelphia post. David Bradford sent his cousin William Bradford, and David Hamilton sent a John Mitchell. The post-rider was stopped on July 26 near Greensburg and the packets containing the mail from Washington and Pittsburgh were abstracted. Benjamin Parkinson delivered the packet to David Bradford in Washington and the two men with Marshall, Alexander Fulton, and a certain Lochry took it to Canonsburg. There they stopped at the Black Horse Tavern kept by Henry Westbay, and retiring to an arbor behind the tavern, according to the tradition, they sent for several local leaders including John Canon and Thomas Speer. The mail was then opened and found to contain no letters from Washington bearing on the disturbances. There were, however, several from Pittsburgh bitterly denouncing the actions of the malcontents. The letters that particularly aroused the ire of Bradford's committee were the ones by Presley Neville to his father-in-law, General Daniel Morgan; by General John Gibson to Governor Mifflin; by James Brison, the prothonotary, to the governor; by Major

The Mingo Meeting

Thomas Butler to Secretary of War Knox; and by Edward Day to Alexander Hamilton.

The tradition is that upon reading the threats contained in the letters someone asked Bradford what would be done to those concerned in the attacks on Bower Hill. "They will be hung," answered Bradford, and went on to advocate the policy upheld by the rioters, that of involving the entire western country in the embroilment in the confidence that the great number concerned would prevent extreme punishment. The result was, at any rate, that it was resolved to take the writers of the objectionable letters and imprison them in the Washington jail and to seize the magazine of Fort Fayette. In order to accomplish these objects the group proceeded to call out the militia from the entire survey, each man signing his name to the circular letter that was sent to the officers. The authors brazenly avowed the robbery of the mail but did not mention the reasons for the call except for the statement that the time had now come for action. The companies were to meet at their usual places of rendezvous on Wednesday, July 30, and were to march on Friday to Braddock's Field, arriving there by two o'clock in the afternoon. Each man was to bring four days' provisions.[5]

The reaction to the call for the assembling of the militia was mixed. The Bower Hill rioters and their proponents were naturally jubilant but many others, particularly the substantial leaders and officers of Washington County, disapproved of it and brought pressure to bear on Bradford to induce him to countermand the order. The man who would have aped Washington was so alarmed by these prophets of evil that he yielded and gave Colonel John Hamilton of the Mingo militia a countermanding order, giving as his reason that the ammunition they had been planning to seize was destined for use against the Indians. "We therefore have concluded not to touch it; I give you this early notice, that your brave sons of war need not turn out till farther notice."

The storm of protest that greeted this order in town and country was tremendous. Men flocked into Washington and demanded of Bradford that the muster be held. A crowd of militiamen gathered in the courthouse and several leading conservatives brought into play their best oratory in an endeavor to stop the movement. James Ross spoke with power and earnestness for two hours, and Congressman Thomas Scott, Thomas Stokely, David Redick, Henry Purviance, and others spoke on the same side. Even James Marshall was anxious to retreat and admitted it in a public address. The popular tide, however, was not to be stemmed, and perhaps Bradford, confronting this sea of faces, was carried away by his ambitions. At any rate he once more changed front and became more radical than ever. He denied that he had issued the countermand and boldly demanded to face the scoundrel who had accused him of it.

It is impossible to discern any leaders of the popular pressure that caused Bradford's *volte-face,* though of course such men as David and Daniel Hamilton and Benjamin Parkinson must have had a hand. They, however, were not educated men nor leaders in legal and political affairs, but were purely local in their influence. Ordinarily they could not have combatted successfully the hierarchy of county leaders who addressed the meeting in the courthouse. The people were at last out of hand, their leaders nothing more than squires or tavern-keepers who found the popular interest theirs or demagogues who were mouthpieces for the popular will. That night the community of Washington had a warning of what might follow, if it continued to obstruct the people, when James Marshall's door was daubed with tar and feathers. Marshall went to Braddock's Field.[6]

Chapter VII: *Braddock's Field*

ON the day of the gathering of the people at Braddock's Field the panicky citizens of Pittsburgh were further stricken by the appearance in their midst, almost like a portent, of a man riding on horseback through the streets with his tomahawk raised threateningly over his head.

"This is not all that I want," he cried. "It is not the excise law only, that must go down; your district and associate judges must go down; your high offices and salaries. A great deal more is to be done; I am but beginning yet."

This man, though his identity has not been ascertained, was of some note in his vicinity and spoke with authority. Whatever the reasons for his attitude, whether disappointment in obtaining office or a genuine resentment at abuse of power and the levying of high taxes, he spoke the popular sentiments. Even those running for election to office were obliged, in order to win the popular franchise, to clamor against excises and taxes and to preach the abolition of the very offices for which they ran. Some people even went so far as to say that they would be better off under the British and suggested that arms and ammunition might be obtained from Canada. It was probably statements such as these that gave rise to the rumor that British soldiers had been seen among the rioters. The atmosphere was charged with revolution, and responsible thinkers saw no way in which it could be avoided. Brackenridge now had occasion to regret the academic brutality with which he had written his "Louis Capet has lost his caput" as the clouds of a revolution, organized and managed on Jacobin principles, began to hover over the western country. In place of a lofty approval of Jacobin sentiments he confessed that he could now scarcely bear to cast his eye over a paragraph of French news.[1]

Rumors of the purposes of the muster at Braddock's Field were not slow in reaching Pittsburgh. Men who were strangers to the townsmen were lounging in the streets and hanging around the fort as if they were spies. An unusual number of countrymen were bringing their produce to the Pittsburgh stores to be exchanged for flints and powder, and blacksmiths found themselves repairing an unusual number of old guns. The threat of fire and plunder was thinly disguised and country people, failing to beat down the prices of goods at the stores, would mutter angrily that they would get them for less in a few days. The sallow, overworked countrywomen, envious of the fripperies and conveniences enjoyed by the wives of the Pittsburgh hierarchy, would remark significantly that "that fine lady lives in a fine house, but her pride will be humbled by and by." Sodom, said the sullen countrymen, had been burned with fire from heaven, but this second Sodom would be burned with fire from earth.[2]

It was to decide upon measures to meet the emergency precipitated by the call to Braddock's Field that the Pittsburgh authorities called a town meeting for Thursday night, July 31. James Ross and other level-headed citizens of Washington had meanwhile been working quietly but persistently to block or at least to modify Bradford's radical program. Their tireless efforts were at length rewarded, and Bradford and Marshall were persuaded to agree unofficially to spare Pittsburgh if the townsmen would exile Kirkpatrick, Presley Neville, Gibson, Brison, Day, and Butler, and then the next day march out to Braddock's Field and join in the display of force that was to be made there. Gabriel Blakeney and William Meetkirk, prominent conservatives, and Dr. Absalom Baird agreed to transmit these terms to the Pittsburghers and at the same time to return to the postoffice those stolen letters for which the insurgents had no use. Henry Purviance, a leader of the local bar, accompanied them. There was some dispute with a party of radicals at the place where the road branched off to Braddock's Field when it became apparent that Blakeney's company was bound for Pittsburgh, the former hurling the accusation that the latter were spies and were really enlisted on the side of the government.

The messengers were besieged for news upon their arrival at Pittsburgh and they made no secret of the circumstances or seriousness of the crisis; they informed the perturbed Pittsburghers that their town was in danger of being burned unless they immediately exiled certain obnoxious characters. Day was among those present and was informed that an unsigned letter to the secretary of the treasury was attributed to him. By this time the landlord had taken their horses and the Washingtonians ascended the stairs to the common room of the tavern. The town meeting, already in session, as soon as it heard of their arrival, appointed a committee composed of George Wallace, Brackenridge, and John Wilkins, Jr., to interview them. Presley Neville was present in the tavern at the conference that followed, and perhaps for this reason he was not mentioned as one of the obnoxious men nor was John Gibson, at that moment presiding over the town meeting.

The committee presently returned to the meeting with the account of what they had learned. The proposal to exile Butler, the commandant of Fort Fayette, was, of course, beyond the power of the town to carry out, but there was little quibbling as to the necessity of complying with the other demands, and that promptly. The chairman named a committee of twenty-one, composed of the most prominent citizens, and for the next week or so this committee in effect supplanted the regular civil government of the town. The committee first appointed men to interview Kirkpatrick, Brison, and Day and suggest that they temporarily absent themselves. The first two acquiesced cheerfully, the latter grudgingly, and they all prepared to leave in the morning.

The committee also drew up a set of resolutions stating the action that had been taken with regard to Kirkpatrick, Brison, and Day. It was also agreed to watch for further disloyalty to "the common cause" and to stamp it out as soon as seen, to appear in force the next day at Braddock's Field, and to send a delegation to the projected meeting at Parkinson's Ferry. It was perfectly understood by all parties, even including the Washington emissaries, that the Pittsburghers were yielding only through motives of policy, and the use of the expression "the common cause" in the resolutions raised a general laugh in the committee. John Scull of the *Gazette* was instructed to print six hundred copies of the resolves in the form of handbills for distribution the next day at Braddock's Field, and he stayed up all night working in the little combination printing shop and post office in the log house on Front Street to finish the task.

It will be noticed that Gibson and Presley Neville had been omitted from the list of those expelled from the town, though their letters had made them obnoxious equally with the others. About midnight, after the committee had dissolved, Purviance, who claimed that he was not a regular representative of the Washington committee, approached Brackenridge and expressed his fears that what the meeting had done would avail the town little unless Gibson and Neville and perhaps also Craig were expelled. Brackenridge, though not the chairman, took it upon himself to reconvene the committee as soon as possible and Purviance was given an opportunity to set forth his fears. The committee finally agreed that Purviance should explain the situation to Gibson and Neville and that they should follow whatever course they thought proper.

There was little sleep in Pittsburgh that night. The people were all stirring about with their houses lit up, the women in tears, and the men busily engaged in hiding their valuables. John Wilkins, Sr., wrote that, when he came home from the meeting of the committee, he found his family in tears. He himself was none too confident of saving his property, as his son General John Wilkins was hated because he would receive at his store only whiskey that had paid the excise, and the store was in one end of the father's house. The elder Wilkins thereupon joined the general activity of burying valuables, hiding in this manner the county records and money as well as his private papers and valuables.

"In the morning," wrote John Wilkins, Sr., "the greatest confusion prevailed amongst the people, all sorts of labour and business ceased, all the men preparing to march, the women in tears, some leaving town, some hiding property, and some so shocked as not to know what to do." At nine o'clock Kirkpatrick and Brison left town. Gibson and Presley Neville, meanwhile, had decided not to leave the vicinity as yet, but were prevailed upon not to go to Braddock's Field. General John Wilkins, declared that he would go, despite the risk involved, hoping thus to avoid banishment and the destruction of his property. The Pittsburgh militia was ready to march by ten o'clock. Just as he was mounting his horse, the elder Wilkins received a letter from the governor requiring him to bring the rioters to justice. With a mental note on the irony of the situation, he hastened to hide the letter and set out after the marching men.[3]

The Pittsburghers halted a mile or two from Braddock's Field to close up their ranks. Brackenridge proposed that the committee advance under a flag of truce and tied a white handkerchief to his riding whip. The committee, however, felt that it would be unwise to show distrust, and it was agreed to send Blakeney and his friends forward to distribute the handbills that Scull had run off in the early hours of the morning. Presently the Washington party returned and reported that the handbills had had a good effect. The Pittsburghers then advanced, the committee of twenty-one in front and unarmed, the remainder armed. They marched a mile or so across the field through the thousands of militiamen already gathered and halted at a spot chosen as headquarters for the day.

Braddock's Field was about eight miles from Pittsburgh, the site of the present boroughs of Braddock and North Braddock, and was located on the eastern bank of the Monongahela River just below the point where Turtle Creek joins it. Here, of course, had occurred the historic defeat of the British in 1755, and here of late years the militia of western Pennsylvania had been accustomed to gather. In 1794 the ground belonged to George Wallace, one of the Pittsburgh committee of twenty-one. Along the river was an open plain elevated above the ordinary level of the water, and the Washington militia probably crossed at the ford used by Braddock's army and ascended to the plain by the old cuts made in the bank by the British engineers for the convenience of the army wagoners. Farther from the river the ground was more hilly, serrated by ravines, and still heavily wooded.[4]

Contemporary estimates differ greatly as to the number of men who turned out. Gallatin, who was inclined to minimize the number, stated that there were fifteen hundred or two thousand. John Wilkins, Sr., said that there were five thousand or six thousand on the march to Pittsburgh. Brackenridge placed the number which met at Braddock's Field at seven thousand, about three-fourths of whom marched to Pittsburgh. Findley took issue with Brackenridge's estimate of the number at the muster, believing that it was not "near so great." Wilkins, who had seen military service as an officer in the Revolutionary army, made his check while the militia was in motion, judging by the length of the line and by the spacing, so it is probable that his estimate was fairly close to the truth.[5] All the local writers, however, agreed that large numbers came through fear or through hope of preventing violence. John Brackenridge, who lived in Washington County and who was a brother of the lawyer, had refused to turn out for the attack on Bower Hill. His life had been threatened by his militia captain, a man named Sharp, and he sat up in his cabin watching for two nights with his ax in hand, since he had no rifle. Now he yielded to the summons to Braddock's Field and appeared armed with only an empty powderhorn. As he went along with his company he saw men threatened with drawn tomahawks and forced to join the march.[6]

It was a day of incongruities. Within two short weeks the "insurrection" had sprung up and now on the day and night at Braddock's Field it reached its full flower. Within two more days it was to wither away and disappear so completely that men would wonder if it had ever existed. It was impossible, however, on the day of the muster, to know that it would prove to be a hollow parade, and perhaps, if the more level-headed among the multitude had not striven so hard, a holocaust would have been loosed from that field. There were locked up in the breasts of these thousands of children of the backwoods vast potentialities of destruction—and reconstruction—which a sharpened sense of injustices suffered bade fair to release. Had there been a competent leader to take the helm it is within the realm of possibility that the current of American history would have been changed. Fortunately for the future no such leader appeared.[7]

This was the day, nevertheless, when the common man had his innings. There must have been a sense of exaltation among the more serious and sincere as they met and discussed their grievances in the half mute, half profane language of the common man and caught as through a rift in the clouds that hid the future a glimpse of a bright day when all men in the western country would live in two-story log houses with verandas —perhaps even brick houses, but certainly with verandas—and their wives could have bunches of bright colored ribbons brought from the iniquitous yet fascinating Sodoms beyond the mountains. It was a day also when demogoguery could strut and rustic intolerance fulminate; the heyday of thoughtless Tom the Tinker and his cronies when they could boast of what they would do to "Sodom" as if, in the words of Findley, they were so many Samsons "who each could kill his thousands with the jaw bone of an ass." It was the day, on another hand, when cautious men walked softly and guarded every word, when men of "respectability" trembled in their doeskin breeches lest the property upon which their social status was founded go up in smoke, and when anxious patriots prayed for a miracle to keep these stalwart western children from falling into the pit that in their blind desperation they had dug for their eastern rulers.[8]

David Bradford was riding high on the wave of popularity. He had assumed the office of major general, and "mounted on a superb horse in splendid trappings, arrayed in full martial uniform, with plumes floating in the air and sword drawn, he rode over the grounds, gave orders to the military and harangued the multitude.... The insurgents adored him, paid him the most servile homage, in order to be able to control and manage him." Brackenridge recorded that several battalions that had just crossed the river were drawn up in rank to be reviewed by Bradford. General Wilkins, still uncertain of his standing with the malcontents, bearded the lion in his den.

"Sir," he said, riding up to Bradford, "have you anything against me?"

"No," answered the Washingtonian, perhaps wary because Wilkins was backed by two hundred and fifty Pittsburgh militia, or perhaps feeling that he could afford to be magnanimous in the hour of his success. He even went out of his way to greet his Pittsburgh brother of the bar, Brackenridge. Had the obnoxious citizens been sent away, was his question, and was there no danger of their return? Brackenridge answered to please his audience, with the addition of a little sulphur to lend conviction to his words. In fact all day long the Pittsburghers were forced to keep the mask of hypocrisy well adjusted, to agree with every seditious sentiment. More than a few insurgents were able to penetrate the disguise.

"You have acted well," they said, "but we understand you. We give you credit for your management."

"What!" the Pittsburghers would reply. "Do you doubt our sincerity?"

The reply was disquieting: "We do not dispute your good policy," they said.

Brackenridge was thrown into terror at one time during the course of the day when Senator Ross in passing spied him sitting with two or three others at the root of a tree.

"You have a great deal of subtlety," said the senator with a smile, "but you will have occasion for it all."

Brackenridge looked about in alarm but was relieved to see that no one who would betray them was near. Ross assured him that he had considered the audience before he spoke and went on to approve the action taken by the town, saying that nothing else could have saved it.

Every man was afraid to speak his mind if he disagreed with the supposed majority. Now and then a word dropped casually, which if not well received could be readily explained away, led to confidences. The great bulk of the people were certainly in earnest, so much so that the talk of tar and feathers had given way to talk of the guillotine. Bradford had been warned before the final call to Braddock's Field of the danger of putting the armed multitude in motion but had answered lightly that he could say to them, "Hitherto shalt thou go, and no further." "Certain it is," wrote Brackenridge, "that his influence was great. I saw a man wade into the river, lift cool water from the bottom of the channel, and bring it [in] his hat to him to drink. Applications were made to him that day for commissions in the service." Yet in spite of this, thought Brackenridge, had Bradford ventured to check the violence of the people in any way not agreeable to them he would have lost his power and would have been hung from the nearest tree. He had invoked the wind and now, perhaps unconscious of the fact, was in the power of the whirlwind.

In spite of the undertone of fear and menace there was a great deal of reckless hilarity. Knots of men dressed in hunting shirts with handkerchiefs tied around their heads lounged about. Numbers of them were shooting at the mark, or perhaps firing charges of powder into the air to vent their emotion. The discharges were almost as heavy as in a battle, and a pall of smoke hung over the field and drifted through the trees as it had thirty-nine years before at the time of Braddock's disaster. The restless Brackenridge, strolling about the grounds, was conjuring up in his mind a picture of the danger should he encounter Andrew McFarlane or Benjamin Parkinson. Suddenly he turned and found the former "dressed in a blue coat, with dark visage, low'ring countenance, and a rifle in his hand" looking at him. The lawyer was so petrified that he did not say a word, only eyed McFarlane in turn until he turned and went away.

Brackenridge some time later happened upon Parkinson seated on the ground engaged in conversation with a group of others who had been at Bower Hill. Summoning his courage the lawyer walked up to them and greeted them with every indication of frankness and good-fellowship, and to his relief was received with cordiality. Brackenridge found a place and sat down. The conversation turned upon the burning of Bower Hill and they expressed rage against Kirkpatrick, blaming him for the resistance that had led to James McFarlane's death, and against Major Butler for sending soldiers to Neville's home. They inquired for young Ormsby, and Brackenridge admitted that he was on the grounds, but added depreciatingly that "he was scarcely worth inquiring after. He was an inconsiderate young man that would go anywhere . . . and it was little matter what he did." They told how, after the battle at Bower Hill, they had taken Ormsby's weapons from him "and put him on the bare back of a colt to ride, as a steed congenial with his years and discretion." The lawyer laughed immoderately and then suggested that the youth had been punished enough— to which the company agreed.

Young Ormsby, however, was in danger at that every moment. A group of fifteen men had blackened their faces and had gone in search of him. He probably would have been caught had not a Zedick Wright of Peter's Creek reached him first and given him warning. Ormsby had only a few minutes start of his enemies when they were seen to pass by in open pursuit. He succeeded in making his way to Pittsburgh by back roads and lay concealed in the fort until the danger was over.

One of the principal topics of conversation during the day was the proposed seizure of Fort Fayette. Numerous methods of accomplishing the desired end were proposed, but all of them were based on the proposition that it was a hazardous undertaking. Two years later, Collot, a French visitor, asserted that four men with a dozen fagots of dry wood could burn the fort and drive out the garrison. The insurgents, fortunately, were not aware of that possibility. The burning of the fort, moreover, might have resulted in the destruction of the ordnance and supplies, the seizure of which was their chief reason for considering the attack. Considerable confusion existed in the minds of the men as to whether or not the intention of seizing the fort had been abandoned, though it was said that men had been sent to Wheeling for cannon to be used in making a breach in the stockade. Now that the rebels were confronted with the possibility of an assault, there was not as much stomach for it as there had been before. Brackenridge and those of like mind worked zealously to aggravate the men's distaste for the undertaking. His method, he later reported, was about like this:

"Are we to take the garrison?" someone would ask.

"We are," Brackenridge would reply.

"Can we take it?"

"No doubt of it."

"But at a great loss?"

"Not at all," the wily lawyer would answer. "Not above a thousand killed, and five hundred mortally wounded."

The Pittsburgh militiamen had not brought provisions with them for an overnight stay, so it was that along toward evening the committee of twenty-one met and decided to risk a return home for the night with the agreement that they return to Braddock's Field early in the morning. The men had scarcely started, however, says Brackenridge, before there was a great clamor in the camp that the Pittsburghers were deserting the cause, and indeed, never had been sincere in it. When the committee saw the effect of the departure Brackenridge was sent posthaste to recall the men, "let their want of food be what it might."

This circumstance demonstrated the peril of the Pittsburghers' situation. Had they left the field it is possible that the town would have fallen the next day before the fury of the malcontents. Brackenridge was thoroughly aware of this and used every effort to spread the word that the Pittsburgh men were staying overnight. He met James Marshall at this juncture and the latter made clear his regret at having had a hand in bringing such peril to the town and readily agreed to help allay the clamor against the Pittsburghers. Brackenridge himself went about through the night conversing with various groups and making a pretense of seeking the Pittsburgh camp. The noise and confusion of the day had died down but there was little sleep, even though the men might be lying about the campfires rolled in their blankets. The air was filled with the continual hum of conversation. Brackenridge found as he rode around that the universal determination was to march on Pittsburgh next day, whether or not it was decided to storm the fort. Coming up to a campfire, the lawyer inquired the way to the Pittsburgh camp. James Miller, an acquaintance in the group, stepped up to his horse and offered him a dram, and another man called out to him:

"Is Kirkpatrick gone?"

"He is gone," Brackenridge answered.

A man started up behind him suddenly. "Why the devil did you let him go?" he demanded angrily.

The Pittsburgher was so startled that for a moment he had no answer, but presently he replied, "It was no fault of mine that he went away; I would rather have kept him here, and punished him by law." This was in one sense true, for at the time Brackenridge was prosecuting him for assault. The answer, however, silenced the enraged man for the moment, and Miller, sensing the tenseness of the moment, whispered to Brackenridge to go, then said aloud, "Come, Mr. Brackenridge, take another dram. We'll not detain you."

The lawyer took the hint and probably the dram and rode on to a range of fires along which was gathered John Hamilton's Mingo Creek battalion called the "bloody battalion" because of its rôle in the destruction of Bower Hill. Hamilton, as has been said, was opposed to the muster at Braddock's Field but had finally come along, hoping to moderate the actions of his men. The battalion had but lately arrived and was fired with a zeal to do something. Daniel Hamilton, who was the first to accost the lawyer, was overflowing with good will toward one who had apparently finally joined the cause.

"This is a true Whig," he called out to the men around him, and then went on talking to Brackenridge. "What do you think of that damn'd fellow, James Ross? He has been here, and all through camp, persuading the people not to go to Pittsburgh."

Brackenridge must have groaned inwardly as he adjusted the mask of hypocrisy a little closer. If this battalion of fire-eaters was determined to march in, there was nothing for him to do but agree and attempt later to prevent extreme measures.

"Damn the fellow," cried Brackenridge, "what business has he with Pittsburgh? The people of Pittsburgh wish to see the army; and you must go through it, and let the damn'd garrison see, that we could take it, if we would. It will convince the government that we are no mob, but a regular army, and can preserve discipline, and pass thro' a town, like the French and American armies, in the course of the last war, without doing the least injury to persons or property."

The men of the "bloody battalion" acclaimed these sentiments loudly and promised that no one should be molested.

When Brackenridge returned to the farmhouse where the committee met he found that the others who had been through the camp had gathered the same impressions as he had of the men's determination to march on Pittsburgh. The members of the committee of twenty-one, as they lay down for a few hours of sleep, had some grounds for hoping that they could save the town but were conscious that the crisis was yet to come with the meeting of the grand committee of battalions in the morning.

Chapter VIII: *The Whiskey Boys in Sodom*

THE next morning the chief officers met and agreed to form a committee composed of three men from each battalion to adopt a plan of action for the day. The Pittsburgh militia was represented on the committee by Brackenridge, General John Wilkins, and Captain John M'Masters. In order that they might be undisturbed in their deliberations, the members of the committee moved some distance to the woods, but a crowd of the curious followed and surrounded them. The chairman, Edward Cook, asked the non-members to leave; some did but others soon filled their places. The conference, therefore, was held before a gallery of radicals and this fact had an influence upon the nature of the decisions. New battalions were continually arriving and sending in delegates. Whether his battalion was among this number or whether he was delayed by other causes, James Ross was among the late arrivals.

David Bradford opened the meeting by stating that the purpose of the gathering was to punish certain individuals who were friendly to the excise; he then read the letters that had been taken from the post rider. Toward Gibson and Brison he expressed particular resentment because they had mentioned Bradford as making a motion at the Mingo meeting to support the perpetrators of the outrages against Neville. He addressed himself to Brackenridge.

"Were you not there? Did I make such a motion?"

Brackenridge looked at the Washington lawyer in astonishment. Bradford, it was true, had not made the motion, but he had violently harangued in its favor. It was well known that he had instigated the robbery of the mail; what profit could there be in seeking to escape the accusation made by Gibson and Brison? All this occurred to the cautious Brackenridge, but he said nothing of it and answered equivocally that the charge was not true, "but that might be the fault of the information given to the writers." Bradford answered that at all events it showed that the correspondents were unfriendly to the popular cause.

Bradford next brought forward the case of Major Craig, whom he accused of saying that, if the Pittsburgh inspection office was closed, he would open one in his own house. The Pittsburghers were called upon to state whether or not they had heard this. They all denied it. Brackenridge, adopting the same tactics he had used at the Mingo meeting, tried to divert the wrath of the insurgents from the major by ridiculing him. Soon after the word of the projected muster at Braddock's Field had gone out, he said, Craig had fallen in with him on the street and had asked the purpose of the gathering. "They have found," the lawyer had replied, whimsically playing upon the soldier's respect for big guns, "some pieces of artillery lost on the retreat [of Braddock] in the channel of the river, and they assemble there to draw them out, and attack the garrison." At this Craig had exhibited considerable alarm, which Brackenridge gleefully described to the committee.

It was then proposed to dispose of the cases of the men under censure by taking up each one singly. Majors Butler and Craig, being army officers, it was agreed should not be interfered with for the present but their dismissal should be demanded of the president and the secretary of war. Gibson and Presley Neville were then brought up. There was some argument over a proposal to banish them when a new arrival on the committee, a Captain Murray, ostentatiously took a stand against Neville, apparently with the sole object of distinguishing himself. Brackenridge, who was standing beside Bradford at the time, turned to him and said warmly, "The sending away [of] the people is a farce; it will be the best recommendation they can have to the government; they will get into office, and be great men by it; it is better to let them stay and be insignificant where they are."

Bradford's answer was straightforward. "The people came out to do something, and something they must do." Brackenridge saw, or thought he saw, that Bradford was convinced by Murray's vehemence that he represented the opinion of the camp and that it was necessary to "throw a tub to the whale." A little before this time the continually shifting ring of spectators was enlarged by the addition of a dozen riflemen, who ranged themselves by a log, leaned upon their rifles, and listened intently. As the debate on Gibson and Neville dragged on the newcomers became restless, and finally one of them peremptorily interrupted the proceedings.

"Gentlemen," he said, "we do not understand your counselling in mystery; do something speedily, or we will go to execution ourselves."

This bellicose declaration reacted upon the assembly like a shock. If the battalions decided to march without a policy having been agreed upon, there was no forecasting what might happen when they reached Pittsburgh. The Pittsburgh members, after hastily consulting, proposed that Gibson and Neville be given eight days to leave Pittsburgh. There was some doubt in the minds of the members of the committee of battalions as to whether the Pittsburghers would carry out the engagement, and there were some expressions of doubt as to the departure of those who had been banished recently. Fortunately, just at this moment a young man interposed with the information that an Indian scout had seen Kirkpatrick and Brison on their way to Sandusky. The report, it later proved, was incorrect but it was most opportune. The further objection that the banished men might return was met by the guarantee by the Pittsburghers that they themselves might be held in that case. The agreement finally stood that Gibson and Presley Neville should be given eight days' grace to prepare for departure.

It may have been at this point that the committee, apprehending injury to Kirkpatrick's property, since he was accused of having been responsible for Major James McFarlane's death, sent for Andrew McFarlane, the major's brother. It was suggested to him that, if he should oppose the destruction of the property, no one else could with good grace insist upon it. He readily acceded to the request and agreed to make his attitude public in the camp; he declared at the same time, however, "that if ever Kirkpatrick and he should meet, one of them should die."

Bradford next moved that the troops start for Pittsburgh. "Yes, by all means," agreed Brackenridge, "and if with no other view, at least to give a proof that the strictest order can be preserved, and no damage done. We will just march through, and taking a turn, come out upon the plain of the Monongahela's banks; and taking a little whiskey with the inhabitants of the town, the troops will embark, and cross the river."

The motion was carried and the members of the committee dispersed to their units. James Ross, happening to pass Brackenridge, paused and said aside, "The veil is getting too thin, I am afraid it will be seen through." A moment later Benjamin Parkinson gave unconscious proof of Ross's comment. "It is well for you," he said, suppressing his anger with difficulty, "that the committee has broke up in such a hurry; you would have been taken notice of, you gentlemen of Pittsburgh. Give us whiskey! we don't go there for your whiskey."

The lawyer was alarmed by the violence of Parkinson's manner and hastened to explain that "I meant no more than that we should drink together, and not any offence whatever; and that it would affect me in the most sensible manner, if any thing, inadvertently said by me, should interrupt harmony, and injure the cause." This mollified the intransigent Parkinson somewhat and Brackenridge managed to escape.

An impromptu meeting of what could be assembled of the Pittsburgh committee of twenty-one hastily outlined a course of action. Some friends of the commandmant of Fort Fayette were sent ahead to inform him that the troops were on the way, but that they had no intention of disturbing the fort. This was to prevent any incident that might lead to the suspicion of collusion between town and fort and cause the insurgents to injure the town. Other members undertook to collect water and whiskey on the plain just east of the town to refresh the troops in order that they might have no excuse to break ranks and wander about the town. All available boats were to be collected on the Monongahela bank so that the men might be sent over the river rapidly and sped on their way. Stores and taverns were to be closed and no liquor was to be sold to the men, though the townsmen were urged to give freely of their whiskey and provisions. A number of Pittsburghers, freshly alarmed at the prospect of invasion, hastily set out for town to hide those papers and valuables that had not already been concealed. Brackenridge had sent orders the day before to have his papers taken across the river to the home of a friend, Lewis Bond, and this was accomplished on the morning of the march.[1]

The drums, meanwhile, had beaten and the men had taken

their places in line. Edward Cook and David Bradford had been appointed commanders and Gabriel Blakeney officer of the day. Daniel Hamilton commanded the advance guard. Brackenridge, by order of the Pittsburgh committee, accompanied him to lead the troops by the best way and incidentally to steer the column away from the fort. The militia marched the eight miles to Pittsburgh in good order. Some of them, an indeterminate number, did not join the march, but went directly home. There were enough left, however, to form a line two miles and a half long—probably about five thousand men, one-third of whom were mounted.

Bradford, unknown to the Pittsburgh committee, had sent David Hamilton to assure Major Butler that the troops meant no harm to the fort and to request that they be allowed to march by it. This suggests that Bradford was not so eager to precipitate a conflict as his words and actions might seem to show. In fact there is every reason to believe that all the more prominent leaders desired to avoid trouble. Cook bore a deserved reputation for levelheadedness and Blakeney had Federalist leanings. The people, however, were in an ugly mood, and there is no doubt that some of them really expected to plunder the town. The cry of the troops was, says Brackenridge, "Huzza for Tom the Tinker." At Braddock's Field a man put his hat on the muzzle of his rifle and twirling it about said significantly, "I have a bad hat now, but I expect to have a better one soon." While the men were marching into the town, numbers of women on the hill across the Monongahela were waiting to see its destruction and to help their men plunder it.[2]

The route of the militia lay along the Monongahela or Braddock's Field Road, which led into what is now Fourth Street. They marched down to the "main street," probably Market Street, turned back, and halted on the plain east of the town. This was probably in the vicinity of the present Baltimore and Ohio Railroad depot. Meanwhile the citizens of the town had been carrying food and water and whiskey to the halting place, the members of the committee of twenty-one setting the example. Brackenridge expressed the situation when he wrote "I thought it better to be employed in extinguishing the fire of their thirst, than of my house." He alone contributed four barrels of whiskey. Bradford retired to a shady place and spent the afternoon resting and expatiating upon the great objects accomplished. Several bodies of men, in the spite of the efforts of the well disposed, left the field and wandered about the town, insulting the inhabitants and forcing the tavern keepers to treat them.

It was obvious that it would take a long time to transport the army across the river in the three or four ferryboats that the committee had been able to collect, so when someone recalled the existence of a ford at the junction of the rivers Brackenridge rode down and found it practicable. The mounted men thus were able to ford the river while the infantry was being ferried across, so that by night the town was clear of all but about a hundred of the troops. These, it was afterward learned, had arranged with some who had crossed that the latter should fire the farm buildings of Kirkpatrick on Coal Hill as a signal for the firing of the houses of Kirkpatrick, the Nevilles, Day, Gibson, and Brison, in town. If this scheme had been carried out, the whole town probably would have been destroyed. Fortunately, perhaps because they had learned of these plans and hoped to exercise a moderating influence, a number of the most prominent leaders of the insurgents had remained in town.

The most active of the insurgents left in town were a company uniformed in yellow hunting shirts and commanded by a Captain Riddle. About nine o'clock in the evening there was an alarm that Riddle's company and some other countrymen were going to burn Kirkpatrick's house. The citizens, with General Wilkins at their head, immediately rushed together and prepared to resist. Brackenridge, seeing the danger inherent in this policy, tried to stop them.

"This will not do," he cried. "It is contrary to the system we have hitherto pursued, and which has been successful. Return, and lay down your arms. If a drop of blood is shed between the town and the country, it will never be forgiven. It will be known, that there is a tumult in the town, between the inhabitants and the country people; and those that have crossed the river, many of them, will return, and we shall fall a sacrifice. If the house is to be defended, it must be by the people of the country themselves."

It is probable that Brackenridge already knew that measures were being taken to prevent trouble. James Marshall, Edward Cook, and Andrew McFarlane arrived at Kirkpatrick's house just as several men were preparing to set it on fire and others were standing around. Cook, thinking that the latter were there to defend the house, called out to them:

"Boys, are your guns loaded?"

"Yes," they answered.

"Then put in a second ball; and the first man that puts fire to the house, shoot him down."

The men were taken aback at this statement. Some of them pretended to have come to defend the place, and others drifted away as unobtrusively as possible. Meanwhile Brackenridge had encountered another group of countrymen headed for Kirkpatrick's.

"Gentlemen," said the lawyer, "you cannot burn this house without burning that of Colonel O'Hara, that is near it; he is a good man, and he is absent. If it is to be destroyed, let it be pulled down, not burned. I will be the first to pull a board off myself; but what necessity to take the trouble now; or to give yourself the trouble at all? The people of Pittsburgh will pull it down, and throw it in the river."

It was known by now that the plot included the destruction of Kirkpatrick's farm buildings across the river, and David Hamilton and Thomas Stokely were setting out to prevent that action just as Brackenridge fell in with them and learned their purpose. The latter seized the opportunity to cross the river and send back the ferryboats that were still on the other side in order to prevent their use in case any of the militia tried to carry out the scheme to return and attack the town. Hamilton and Stokely were apparently too late, for Brackenridge saw the glare from Kirkpatrick's blazing barn and grain stack as he recrossed the river.[8]

The firing of Kirkpatrick's barn was the last flare-up of the insurgents in that section, though the crisis was to last for weeks and loyal backbones were yet to be shaken by many a rumor and threat. The very next day, so it was said, a body of nearly a thousand men who had spent the night four or five miles from Pittsburgh halted as they argued as to whether or not they should return to the town to carry out their original intentions; they were dissuaded only with difficulty. The troops who passed the house of the former collector, Robert Johnson, near Woodville, not only stopped to consider the advisability of plundering and burning the house but also threatened to shoot Mrs. Johnson.

Bradford magniloquently summed up the results of the march on Pittsburgh in the statement that there had been "a glorious revolution accomplished without bloodshed." A correspondent writing in the *Gazette* complimented the militia upon the perfection of its behavior and went on to say that principle supplied the place of discipline and that "it was the cause, not the hope of plunder or rapine, that brought them to the field." It was a disgrace not to have appeared at Braddock's Field and John M'Donald, the secretary of the Mingo Democratic Society, felt obliged to excuse his absence on the score that the mustering orders had been countermanded and that two members of his family had been sick. Even the venerated William Findley was warned to be cautious about speaking of "rebels."[4]

Findley's own bailiwick of Westmoreland was affected by the contagion of violence soon after the review at Braddock's Field. Benjamin Wells's son, John, had been appointed collector for Westmoreland County and had established his office in the house of a deputy collector, Philip Reagan. A first attack made at night upon the house was signalized only by a harmless exchange of shots and the firing of Reagan's barn. A few days later, during John Wells's absence, a large band of men returned and the attack was renewed. Reagan finally agreed to surrender his commission on the condition that the rioters would not injure his person or his property. The terms were written out and signed by both parties, then Reagan opened his door and brought out a keg of whiskey and treated the crowd. As the effects of the whiskey began to be felt, some of the assailants declared that Reagan had been let off too easily, and after some squabbling the rioters decided to carry him off, to seize Benjamin Wells, and to court-martial the two together. When they arrived at Wells's place he was absent, so they burned the house to the ground and set an ambush to catch him upon his return. That night Reagan escaped, probably by connivance of some of his captors. Wells was taken the next morning but was allowed to go when he meekly agreed to all his captors' terms.

The next expedition was against John Webster, collector of Bedford County. Most of those engaged in it were from adjoining parts of Westmoreland, and some of them, it was said, had suffered from Webster's practice of seizing liquor on the road. The collector was captured without difficulty and submissively tore up and trod upon his papers. The usual argument then occurred over what to do with him. Fire was set to his haystacks and stables and then extinguished. Finally he was taken to Westmoreland and lodged overnight, then released by the moderates among his captors, after they had forced him to mount a stump and hurrah three times for Tom the Tinker. Benjamin and John Wells and John Webster all passed through the "insurrection" unscathed and retained their positions as collectors for some years.[5]

Brackenridge's equivocal stand was not long in bearing the fruit of suspicion on both sides of the controversy. Two days or so after the march on Pittsburgh, Presley Neville confided to Henry Purviance of Washington that he believed Brackenridge had been privy to the robbing of the mail, with the object of effecting the expulsion of those whose letters had given offense. Purviance countered that Brackenridge, unless he had supernatural powers, could not have known beforehand what these men would write. Neville then answered that at least Brackenridge was pleased that the robbery and consequent banishments had taken place.

The evening of the day after the march there was an alarm that a body of men was waiting in the woods to complete the destruction of Kirkpatrick's farm buildings, with the further intention of crossing the river to burn his town house. A call was issued for the assembling of the committee of twenty-one just as word was brought that Kirkpatrick had returned that evening and was even then in the fort. As if to confirm the report Presley Neville and Isaac Craig appeared, coming from the direction of the garrison, as the committee was about to convene in a public house. The two were questioned and they acknowledged that Kirkpatrick was in the fort, alleging that he had returned only because his course had been dogged so persistently by disaffected men as to endanger his safety. When asked by the committee why he had not reported to it at once and asked for an escort, Neville answered shortly that he had known of Kirkpatrick's return for only half an hour; he then abruptly left the tavern.

The committee, believing that Kirkpatrick had never been out of town and that Neville and Craig had been privy to the deception, gave orders for the immediate seizure of Neville and Craig, who were to be sent to Washington as forfeit for Kirkpatrick. Craig made his escape to the fort, but Neville promised upon his honor to appear within half an hour. He came, sauntering in with an irritating air between contempt and amusement, puffing unconcernedly at a cigar and every inch the polished and self-possessed man of the world. Perhaps he was secretly shaken to find that the committee was in earnest in its decision to go to any length to avoid a rupture with the country people; at least he discreetly gave assurance that Kirkpatrick would leave at once if provided with an escort.

By this time night had fallen and there was a promise of rain. Some townsmen, meanwhile, had invested the fort, determined to seize Kirkpatrick as he came out, or at least to prevent the entrance of Kirkpatrick's escort. John Wilkins, Sr., heard of this and went out and persuaded the men to disperse. He then returned home, saddled his own horse, filled his saddlebags with provisions, and sent them to Kirkpatrick under the charge of Henry Woolf, who had volunteered to be one of the major's guard. The fort had been reinvested but Woolf managed to steal in under cover of the rain, which had just begun to fall, and then to get out again with Kirkpatrick. The rest of the guard failed to appear. It was said that a shot was fired after the two as they were leaving, but they escaped unscathed and made their way by a circuitous route to the Allegheny Mountains.

The attempts to prevent Kirkpatrick's escape resulted in the calling of a town meeting the next evening in order to impress upon the people that the laws were still to be obeyed. John Wilkins, Sr., aptly expressed the situation by saying to them, "It is only the excise law that is repealed." Brackenridge was also called upon to harangue the meeting.

The remainder of the proscribed men were leaving Pittsburgh or had already left. Day went down the Ohio to Fort Washington and Gibson started east within the allotted time. During Gibson's first stop, at Greensburg, a crowd surrounded the tavern and gave him half an hour to move on, and a somewhat similar incident occurred at Carlisle. Brison, on his first night out, stopped at the home of a state deputy attorney. The next night the house was surrounded by a mob, an entrance forced, and search made for the prothonotary. The attorney's wife having fainted from fright, a mulatto woman was sent to the spring for a glass of water; she was mistaken for Brison trying to escape in disguise and was pursued into the woods.

It was a more difficult problem for the committee to get rid of Presley Neville. He addressed a note to Brackenridge, as chairman, in which he demanded a passport and an escort. The lawyer thought he saw more than a hint of ill-humor and a certain promise of future trouble in this gratuitous address, for he had never been the chairman. Brackenridge, however, swallowed his resentment and got the committee called together, wishing meanwhile that it were he in place of Neville who was to make the journey. Two passports apiece were made out for Gibson and Neville by James Clow; one was to serve them in going east and the other, a complete statement of the grounds upon which they had been expelled, was intended to win them a welcome in Philadelphia. After Gibson had gone and Brackenridge had been elected a delegate to the Parkinson's Ferry meeting, Neville came to the latter and demanded that his case be carried before the meeting and a repeal of the sentence of banishment be obtained. His attitude was that he had a right to expect this since it was to save the town that he was being banished.

Brackenridge pointed out to him that he had the wrong conception, that the town would have been in no danger save for the presence and actions of Neville and some others, and that it was for his own sake as well as for that of the town that he was being sent away. In truth Neville seems to have fallen into the error common among men of his class—that popular movements, if they are treated with the proper mixture of contempt and gunpowder, will quickly subside. Brackenridge labored, therefore, to show him that it was really a serious situation that confronted the region and that only diplomacy and a certain amount of yielding to the popular will would avert bloodshed if not real revolution. The argument probably strengthened Neville's opinion that the lawyer was really in sympathy with the insurgents.[6]

The month of August, 1794, was a time of extreme tenseness in the Monongahela country. There was a widespread idea that law was at an end in the region, and some even proceeded to settle their disputes by direct action. There was no attempt at secession, though many toyed with the idea that it might be better to be under the British than a part of the United States. The new-state project was revived and there was talk of making Bradford or Brackenridge governor. The latter wrote that "the people acted and spoke as if we were in a state of revolution," even though there was no plan as yet for carrying one into effect. John Wilkins, Sr., wrote that the country was in a more dangerous situation than before the march on Pittsburgh and gloomily forecast that it would soon "be involved in the horrors of a civil war." Liberty poles bearing devices such as the familiar revolutionary emblem of a snake divided, or with inscriptions such as "an equal tax, and no excise," were being erected at many places in the Mononga- hela country. They were even beginning to appear east of the mountains, a sign that encouraged the westerners greatly. Those who considered themselves in danger wanted to find refuge in Pittsburgh, but Brackenridge discouraged this, see- ing that it would only serve to arouse the country against the town again.

Orders came to Major Craig from Philadelphia instructing him to send the war materials intended for Wayne down river as soon as possible lest they fall into the hands of the rebels. Fort Fayette was put into as good a state for defense as possible; a blockhouse was constructed and provisions were laid in for two months. Major Butler applied to a biscuit baker of the town for all the biscuits he had on hand, but the baker, fearful of the consequences were it known that he was furnishing supplies to the garrison, consulted with Brackenridge before he would sell his stock.

Brackenridge himself began to ponder ways of getting out of the country and finally hit upon the expedient of having the Pittsburghers appoint him as an emissary to the president to explain their conduct during the crisis. He got James Ross to agree to the project but General Wilkins objected, as "he was in the same situation himself, and did not like to lose company." Just about this time Brackenridge received a letter from Tench Coxe, the supervisor of the revenue, relative to a packet of papers on agriculture to be distributed to the people or reprinted for their use, and it struck him that by writing to Coxe he might give the government a just idea of the excise controversy and thereby promote pacification. Perhaps he also hoped to justify his own conduct in the estimation of Coxe. Brackenridge attempted to show in his letter that the opposi- tion was not to the federal principle but only to the excise, and he expressed the opinion that that law could not be enforced in the Monongahela country. He gave an outline of what had occurred and pled for delay until the controversy could be settled peaceably. His fear of another mail robbery, however, caused him to use some equivocal expressions. One of these was: "Should an attempt be made to suppress these people, I am afraid the question will not be, whether you will march to Pittsburgh, but whether they will march to Philadelphia, accumulating in their course, and swelling over the banks of the Susquehanna like a torrent, irresistible, and devouring in its progress. There can be no equality of contest between the rage of a forest, and the abundance, indolence, and opulence of a city."

This was one of the statements that was later to be brought up as proof of Brackenridge's disaffection.[7]

Chapter IX: *The First Parkinson's Ferry Meeting*

WITH the passing of the Braddock's Field crisis the attention of the Monongahela country passed to the forthcoming meeting at Parkinson's Ferry on August 14. By the terms of the call, not only the four western counties of Pennsylvania but also the neighboring counties of Virginia were to send delegates. It was apparent to everyone that here was to be made the grand attempt by the disaffected to force the people of the region into open and united resistance to the laws, to lay down an ultimatum to the government that was to be backed by more than threats and desultory riots.

The resistance hitherto had been leaderless or headed by vacillating demagogues or more substantial men who went along only because they hoped to deflect the direction and dissipate the strength of the movement. The advocates of rebellion were, considering everything, remarkably naïve and aboveboard in their methods. As Brackenridge felt justified in writing later, "the intriguers here were all on the side of government; there was nothing but open force against it." The danger of a unification of radicals for the purpose of promoting a revolt was by now so apparent that the more moderate elements felt impelled to unite in support of those of their number who had already been working to avert trouble. The tactics followed were to capture the Parkinson's Ferry meeting from the radicals by packing it with delegates known to favor a moderate policy. There seems to have been no collusion between counties; the program, pointed out by the necessity of the case, was developed independently in each county.

Brackenridge at first favored a policy of lying low to avoid antagonizing the radicals further, but Ross and General Wilkins persuaded him that it was much wiser to bore from within. Efforts were made to have the proper persons announce their candidacy for election as delegates, and Brackenridge became the foremost candidate in Pittsburgh. The election in that town was held with form and ceremony. John Wilkins, Sr., who acted as judge of the election, humorously made it a test of the right to vote that a man must be for Tom the Tinker. Some who failed to catch the burlesque hesitated to declare themselves. When Brackenridge came in, Wilkins waived the question, jocosely saying, "I need not ask any test from you, for you are Tom the Tinker himself." Brackenridge, General Wilkins, George Wallace, Peter Audrain, and John Lucas were the delegates selected. A set of instructions was drawn up containing suggestions that they were to present to the meeting. First, it was proposed that the meeting impress upon the public that the civil law was still in force; second, that the president be asked for "a suspension of force" and for an amnesty; third, that a committee of safety be appointed (with the ulterior object of taking the guidance of affairs out of the hands of the people); fourth, that the people be apprised of the actions of the meetings with the reasons therefor.[1]

Mifflin Township's election was punctuated by a brawl when some citizens broke in at a window to prevent a committee from instructing the township's delegates to ask the Parkinson's Ferry meeting to petition the president. A declaration was finally drawn up disavowing any desire for secession, but insisting that the people would never submit to the excise law.[2] Ross in Washington County and Findley in Westmoreland labored to have moderates elected to the meeting. The more cautious part of the citizenry had at first hesitated, as in Pittsburgh, to take part in the election, and the shortness of the time prevented a full consolidation of their strength on the plan to capture the meeting. Many townships, where the moderates had not learned of the new scheme or where the violent were numerous enough to control, elected radical delegates. In fact it is probable that in most cases only a minority of those qualified participated in the election, so it cannot be said with any certainty that the Parkinson's Ferry meeting really represented the opinion of the region.[3]

Parkinson's Ferry (now known as Monongahela City) was situated on the west bank of the Monongahela River at the mouth of Pigeon Creek, a few miles up the river from the mouth of Mingo Creek. Its name was taken from that of a brother of the fiery Benjamin Parkinson, who operated there a ferry and combination tavern and store and who could be easily persuaded to sell lots in the town that he believed was about to spring up on the site. Parkinson's Ferry was chosen for the meeting because of its central location, roads from most of the adjacent centers of population intersecting there. At the same time it was close enough to the disaffected Mingo Creek region and to the home of the McFarlanes to increase the danger of the meeting's being swayed by the radicals. The place where the conference met on the appointed day was a wooded bench on the shoulder of a hill overlooking the river, a spot still sometimes known as Whiskey Point. Here the delegates accommodated themselves as best they could on stumps and fallen trees or on the grass; the leaves and the sky were their canopy, the hill behind them was their sounding board, and the turbid Monongahela with the abrupt green heights beyond was a scene inspirational enough for any congress of rebels.

There were in all two hundred and twenty-six delegates: forty-three from Allegheny County, ninety-three from Washington, forty-nine from Westmoreland, thirty-three from Fayette, two from Bedford, and six from Ohio County, Virginia. The inevitable gallery was present, more numerous even than the delegates and observant but not always silent, an ominous threat to those whom it might consider lukewarm.[4]

A little before the meeting began Brackenridge met James Marshall and, anxious to gain his favor, observed that the muster at Braddock's Field, though a rash act, might have the good effect of impressing the government with the strength of the movement against the excise. Marshall then, willing to go halfway, admitted that Bradford was hasty in undertaking projects without the ability to retain control of them. Marshall went on to exhibit a five-point program he planned to present to the meeting and Bradford, coming up at this moment, produced a plan for the raising of war supplies and the appointment of a committee of safety to rule the country and direct the war in case one arose. Brackenridge, in turn, concealing his alarm at the boldness of these fire-eaters, showed his resolutions, which on some points agreed with Marshall's program. The conversation shifted then to other and lighter subjects, with Major Craig again furnishing a butt for the laughter. Such was the *camaraderie* developed that Bradford urged Brackenridge to open the meeting by summarizing the events since the march on Pittsburgh and offered him the intercepted letters to read aloud. Brackenridge thought fast and excused himself on the ground that, because of living in the same town with the families of the banished men, the task would be of greater delicacy for him than for Bradford.

The conference selected Edward Cook as chairman and

Albert Gallatin as secretary. After the delegates' credentials had been received, Bradford made an introductory address, then Marshall presented his resolutions. The first resolution, adopting the western view that the county was the vicinage, characterized the taking of citizens from their vicinages for trial as a violation of their rights. Brackenridge spoke, pointing out that constitutionally the entire state was the vicinage of a federal court, but he candidly acknowledged that it was a hardship for a citizen to be forced to attend a court at the opposite end of the state. He therefore approved the substance of the resolution but, taking advantage of Marshall's apologies for his awkwardness of expression, suggested that it might be improved in form and that it would be well for the meeting to approve the sense of this and the succeeding resolutions, then turn them over to a redrafting committee to whip them into final shape. The suggestion was adopted and Marshall took up his resolution which called for a committee of public safety to guard against any invasions of the rights of the people.

Despite the fact that this resolution expressed the view of most of the delegates as well as of the gallery, the courageous Gallatin lost no time in grappling with it. "What reason," said he, according to Brackenridge's report, "have we to suppose, that hostile attempts will be made against our rights? and why, therefore, prepare to resist them? Riots have taken place, which may be the subject of judiciary cognizance; but we are not to suppose a military force, on the part of the government."

Brackenridge, though admiring the courage of the scholarly Genevan, felt that nothing was to be gained by a frontal attack upon this citadel. He preferred to gain his end by pretending to agree with the popular prejudices while at the same time actually undermining them by presenting reasonable policies that, once adopted, would open the way to procrastination and radical alteration. He accordingly affected to oppose

Gallatin, agreed that it might be well to adopt the resolution, but suggested that, to insure a proper phrasing, it should be referred to the projected redrafting committee. Marshall agreed to this and went on. The third resolution, which called for yet one more remonstrance to Congress, was carried. The fourth called for the formulation of a statement and explanation of the motives that had actuated the people of the western country in the late unhappy disturbances. It was referred to the subcommittee. The fifth pledged the West to the support of the laws save for the excise and the removal of citizens for trial outside their vicinages.[5]

Bradford's plan of defense was now called for and presented. Several speakers warmly approved it, Gallatin again being the only one who dared to oppose it, but seemingly with the effect only of making the delegates more set upon taking definite favorable action. Brackenridge once more stepped in, apparently opposing the secretary. The appearance of being ready and eager to fight, he said, might make it unnecessary to do so by scaring the government into giving way. But then why not leave the details to the committee of safety or whatever it might be called? This compromise saved the faces of both sides and gained the devious Brackenridge a reputation with the gallery of being for war. The prestige he had lost at Mingo was returning.[6]

With Bradford, however, he soon lost ground. The banishment of the prothonotary, Brison, was a serious handicap to the transaction of legal business in Pittsburgh, and the delegates from that place urged Brackenridge to solicit Bradford's approval of his recall. Brackenridge finally undertook the task as diplomatically as he could, but Bradford only answered that he would not oppose it but that the people would be dissatisfied at this undoing of what had been accomplished at Braddock's Field. Nothing came of the proposal except that Brackenridge's mask had slipped for a moment and Bradford, now aware that he was being managed, began to feel a definite distrust of the Pittsburgher's loyalty to the insurgent cause.[7]

The committee that was to new-model Marshall's resolutions consisted of four or five, including at least Gallatin, Brackenridge, Bradford, and Harmon Husband, and was to meet early the next morning. That night Brackenridge stayed at a nearby farmhouse with a hundred or so other men about. The coming war was the whole subject of conversation and the Pittsburgh lawyer found himself the center of popular approbation. "Stand by us," was the word, "and we will stand by you." The lawyer lay down upon the floor of the cabin with his head upon a saddle and give himself up to reveries. Suppose that war should come, what should he do? He did not agree with the people that they were in the right, yet he was not sure where his own interest lay. "It is a miserable thing to be an emigrant; there is a secret contempt attached to it." What chance was there of independence? The mountain passes might be defended even if an army could be raised in the East. The people "are warlike, accustomed to the use of arms; capable of hunger and fatigue; and can lie in the water like badgers. They are enthusiastic to madness; and the effect of this is beyond calculation." Even with independence won, however, the region would for a long time be miserable and poverty-stricken. After all, the only solution was an amnesty, but could the president be brought to see that? "The excise law is a branch of the funding system, which is a child of the secretary of the treasury; who is considered as the minister of the President." The secretary would be bloody-minded toward any who opposed his pet measure, and even the president would "be disposed to apply . . . desperate remedies. . . . Nevertheless, the extreme reluctance which he must have, to shed the blood of the people, with whom he is personally popular, will dispose him to overtures of amnesty."[8]

The next morning a liberty pole was raised bearing a flag with six stripes, one for each of the six counties represented at the meeting. Benjamin Parkinson appeared presently with a board, which he fixed upon the pole. Boldly lettered upon it appeared the words, "Equal taxation, and no excise. No asylum for traitors and cowards." There was a feeling in the air that the revolution was on the verge of being accomplished. Other things besides those named the day before were the objects of proposed attacks. Torrence Campbell, of Westmoreland County, innocently sure of a welcome, approached Brackenridge and handed him a set of resolves, which the lawyer after a hasty glance took to be proposals to do away with high salaried officers and to abolish judges learned in the law and substitute justices, as had formerly been the rule. Brackenridge, who as a worshipper at the shrine of the legal mysteries had a horror of practicing before justices, smothered his impatience and shamefully hoodwinked the trusting Torrence. "I took him aside into the bushes," said he, "as if to communicate some great state secrets, and informed him, that the plan agreed upon, was not to take up more things than one at once; —let us bull-bait the excise law for the present, and, in due time, we will knock down everything else." Campbell departed, probably highly honored at this confidence, and perhaps became a loud advocate of gradual reform whenever his fellow commoners appeared too hasty.[9]

The redrafting committee, because of the work of the astute Brackenridge on the previous day, was now in a position to draw the teeth of Marshall's resolutions. Harmon Husband, it will be remembered, was an unkempt, barefooted, backwoods preacher with a farfetched interpretation of Ezekiel's vision of the temple as applying to the western country. Brackenridge attempted to draw Husband out concerning this scriptural interpretation, hoping thus to relieve the tension of the situation. Bradford, however, was too intent upon the purpose of getting a provisional declaration of war in the resolutions to appreciate humor and complainingly asked the Pittsburgher to stop laughing and be more serious. Gallatin, failing to perceive the motive behind the action, acidly commented that "He laughs all by himself."[10]

The nub of controversy, of course, was the authority to be given to the committee of public safety, now renamed the standing committee. Bradford's plan to prepare for war was finally voted down, but Gallatin was forced to allow the inclusion of a sentence that gave the committee the right to take temporary measures in case of sudden emergency. The resolutions as reported to the reassembled meeting were practically the same as they were when first presented save for the arrangement and for the emasculation of the committee.

The original plan had been to have the standing committee composed of county representatives but Brackenridge moved before the meeting that it be composed of two members from each township and put up a specious argument for his proposition. His real purpose was to scatter responsibility and to delay action; and, though there were those who saw through it, the provision (perhaps because of that) was adopted. He also succeeded in giving the standing committee the right to call a meeting of new representatives, his object being to afford himself a loophole for retreat in case the opposition to the government got beyond control. The alacrity with which this amendment was adopted showed that its significance was understood by many and gave some clue to the real attitude of the delegates toward encouraging resistance.[11]

The meeting now adjourned to enable the township representatives to choose members of the standing committee. William Findley had arrived at Parkinson's Ferry at some time during the meeting with the word that commissioners appointed by President Washington to treat with the westerners had arrived at the mouth of the Youghiogheny. There came to hand, probably brought by Findley, a proclamation issued by Washington on August 7 that summarized the troubles in western Pennsylvania and announced that he had determined to call out the militia to combat the treasonable activities in that region. The reading of this proclamation to the reconvened assembly "had a bad effect, seemed to produce anger; the idea of draughting the militia and the charge of being guilty of treason" added strength to the arguments of the militant element. There was a pause when the secretary had finished; then Marshall commented that the proclamation could kill nobody and that, since the business was over, it was best to go home.[12]

The proposal to adjourn met with a stout opposition. The curiosity as well as the suspicions of members of the convention made them feel that the commissioners should appear before them. This would never do. Brackenridge, anxious to avoid a meeting between the commissioners and the temperamental delegates of townships, especially when ringed around by a gallery of commoners, proposed that a committee be appointed to meet the commissioners and report results to the standing committee. The movement to hold the conference in session was opposed by every possible argument: there were no accomodations to speak of, the business would take a long time and would consist of conference and correspondence, and there were no writing conveniences present. Inch by inch the friends of order fought their way and finally won.

The defeated party then moved that the delegates should wait at Parkinson's Ferry until the special committee could confer with the commissioners and report. The old ground was then to be fought over again and the disguise of such men as Gallatin must have worn thin in the struggle as they exerted

themselves mightily but to no effect. James Ross, who unknown to most had just received his appointment as a federal
commissioner, was present. He found Brackenridge walking
on the outside of the circle and urged him to take up the cudgel
and bring a favorable conclusion. "This is the turning point;
you must now speak," he concluded.

"I do not see that I can do anything," said the Pittsburgher.
"Gallatin, and others, have said all that is reasonable in the
case, and yet have failed."

"You can do it," insisted Ross.

Aware that it was mainly curiosity that made the delegates
so eager to remain, Brackenridge stepped into the circle and
struck the proper key at once by depreciating the possibility
that the commissioners had anything of much consequence
to propose. Convinced at last that they would only be wasting
their time by staying, the delegates voted to adjourn.

But the radical party was not yet out of ammunition. There
was still the question of what instructions, if any, should be
given to the special committee. The weary intriguers parried
and thrust again and finally convinced the conference that
instructions could not be given upon the commissioners' propositions before it was known what those propositions were. As a
last concession the standing committee was left to set its own
date for meeting and the conference then adjourned, *sine die*.
The standing committee met at once and fixed the day of its
next gathering as September 2 and Brownsville as the place.

The wearied friends of order must have breathed sighs of
relief as the last bullet of the opposition was spent and the
delegates scattered to their bailiwicks. The tactics of boring
from within had proved successful, with only slight qualifications. But there were still the commissioners to be dealt with,
and a critical and intransigent people looked on ready to take
advantage of the first false step.[13]

Chapter X: *The Commissioners to the White Indians Come and Go*

DEVELOPMENTS in the Monongahela country had been watched with ever increasing anxiety in the East. There were no illusions in official circles in Philadelphia as to the importance of this crisis in the attempt of the federal government to build up its power and prestige by an enforcement of the funding system. The cry was that if the government was to survive, the democrats must be scotched, and what better and more defensible opportunity could be presented for effective scotching than this heaven-sent rebellion in the West.

Washington called a meeting at his home in the Morris House on Market Street for Saturday, August 2. This, of course, was before the news of the march on Pittsburgh had reached Philadelphia. Besides the president, there were present most of the high officials of the federal government and of Pennsylvania—Randolph, Hamilton, Knox, and Attorney-General William Bradford of the former; and of the latter, Governor Mifflin, Chief Justice Thomas McKean, Attorney-General Jared Ingersoll and Secretary of the Commonwealth Alexander James Dallas. The president opened the meeting by calling attention to the gravity of the crisis and asserting "that the most spirited & firm measures were necessary" to prevent the overthrow of the constitution and the laws. He expressed "his determination to go every length that the Constitution and Laws would permit, but no further." The actions of the general government would necessarily be slow, he said, since it must wait for a judicial certification that the disorders were beyond control by judicial authority, and he inquired if there was not some way in which the state could coöperate by adopting preliminary measures.

The state officials were silent, probably each reminded of the prophecy that the federal government would swallow up the states and interpreting this proposal as a step in that direction. Bradford finally broke the tension by reading a law of 1783 authorizing the governor to call out the militia in sudden emergencies, but Dallas quickly pointed out that the law had been repealed. In answer to Bradford's questioning, he gave it as his opinion that the governor, like the president, was obliged to wait for a judicial certificate before he could call out the militia. Washington made it clear that it was his intention to proceed against the rioters by military means; McKean countered with the statement that "the judiciary power was equal to the task of quelling and punishing the riots, and that the employment of military force, at this period, would be as bad as anything that the Rioters had done—equally unconstitutional and illegal." Hamilton then cited the various causes of western discontent and insisted that the crisis be met by an immediate resort to arms. Dallas commented that in the opinion of Judge Addison force would only promote resistance to what would be taken as an attempt to dragoon the people into submission. Hamilton answered that Addison himself was one of the most insidious promoters of the opposition and that his own report to the president contained particulars of the judge's conduct.[1]

On the fourth of August Justice James Wilson issued a certificate stating that the enforcement of the laws in western Pennsylvania was being "obstructed by combinations too powerful to be suppressed" by judicial proceedings, and the next day Hamilton issued his report, giving a history of the disturbances. The split between federal and state officials was emphasized by a letter to the president from Mifflin, prepared by Dallas, arguing that the powers of the courts had not yet been tried and specifically opposing the use of an army. Circular letters, he said, had already been sent to local officials exhorting them to support the laws. Randolph replied for Washington, stating the president's regret that Mifflin saw "Pennsylvania in a light too separate and unconnected," a delicate way of accusing Mifflin of uncoöperativeness. The correspondence dragged on and on, and there is no reason to believe that the state officials ever sincerely abandoned their feeling that that federal government was following a high-handed course.[2]

Washington on the seventh of August issued the proclamation that was later to incur the westerners' anger at the Parkinson's Ferry conference; Mifflin followed suit the same day with a proclamation of his own couched in milder terms than Washington's but announcing a determination to bring the offenders to justice and to give full coöperation to the federal government in the carrying out of its punitive measures. Coincidentally with Washington's proclamation Knox transmitted to the governors of Pennsylvania, New Jersey, Maryland, and Virginia orders to call out thirteen thousand militiamen and to hold them in readiness to march. One more pacific move, however, was decided upon—that of sending commissioners from both Washington and Mifflin to the Monongahela country to seek to heal the breach. The delegation appointed by the president, which of course was the more important, was composed of William Bradford, James Ross, and Jasper Yeates, the last a justice of the Pennsylvania supreme court; Mifflin appointed McKean and General William Irvine.[3]

Bradford lost no time in setting out upon his mission and left Philadelphia on the seventh. The next day at Lancaster he found General Neville and Lenox, who painted dark pictures of conditions in the West and prophesied that the mission would be unsuccessful. Here also Bradford picked up Yeates. On the ninth they met Brison at Carlisle, in company with a young man identified only as Mr. Henry. Addison, said Henry, was discredited in the opinion of the West because he had discountenanced illegal opposition to the excise. He also told them that Mifflin's circular letters to local officials had been treated with ridicule and that some magistrates had contemptuously torn them up.

At Littleton, on the eleventh, the commissioners sent an express to Ross asking him whether or not they should go to Parkinson's Ferry. At Bedford they met Gibson and at Greensburg Presley Neville, from whom they received blacker and blacker accounts of the rebels' actions. Gibson was convinced that the object of many of the people was "a declaration of independence." The common challenge, he said, was, "Are you for Congress or for liberty?" The canny Bradford, however, took hope in the thought that perhaps all the commotion was stirred up for the purpose "of rendering punishment inexpedient and securing an act of Oblivion." The report of the mob's attack on Webster gave rise to the reflection that there was now no office of inspection in the fourth survey.

On the fourteenth the commissioners arrived at Colonel Thomas Morton's home near the mouth of the Youghiogheny, and from there they again wrote Ross, advising that the conference at Parkinson's Ferry, which was only seven miles from Morton's should appoint a small committee to meet with the commissioners in a safe place. Fortunately this very course had already been adopted. Bradford and Yeates, however, unaware of the action taken, drew up a strong letter couched in threatening terms and proceeded to the meeting place to present it to the conference. It was undoubtedly a fortunate circumstance that the conference had adjourned before their arrival. They then went on to Pittsburgh to await the committeemen appointed by the conference. They arrived on the sixteenth and put up at "The Sign of General Butler" on Market Street, kept at the time by the buxom widow, Molly Murphy.[4]

The several days that elasped before the committee was assembled were spent in informal conferring and note taking. This period was also not without excitement as some of the citizens had their own ideas of entertaining commissioners. A number of them got together and raised a liberty pole and were about to hoist a six-striped flag when others intervened and persuaded them to substitute the fifteen stripes of the United States. Brackenridge was among those who called upon the federal commissioners at their tavern soon after their arrival. He found Major Craig giving them a "tragical" account of the treatment of the Nevilles, Kirkpatrick, and others, and as usual casting the blame upon the Pittsburghers. Brackenridge indignantly attacked the major's statements and silenced him by a display of cogent rhetoric. He was not long in discovering what appeared to be unfavorable sentiments in the minds of Bradford and Yeates concerning his loyalty. This revelation was a bitter blow, especially since he and William Bradford had been roommates at Princeton and had been friends ever since. It seemed to the Pittsburgher that his friends, at least, should have known him well enough to realize that if he had been an insurgent he would have had spirit enough to avow it. His immediate thought was to blame the Nevilles, and the fact that Craig was against him lent color to the thought.

The mercurial lawyer plunged into the depths of despair. If the Nevilles continued to hound him upon their return he would be ruined. The alternative of standing with the insurgents presented itself. Could independence be gained? Perhaps. He reviewed the possibilities: "Collect all the banditti on the frontiers of the state . . . tell the Spaniards to come up to the mouth of the Ohio, and give us a free trade; let the British keep the posts, and furnish us with arms and ammunition; get the Indians of the woods to assist us; tell them, that the people on the east of the mountains want our whiskey, and their lands;—we might wage war, and perhaps succeed. . . . These were the thoughts of a night. When I saw James Ross in the morning, I explained to him my chagrin of the preceding day, and my reflections in consequence of it; and gave him to understand, that I had half a mind to become an insurgent. He took it more seriously than I intended it; his expression was, 'The force of genius is almighty; give them not the aid of yours.' I told him, that nothing but self-preservation would lead me to think of it; or the being unjustly suspected. He soothed my mind, by assuring me, that no suspicion could possibly fall on me; that the commissioners, the preceding day, were perfectly satisfied with the explanation I had given in the presence of Craig; and that what he had said, had not left the least impression."

During this period of waiting Brackenridge had his first conversation with Gallatin. Feeling that the latter might have misunderstood his pretense of opposition at Parkinson's Ferry, the lawyer addressed him:

"You understand me, Mr. Gallatin?"

"I do, perfectly," answered the Genevan. He had been puzzled by Brackenridge's actions but Ross had since explained them to him.

Now that the federal commissioners had come and there was a fair chance of an amnesty being arranged. Brackenridge felt it safe to abandon his equivocal position and to come out for law and order. At the first opportunity he broached the subject to David Bradford and James Marshall. The first was angry, the second alarmed. Bradford, indeed, was probably the committeeman least likely to acquiesce to the government's demands, and Irvine and McKean, the state commissioners who had arrived on the seventeenth, undertook to labor with him in order to bring him around.[5]

By this time William Bradford had a number of points on which to report. He pointed out that Brackenridge, who now showed zeal in the cause of good order and the laws, declared that nothing would save the country from the horrors of civil war but waiting till Congress convened. The militia west of the Susquehanna, Bradford said, could not be relied upon. Westerners were not ignorant of what was going on in the East, for they were always corresponding with their friends. Pennsylvania should raise a regular force. The westerners were not much afraid of eastern troops but they did fear that General Morgan and his Virginia mountaineers would be sent against them. There was little ammunition in the West, but Dr. Baird, brigade inspector of Washington County, had seventy-one barrels of powder and five hundred stands of arms, and when the insurgents had demanded them he had parried by saying that it would be "time enough to take them when things came to extremity." Furthermore there was danger that the troops at Fort Le Bœuf, recruited in the West, would bring their field pieces to Pittsburgh and bombard Fort Fayette. Pittsburgh had been forced to affect zeal for the insurgent cause, and Brackenridge and the Wilkinses had been playing a double part—anyone recommending obedience ran the risk of assassination. Bradford believed that firmness on the part of the government in the matter of the navigation of the Mississippi would placate Kentucky, and he stated that there was no evidence that the insurgents had made overtures to the British for an alliance, but that two men from Detroit had appeared a month before in Washington County and had persuaded four hundred signers to undertake to go to a new settlement at the mouth of the Cuyahoga River. The men were now on Buffalo Creek.[6]

Irvine, once the commanding general in the West and now a congressman and resident in Carlisle, was, next to Ross, probably better acquainted than any of the other commissioners with the western mind. He had no sooner reached Pittsburgh than he wrote to Dallas that nothing could be done unless the president would suspend the excise law until the meeting of Congress, or at least connive at its suspension. He agreed with William Bradford that time was essential and that the dead line of September 1 for receiving the westerners' submission was far too early. A few days later he wrote again expressing his sympathy with the western viewpoint, particularly with regard to the trial in York or Philadelphia of law suits involving westerners.

A rain on August 20 delayed the arrival of the committeemen, and the Fayette delegates did not arrive for another day. There finally assembled three committeemen from each of the western counties: Bradford, Marshall, and Edgar from Washington; Morton, Lucas, and Brackenridge from Allegheny; John Kirkpatrick, George Smith, and John Powers from Westmoreland; and Cook, Gallatin, and Lang from Fayette. Ohio County, Virginia, had sent William McKinley, William Sutherland, and Robert Stephenson. Those who were present on the twentieth met and, as was by now almost the habit, proceeded to place Edward Cook in the chair. It was then arranged with the five commissioners that conferences should be secret and at first verbal. As they proceeded to final terms communication should be in writing. The conferences, as might have been expected, began with rhetorical discourses. In answer to the commissioners' demand for assurances that the country would submit to the law in exchange for an amnesty, the committeemen stated that they did not have the power to bind the people to any certain course of action. They could, however, give their personal opinions, which were to the effect that submission was the best course, but they did not dare to recommend this course openly lest they imperil the safety of their persons and property. After this interview the negotiations were carried on by correspondence, the two sets of commissioners drawing up separate communications, which, however, agreed on the main points.

The committeemen were urged, in order to prevent the spread of disaffection, to call together the standing committee at an earlier date than September 2, to recommend to it that assurances of submission be given, and to provide for the holding of meetings in each election district or other convenient places at which the people should give satisfactory evidences of a determination to abide by the law. The committeemen agreed in the end, hedging with the people by stating that they did it to prevent civil war. The commissioners, appreciative of the willingness of the committee to oblige and conscious that the allotted time was too short, promised to hold off the army until further arrangements could be made. The conferences ended on August 23, and the standing committee was called to meet at Brownsville on the twenty-eighth.[8]

The yielding of the conference committee did not by any means end the uncertainty. The people were yet to be convinced. Brackenridge was so pessimistic over the chances of pacification that he sent a friend out to collect money owed him in order to finance his removal to Philadelphia in case of necessity.[9] This action may have been hastened by the appearance in the *Pittsburgh Gazette* of August 23 of "a savage satire" entitled "Speeches intended to be spoken at a Treaty now holding with the Six United Nations of White Indians." The term "White Indians" was then in common use by the government party to designate the insurgents. The satire, which appeared to be an attack upon the supporters of the government, was composed of speeches, each representing an attitude supposedly held by a faction of westerners. In one a Captain Blanket asked for a bribe of blankets and ammunition. In another Captain Whiskey stated that he was willing to go to any length to defend his favorite tipple. "Brothers," he said, "you must not think to frighten us with fine arranged lists of infantry, cavalry and artillery, composed of your water-mellon armies from the Jersey shores; they would cut a much better figure in warring with the crabs and oysters about the Capes of Delaware." Captain Alliance threatened to bring the Kentuckians and the British to the aid of the insurgents, and Captain Pacificus proposed a suspension of hostilities and excise until the meeting of Congress.[10]

The skit enjoyed great popularity in the West and great odium in the East, particularly in New Jersey. Brackenridge, as usual in such cases, was credited with the authorship, and though he publicly disavowed it, there were few who believed him. The sarcasm continued to rankle with easterners and in the end almost led to Brackenridge's assassination. The actual author never had the courage to confess, though he did publish in the *Gazette* of November 1 an explanation that he had intended the article as an *exposé* of the westerners' weakness and corruption rather than a defense of their actions. Whoever he was, he had used a blunderbuss rather than a Kentucky rifle.

The conference committee may have been convinced of the wisdom of submission, but the people were not. The Allegheny County delegation to the standing committee, as it rode to Brownsville, had thorough proof of the popular attitude in the many liberty poles that they saw along the highway. The grape-vine had already conveyed to the people the information, supposed to be secret, that the committee was going to advise submission and the acceptance of an amnesty. A rumor had at once started that the commissioners had come West with their saddlebags laden with gold and had bought off the committee.[11]

It was accordingly not a very sweet-tempered standing committee that gathered at Brownsville on the morning of August 28. A note of relief, however, was furnished by an amusing incident that was turned to advantage by the resourceful Brackenridge. A certain Quaker named Samuel Jackson, resident near Brownsville, had been accused of calling the Parkinson's Ferry meeting a scrub congress, and a company of about seventy armed men from Washington County had come to town to punish him by burning his farm buildings and house. The delegates, after considerable effort, succeeded in persuading the men that, by the arrangements made at Parkinson's Ferry, such cases as this should come before the standing committee. A file of men was sent after the Quaker, and the committee meanwhile met under a temporary board shelter and organized, making Edward Cook chairman and Gallatin secretary. Samuel Jackson proved to be a tall man of a composed and meek air, who stood quietly while the charge against him was proved by two witnesses. The matter was heard with gravity, as befitted the seriousness of the charge; for such dangerous language was an indignity to the new authorities—the gentlemen of the standing committee present—as well as a betrayal of the popular cause. There is no telling what might have followed had not Brackenridge, when it came time for a decision, risen and observed dryly: "This Quaker has called us a Scrub Congress; let our sentence be, that he shall be called a Scrub himself." The crowd's humor suddenly changed and it burst

into a loud laugh. The troop took Jackson off to make a ceremony of bestowing the epithet of "Scrub Quaker" upon him,
while he produced a bucket of whiskey and water to seal his
forgiveness.[12]

The conference committee had had its report printed and
now distributed copies among the members of the standing
committee. The secretary then proceeded to read it to the committee and the large gallery, which included the armed party
that had come for Jackson. As it became apparent that the report was recommending submission, there rose an undertone
of protest from the assembly, as when the congregation in a
church stirs uneasily beneath the ministerial barb. The dissatisfaction was so pronounced that those in favor of the report
decided to ask for an adjournment until the next day. David
Bradford, encouraged or perhaps intimidated by the gallery,
moved for an immediate vote, expressing his surprise that
anyone should require time to decide. He might have had his
way had not James Edgar had the courage to oppose him.
Brackenridge describes Edgar as a "kind of a rabbi" in the
Presbyterian churches of the western country. A devotee of
fasting and prayer, with hair prematurely gray and a thin,
ascetic face, he resembled a Puritan of the Long Parliament.
A veteran also of committees, conventions, and legislative as-
semblies almost without number, he was a man of experience,
eloquence, and judgment, a man to be reckoned with. Rising
to the occasion, he paid ironical compliment to Bradford's
strength of mind and decision of character and begged for a
delay to enable weaker-minded men like himself to make their
choice. He carried the day, the vote being put off till the mor-
row. Bradford immediately seized the opportunity to call a
meeting of the Washington County members for that evening.
The session was a lively affair characterized by blazing oratory
interspersed with talk of guillotining.[18]

The Commissioners to the White Indians

Brackenridge put the Monongahela River between himself and Brownsville for the night, his mind filled with visions of the standing committee, led by such demagogues as Bradford, seizing the submissionists and putting them out of the way. The next morning the committee met in the midst of its attendant gallery (though fortunately the armed party had gone home), and Gallatin, as had been previously decided, addressed the chair. He spoke for some hours, deliberately and didactically, yet with animation, appealing to his hearers' patriotism, covering the situation so completely that there was not much left to say, yet in spite of his bias receiving the most profound attention.[14]

Brackenridge followed, speaking, as he said, more for the sake of showing that he had the courage to speak than with the idea of adding anything of value. His appeal was to the consciences and fears of the people, particularly the latter. He pictured the isolated situation of the region, which would make it almost impossible to maintain an independent existence, and he contrasted the resources in man power of East and West. He ruthlessly punctured the optimistic viewpoint that the westerners were a band of patriots united unto death in the defense of the common liberty:

"But do you know, that you are mistaken in your support at home? Do you think that all are sincere, who have been clamouring for war? Some clamour, because they are cowards, and wish to be thought brave; because they are ignorant enough not to expect a war. Others, because they have not estimated the fatigues of campaigning, and do not consider how soon they will be tired. Others, because they have contracted for the sale of their lands, and are about to remove to Kentucky, or elsewhere. Others, and this class numerous, because they have nothing to lose, and can make their escape by the floods. If you depend upon these, you will by and by have to take the same course, *and descend the current with the frogs.*

"But men affect to be for war, because they are afraid to speak their real sentiments. I have my eye upon those, here present, and could name them, who are thought to be strenuous for the most violent measures; and yet, in the course of our committeeing, have acknowledged to me, what they really think; and it is their earnest desire, to get out of the scrape, upon almost any terms. After what has happened, any terms, short of life, ought to be accepted."[15]

James Edgar came next and advocated submission. He had been the choice of the submissionists for first speaker but had declined; he now spoke at length "with great earnestness, and with the solemnity of an evening sermon." David Bradford then rose and, throwing aside his agreement to support the decision of the conference committee, launched into a harangue against the report and directly advocated resistance. He brushed aside Brackenridge's warnings.

"We will defeat the first army that comes over the mountains," he said, "and take their arms and baggage."

"Not so easy neither," retorted an old Indian fighter in the gallery. Bradford seems to have been in fear of the people and willing to go to any length to escape immediate loss of popularity or perhaps even bodily injury.[16]

When Bradford had finished speaking Gallatin moved to vote on the commissioners' offer. The body refused to vote even by ballot lest the handwriting of those voting for acceptance be recognized. It seemed that the terms were about to be rejected by the simple expedient of preventing a vote, when it was proposed that the secretary write on slips of paper the words "yea" and "nay" and that the delegates tear off their choice, cast their vote in the secretary's hat, and tear up or chew the remaining part. The suggestion was adopted, each man dropping his ballot with great care so as to conceal the word it bore. When the votes were counted, there were found to be thirty-four for acceptance and twenty-three against, and six men later claimed they had voted "nay" under a misapprehension. The opinions held by individuals in committee and gallery were clearly discernible in their faces; most of the committeemen were relieved, the members of the gallery were disgusted and even angered. Bradford took advantage of an intermission in the proceedings to go home.[17]

When the committee convened again the question arose as to whether or not more favorable terms than those laid down at Pittsburgh could be obtained from the commissioners. The conference committee thought not. The standing committee had hopes that something could be done, and some aspersions were cast upon the sincerity of the men who had interviewed the commissioners. In the end a new conference committee was appointed, and the old one yielded up its duties with relief. It was also resolved to adopt the democratic method of ascertaining the will of the people by permitting them to vote for or against the acceptance of the commissioners' offer.[18]

The gallery had been small at this last session, but upon the adjournment of the committee it had became apparent that the men were still on hand, broken up into small knots and engaged in close conversation. Brackenridge, as he passed by, spoke to various men who were or had been his clients, but he was received with silence and angry looks. One of his companions, not of the committee, assured the lawyer that something was up. The latter lost no time in crossing the river, and, as soon as some of the other delegates from Allegheny County had joined him, he set off for home, riding far enough that night to get through the most of the Mingo Creek settlement. There actually had been a project to seize Brackenridge and Gallatin, but lack of decision had prevented it.[19]

The size of the vote against submission in the standing committee and David Bradford's fiery advocacy of violence did not prepossess the commissioners in favor of moderating their terms. The United States representatives reported to Randolph that the only Washington County delegate to vote for compliance was James Edgar and that the county sheriff, Colonel John Hamilton, though personally disposed toward peace, let himself be swayed by his battalion. Parts of Allegheny and Westmoreland counties, they wrote, were still disaffected but Fayette was wholly inclined to submit. "We regret," the report continued, "that we have still much Reason to apprehend, that the Authority of the Laws will not be *universally* & *perfectly* restored, without military Coercion." The commissioners apprehended that little good would result from the meeting with the new committee, as it included "some of the Men most violent for Resistance, particularly Corbley & Philips, two Baptist Preachers." William Bradford wrote that he had been told that two packtrains of five hundred horses each had departed for the East. It was announced that they were going for salt but it was too early in the season for that so the implication was that they were going for ammunition. The majority of the residents of Washington County, reported the Pennsylvania commissioners to Mifflin, preferred civil war to submission, "so infatuated and frantic are the Leaders in opposition."[20]

The second conference between commissioners and committee took place on the first and second of September. A feeble attempt was made to obtain better terms, but without success. The committee capitulated without more ado and signed an agreement providing for a popular referendum to be held upon the eleventh of September. The citizens eighteen years of age and over were to meet and vote "Yea, or nay" to a statement of submission to the laws of the United States and those voting in the affirmative were to sign the following ironclad declaration: "I do solemnly promise henceforth to submit to the laws of the United States, that I will not, directly or indirectly, oppose the execution of the acts for raising a revenue on distilled spirits and stills; and that I will support, as far as the law requires, the civil authority in affording the protection due to all officers and other citizens." In exchange for this conformity they were to receive on the tenth of the next July a pardon for past offenses.[21]

The wording of this promise raised a storm of protest. Some Presbyterians objected to the word "solemnly" on the ground that it made the declaration an oath, which could not be conscientiously taken. "Henceforth" implied that the signers had previously broken the laws, a supposition that, said many citizens indignantly, was not true. "Indirectly" was thought by some to preclude the signing of petitions for repeal of the excise. The commissioners allowed the words "solemnly" and "henceforth" to be omitted, but their decision, published in the *Pittsburgh Gazette,* came too late to many sections to afford relief. The great fault in the procedure was that circumstances did not permit the commissioners to allow sufficient time for the people to reflect, and in fact many did not know the terms of the submission until they came to the polls to cast their votes.[22]

The commissioners were not to get out of the region without a taste of western direct action. McKean, it was rumored, had been the stiffest in his demands and had even insisted upon the recall of the exiles. When the commissioners stopped at the house of Simon Drum in Greensburg on their way east, a rioter, attempting to force a quarrel, accused McKean's servant of stealing his boots and spurs and tried to gain admittance to the house, but he was driven away under threat of being fired upon. A party of semi-intoxicated men then gathered and took turns in shouting insults at the sleeping commissioners. Several stones were thrown, one of which broke an upper window, and General Irvine, who was in the room, put his head out and threatened to fire, whereupon the assailants incontinently fled. The rest of the commissioners were not awakened. Thirteen of the rioters were later indicted and punished.[23]

The United States commissioners, at least, seem to have been encouraged by the results of their mission. "The Issue on which we have at last been able to put the Business," they wrote, "is a more favorable one than we hoped for." There was an ominous note, however, in Randolph's letter in which he conveyed Washington's thanks to the commissioners for their services. "He ascribes to your conduct," the letter read, "the prospect of finding but a feeble opposition; and let the opposition be what it will, you have at least amply prepared the public mind for the support of any measures, which may be necessary on the occasion."[24]

Chapter XI: *The Solemn Promise*

THE town of Pittsburgh was still buzzing with talk of the Brownsville meeting when on September first the Allegheny County court convened under the presidency of Judge Addison. He had stopped in Bedford on his way from the court of errors and appeals in Philadelphia, fearing to go to his home in Washington, but had finally decided to go on to Pittsburgh even at the peril of his life. The common room of Andrew Watson's log tavern at Front and Market streets was then used as town hall and courthouse and it must have been filled to overflowing by those curious to learn for themselves what the doughty, thick-tongued Scotchman would have to say concerning recent events.

His hearers must have gasped at the boldness of his words, even spoken as they were in the supposed western stronghold of federalism. He did not qualify nor palliate. He castigated those who would pretend to dictate to the vast majority and warned them that if they succeeded no law would have any force. The course of reason and humanity demanded a submission to the excise law on any conditions, especially such mild ones as those laid down by the commissioners. "A rejection of the conditions," said he, "is a declaration of war; and war is the sure road to ruin." The westerners' boasts that the government would not dare to send troops against them and that if it did, the troops could easily be routed in the mountain passes, were characterized as delusions. Delusions also were the hopes of aid from Britain or from any other source. The Monongahela country could not be counted upon to act as a unit, but on the contrary it would be divided into factions, and murder, rapine, and famine would lay it prostrate before an army could reach its borders.

The judge declared that the cry of tyranny and discrimination on the part of the government against the West was no longer valid, if it ever had been. He proceeded in a few expressive sentences to cut the ground from under the feet of the opposition: "The progress of this country to wealth has been amazingly rapid.—There have been more public and private buildings raised and fewer sheriff sales for debt, within this period, than for nine years past preceding.—Three years ago, I believe, there was hardly a burr millstone in this country: now there are perhaps a dozen. The quantity of money circulating among us is since greatly increased; and the value of all property is thereby greatly increased; in other words the value of money is greatly lessened, and thereby the value of the excise to be paid by us is greatly lessened. *Then* there was hardly any trade to the Spanish settlements on the Mississippi; it was, at any rate, small, and confined to a few adventurers: the quantity of grain exported was but little; of course but little was withdrawn from our own consumption; and this little was generally bought with goods.

"*Now* a very respectable trade is carried on to the Spanish settlements; our traders are treated with great civility by the Spaniards; the duty on our trade is reduced to a mere trifle; and there is very little difficulty in bringing away dollars in return. We shall soon have the whole supply of that market to ourselves. Last spring, our best flour was sold there a dollar each barrel dearer than flour from New York.—None of the traders now depend on goods for the purchase of wheat; but must purchase, at a reasonable price, in money. From this increased exportation of our grain, the necessity of distillation is greatly *lessened in degree,* and will every day lessen. Government does not *now,* as *formerly* supply the army with whiskey, through contractors purchasing with goods; but employs agents to purchase it with money. Last year ten thousand dollars was laid out, in this way, by one agent in this country; and the execution of an order for ten thousand more, was stopt only by the present troubles. The contractors themselves have, these two last years purchased their supplies with cash. From these circumstances, and the pay, and other expenses of the army, government sends *far* more money to this side of the mountains, than it would draw back by the excise. At the commencement of this law, a very great quantity of foreign spirits was consumed in this country. But so severe is the duty which this law lays on foreign spirits, that the people on the east side of the mountains drink such spirits at a very increased price, and our store keepers cannot afford to bring foreign spirits, in any considerable quantity, over the mountains."

Perhaps, he admitted, these facts did not entirely remove the objection to the excise, but they certainly lessened it. The only way to get the law repealed, moreover, was to submit and by this means obtain the right to have protests heard. The approaching end of the Indian war would obviate the necessity for extraordinary expenses and incline Congress to listen to proposals for repeal. The discourse ended on a high note of patriotism and piety: "They [*the sentiments expressed*] are mine—" the judge declared, "and were an angel from Heaven to charge me, to make to you, as I should answer it at the tribunal of God, a faithful declaration of my opinion of the interests of this country, at this important period, I would, were it the last moment of my life, address you, as I have now done. And, O! may the God of wisdom and peace inspire this people with discernment and virtue, remove from their minds blindness and passion, and save this country from becoming a field of blood."

The grand jury's attitude was not such as to encourage the judge. "The above sentiments, of peace and obedience, to the laws," according to a note attached to the address as printed in the *Gazette*, "would have received the sanction of the Grand Jury; but as a few members declined their assent, silence was thought better, than an approbation not *unanimous*."[1]

The loyalists among the Pittsburghers felt that the propositions of the commissioners had set up a standard "round which those, opposed to the insurrection, could rally" and proposed that they now form an armed association for their own defense and the support of the laws. The ever cautious Brackenridge feared that such an organization might be taken by the country people as evidence of the townsmen's distrust of them and might lead to a march that could not be diverted so easily as the last one had been. General Wilkins, however, who had lost patience, was in favor of organizing and stated that "he would lose his life, rather than to be bullied any longer." A town meeting was therefore called for the sixth of September. The majority of the citizens decidedly disagreed with Wilkins as to the expediency of organizing, and the meeting was adjourned until evening to allow time for reflection. During the interim several of the leading citizens met and at Brackenridge's suggestion drew up a compromise, by which an organization was proposed to preserve the town's neutrality. This met with popular approval, the articles of association were signed by most of the inhabitants, and plans were formed for defense in case of necessity.[2]

The period intervening between the departure of the commissioners and the day appointed for the signing of the solemn promise was one of turmoil. Some now dared to stand by a program of submission, but the recalcitrant elements became even more stubborn. Tom the Tinker renewed his literary activities, and John Scull did not dare refuse to grant him space in the *Gazette*. Tom announced that he was obliged to take up his commission again because the men chosen by the people as leaders, having been scared by four or five big men from below, had turned out to be traitors. His friends were urged to keep up their spirits and traitors to take care "for my hammer is up, and my ladle is hot."[3] Prudent men continued to urge a compliance with the terms of the commissioners. Foremost among them were the Presbyterian clergy, who had boldly denounced violence from the very first, though they had no sympathy with the principle of an excise. McMillan had the temerity to postpone the date for administering communion to his congregations until after the eleventh with the expressed intention of barring those who did not sign; and the presbyteries of Redstone and Ohio at the suggestion of the Synod of Virginia called "a day of fasting and prayer to confess our own sins and the sins of our land, to mourn over them before God, and to deprecate the divine wrath manifested in the many judgements [*sic*] which hang over our land in general, and which more especially threaten this country because of the late very sinful and unconstitutional opposition which has taken place to some of the laws of the United States."[4]

By this time the violent elements were receiving encouragement from sympathetic riots in western Virginia and even east of the mountains. Doubtless this had much to do with the stiffening of the resistance of the malcontents in the Monongahela country, for it actually began to look as though they were justified in their boasts that even the people farther east would take their side.

The members of the conference committee from Ohio County, Virginia, to their chagrin and alarm, had been specifically excluded by the commissioners from the negotiations at Pittsburgh, and they proceeded to write a letter protesting such treatment and asking also that Ohio County offenders against the law be given the same consideration as Pennsylvanians. A recent attack, however, had been made on Zacheus Biggs, the Ohio County collector, and certain bonds had been taken from him. The commissioners finally offered to recommend clemency except for the perpetrators of this attack, but the Ohio County delegates in a delightfully misspelled letter, refused to accept the qualified offer until they could consult with their constituents. It was probably in pursuance of their decision that a meeting of delegates of the militia of Ohio County was held at West Liberty on the eighth and ninth of September and a set of resolutions was adopted condemning various policies of the federal government and ending with a veiled threat against those "whose interests is different from that of the people at large."[5]

Monongalia County, Virginia, was the seat of some disturbances in August. The collector, stationed at Morgantown, was warned by letter that if he did not resign he would be forced to give up his commission and his property would be destroyed. Sentiment against the enforcement of the excise was so strong in the immediate region that he considered discretion the better course and decamped, leaving his resignation posted on his door. The rioters appeared, about thirty in number, with blacked faces, but finding their victim gone they went off peaceably. There were some later minor disorders, but some of the citizens organized and cleared the town of trouble makers. Morgantown did well to preserve a state of neutrality during the period of turmoil in the North, and one inhabitant wrote that the town was "much threatened even for lying still by our Powerful neighbors." Governor Lee issued a proclamation on August 20 attributing the disturbances in the county to Pennsylvanians, but it later appeared that they were perpetrated by Virginians.[6]

A gathering held near Martinsburg in the Shenandoah Valley on September 4 for the purpose of erecting a liberty pole was attacked and scattered by a militia detachment. Several of the leaders were caught but were later admitted to bail on promise of future good behavior.[7] In nearby Winchester some citizens and a number of volunteers gathering for the western expedition put up two poles in the public squares in opposition to the insurgents and hoisted banners inscribed "For Liberty and the Laws of our Country." The people marched around the poles after a military band and partook of the spirituous offerings of some generous citizens. The celebration in some quarters seems to have been credited to sympathizers with the insurgents, much to the discomfiture of those responsible for the raising of the poles. Perhaps because of this demonstration the Winchester paper was particularly venomous in ridiculing the idea that western Pennsylvania was peaceably inclined. "Chaste republicans" knew better, and "the mighty arm of an offended people is uplifted against them."[8]

The first part of September was punctuated by a number of riots in Maryland. Most of them were the result of opposition to the draft, which had already proved necessary in the raising of the army to be used against the westerners. An exception was an attempt about the first of September to force Collector Selby of Cumberland to give up his papers, but the attempt was foiled by the presence of a militia company. Several poles, each bearing a flag carrying the inscription "Liberty or Death," were erected near Middletown, west of Frederick, but they were cut down by troops from the latter place and the flags were burned publicly under the pillory at Frederick.[9] Disturbances in Hagerstown were more difficult to control. When the militiamen were called into service they beat off their officers and celebrated the victory by putting up a liberty pole in the courthouse square. The next morning the pole was cut down by the magistrates, whereupon the militia, aided by friends from the country, put up another pole and swore to kill anyone who disturbed it. The malcontents even decided to march upon Frederick and plunder the arsenal located at that place, but desisted when the citizens of Frederick armed and intrenched themselves to withstand attack. Troops were dispatched to Hagerstown from Baltimore, Frederick, and Montgomery, and the ringleaders of the mob were hunted down and imprisoned.[10]

The rioting in central Pennsylvania also seems to have arisen partly from an opposition to the draft. The road near Bedford was said to have had a liberty pole every four or five miles, and three hundred men erected one in the middle of the town itself, though the court was in session at the time. The judges prudently took no notice of the event. Some Chambersburgers who were censured by a town meeting for raising a pole penitently chopped it down and hauled it away. The excise and the draft were odious all through central Pennsylvania, and the resistance to them was everywhere expressed by the erection of liberty poles.[11] At Northumberland a pole studded with nails was erected at one of the principal corners. The arsenal was broken open and the weapons were seized by the insurgents, who held possession of the town for several days. A company of militia from Lancaster finally arrived and dispersed the guardians of the pole with a bayonet charge. The destruction of the pole was preceded by a skirmish over the possession of an ax between two sisters who took opposite stands on the excise question. Some of the ringleaders were arrested and sent to Philadelphia for trial.[12]

Carlisle seems to have had the liveliest time. The collector for Cumberland County was visited by a party of men with blackened faces on the evening of August 28 and was forced to resign. On the night of September 8 or 9 a pole was erected in the public square of Carlisle bearing the inscription "Liberty and No Excise, O Whiskey." The next morning it was cut down. The angry rioters thereupon reassembled in even greater number and put up another. The pole became the scene of a nightly celebration accompanied by much noise and shooting. Peaceable citizens who ventured out were stopped and forced to contribute money for the purchase of whiskey for the crowd.[18]

As the day for the signing in the five western counties came nearer it was apparent that the opposition was still uncowed, though more disorganized than it had been during July and August. It is conceivable that the news of Wayne's victory over the Indians at Fallen Timbers on August 18 had done something to pacify the fears of the residents on the exposed portions of the frontier and to weaken their support of violent opposition to the government, and moreover the timid feared the might of the army that was gathering in the East. "A Friend to Peace" wrote to the *Gazette* pleading with the people to sign and suggesting that in case of civil war the innocent would thus be known and protected. The innocent, however, were canny about making themselves known. The threats of Tom the Tinker were still too potent to be disregarded. The eleventh dawned, a day of confusion and misapprehension, not to mention threats and violence. Some officials had not received the necessary forms and so wrote out extemporaneous oaths, which the people signed. In one settlement, after the people waited all day for the papers, a petition appeared praying for a repeal of the excise, the first two lines of which seemed to be a promise to submit to the laws. Misapprehending its true nature, the great "magourity," who were in favor of submission, proceeded to sign the petition. In some township meetings the people decided that since they had never broken the law they were not obliged to sign. Numerous absentees authorized others to sign for them. Results more favorable to submission might have been attained everywhere if the voting had been by ballot rather than by voice.[14]

The meeting in Unity Township, Westmoreland County, the home of William Findley, was terrorized by insurgents, and the paper bearing the signatures of the submissionists was snatched from the hands of the presiding official and destroyed. The next Saturday a number of the citizens met and signed again. At Greensburg only eighty out of three hundred dared to sign, and they were in danger that night for having done so. In Elizabeth Township, Allegheny County, at the junction of the Youghiogheny and Monongahela rivers, it was proposed that "every one should be at liberty to speak his mind freely, without danger of having his property burnt for so doing—but this motion was over ruled, and on putting the motion for submission the majority was for war." In another Allegheny County district an armed party, hoping to prevent the voting, took the forms from the official who had agreed to distribute them.[15]

The people of Canonsburg signed, apparently without trouble. Bradford advocated submission in Washington, saying that he had been deserted and could not hold out alone, and he defended his action in a two-hour speech to a courthouse gathering. Nottingham Township in Washington County had been one of the most recalcitrant, and when the venerable Judge Edgar attempted to speak to the people gathered at the polls he was hissed and pelted with mud and stones. The table provided for official use was carried away and the meeting was broken up. There is a tradition that the Reverend Samuel

Porter preached a powerful sermon on the passage in Romans 13:1-7 beginning, "Let every soul be subject unto the higher powers," and brought peace and submission. At Mingo Creek the militia appeared, ready for combat. Only a few had signed when the paper was seized and torn up. That night a number of people gathered and signed a duplicate paper. The inhabitants of the upper part of Washington County, who had been involved little or not at all in the disturbances and who did not receive notice of the test oath until a late date, did not turn out in very great numbers. In fact the general attitude of the people of the frontier townships was that they had nothing to do with the disturbances and therefore did not need to take the oath. The inhabitants of Fayette County did not sign the oath prescribed, because of a misunderstanding among the people concerning the agreement between the committee and the commissioners, but some of them did sign an assurance of submission. Only a fraction of the qualified electors turned out, and the townships of Tyrone and Bullskin rejected submission.[16]

There were indications that the spirit of the opposition was hollow, supported in many places only by mutual fear. James Ross, who had remained in the West to receive the lists, when he started east was pursued by two men, who gave out that they intended to seize the papers from him. When they overtook him, it transpired that they simply wanted to add their names to those who had agreed to submit. The same thing was said to have occurred to many local election officials as they left the polling places.[17]

Brackenridge has left an account of his experiences in the heart of the insurgent country upon the day of the vote. He had attended the Greensburg court and had been urged by some of his Westmoreland friends to run for Congress in that district against Findley. He had declined, however, since he and Findley had become reconciled at the Redstone meeting during the effort to avert a civil war. A young man named Parker who lived near Parkinson's Ferry planned to leave Greensburg the day before the voting in order to be at home in time to sign the submission papers, and Brackenridge, feeling, as he said, a passion for risking his own safety in the good cause, decided to go along.

They arrived at Parkinson's Ferry the next morning and inquired of a ferryman concerning the feeling of the country toward the oath and were referred to a Major Scott who was loading his rifle near them. Scott answered that he was over "the other day, on Mingo creek, when there were about 200 present, and they all, to a man, pledged themselves not to sign, and to shoot any man that will. I am going to the meeting in the forks of the rivers, and I will take care that nobody shall sign there." Brackenridge's heart failed him at this recital and he proposed to his companion, as soon as they had crossed the river, that he make his way directly to Pittsburgh.

Inquiry at the ferry house of Joseph Parkinson revealed, however, that Scott had exaggerated the hostility of the people. Parker then urged the lawyer to go on with him to Benjamin Parkinson's, and upon Brackenridge's protest that Benjamin Parkinson and Andrew McFarlane, neighbors, were the two men most disposed to assassinate him, Parker pledged himself to defend him with his life. When they reached Parkinson's they leaped the fence into the barnyard and rode up to the house. A horse stood there, saddled, and Brackenridge was far from reassured at the sight of a rifle at the door. Entering the house he was appalled at the sight of Parkinson and McFarlane together, with another rifle standing near McFarlane. Concealing his confusion, the lawyer addressed Parkinson with apparent confidence and was answered with evident good humor and even pleasure. Parker and Parkinson then went out of the room, leaving Brackenridge seated near McFarlane.

Brackenridge, measuring the distance to window and door, turned to his companion and, assuming a frankness that he did not feel, observed:

"Mr. McFarlane, these are disagreeable times."

"Indeed they are, Mr. Brackenridge," McFarlane answered, with every evidence of cordiality, "I have been for these two days afraid of my life because I recommended submission. I have been afraid to sleep at home, and I am obliged now to go with my rifle."

Parkinson entered at that moment and, expressing his happiness that Brackenridge had been interested in coming over to serve the settlement, said that he intended to sign the oath. McFarlane then advised Brackenridge that it would not be safe to go to the Mingo meeting, but agreed to carry a letter to David Hamilton. The lawyer thereupon hastily indited a note to Hamilton, stating that the rest of the western country was disposed to submit and warning the people of the Mingo Creek settlement against standing out alone.

Brackenridge left for Pittsburgh by a roundabout way in order to avoid the Mingo meeting. He met numbers of people bound for that place, all of them armed. He stopped at a cabin to inquire the way and found John McDonald, the secretary of the Mingo Creek Democratic Society. McDonald during the ensuing conversation advised him not to go to the meeting, saying, "Let them go to the devil their own way." He then pointed out a road that would avoid the meeting place but that led past the house of John Holcroft.

"That is the very man," said Brackenridge, "that I am the most afraid of; he is Tom the Tinker. I was obliged to put up with the insulting language of one of his sons, the other day, in Pittsburgh; not thinking it safe to resent it, in the present state of things. He threatened the town with Tom the Tinker."

McDonald thereupon gave him directions as to how, by taking a woods path, he could avoid Holcroft's house. Before Brackenridge could reach the path, however, he met two men on horseback, one of whom accosted him by name. The man expressed his sorrow that he had set out before Brackenridge had reached his house, as otherwise he could have provided a drink of whiskey for him and a bait for the horse. In the end the strangers turned around and accompanied the lawyer, who, not knowing with whom he had to deal, dared not beg off. Presently when they arrived at the house Brackenridge recognized it as one that had been sold to John Holcroft some years before. The man who had insisted upon turning back to proffer his hospitality was none other than Tom the Tinker in person.

The conversation turned upon the business of the day, and Holcroft stated that the people of the neighborhood threatened death to signers.

"That is unreasonable," said the second man, "it is not so with us, in our settlement. We allow free liberty of conscience, and molest no man for doing what he pleases. Every man that chuses to submit, let him do it; and we give him five weeks, to sell off his effects, and move out of the country."

Holcroft was uncertain whether or not to sign, and Brackenridge gave him his opinion of the way the country would act. Presently the lawyer continued on his way. A few miles farther on toward Peter's Creek he found the people signing the submission papers in spite of the opposition of William Miller's militia company, which was standing by in a grove. Brackenridge gave an account of affairs in general to those who came around him, and he then set out for Pittsburgh. When he arrived there he found that the people had nearly all taken the oath, but since the hours for signing were over he waited until the next day to add his name to the list.[18]

The report of the United States commissioners was made

on September 24, and the status of the various counties was outlined therein. No official information had been received from Allegheny County, and though it was understood that Pittsburgh had submitted there was no reason to believe that the rest of the county had. The election superintendents of Washington County had certified that a majority would submit to the excise "under a hope and firm belief that the Congress of the United States will repeal the law." They did not, however, "state the number of the yeas and nays" and they refused to express an opinion as to the feasibility of reëstablishing an office of inspection. Westmoreland's report also failed to give the vote, and the superintendents asserted that an excise office could not yet be set up with safety. Fayette had not voted in the form prescribed but was largely in favor of submission in spite of the intransigence of certain sections. Bedford had not been heard from. The commissioners concluded the report by stating their belief that the majority of the citizens favored submission but were intimidated by a violent minority. They saw no possibility of enforcing the law without extra-judicial help. The report thus caused the acceleration of the military preparations that were already well under way.[19]

John Woods, who will be remembered as the attorney of the Neville connection and the enemy of Brackenridge, had been absent from Pittsburgh during the late disturbances but had returned early in September. According to Brackenridge, Woods had scarcely had time to take stock of the situation before he began a whispering campaign with the object of making it seem that Brackenridge had been a conspirator with David Bradford in planning the outrages of July and August. At a town meeting held on the seventeenth at the instigation of Woods and a relative of Kirkpatrick, a proposal to recall the exiles was made, and a resolution to that effect was boldly published in the *Pittsburgh Gazette*. Brackenridge, still fearful of arousing the country, was opposed to both the resolution and its publication but, wary of being caught between two fires, refused to make an issue of the matter.[20]

The passing of the eleventh of the month brought time for meditation and the consequent growth of apprehensions as to the future. Citizens now found courage to band together and pass resolutions favoring submission, and Greensburgers organized a special troop to be held in readiness to protect those who might be in danger. General William Jack and William Findley had already jailed one of the insurgent ringleaders, a militia officer named Straw, and with a large party had marched to disperse a gathering of his followers. Findley and Jack then hastened to inform their correspondents that the county was now pacified except for the Germans, who, ignorant of English, were easily imposed upon and who were still inclined to be turbulent.[21]

Fayette County was not, in spite of its independence on the signing day, disposed to resist. Meetings of distillers were held during the summer, and even those who had been served with processes by Lenox saw no reasonable course but to submit. It was discovered that the processes had been made returnable on a day on which no court was to be held and therefore they were held to be void. As a matter of fact a special session was held on the day and the writs returned. Fifteen of the cases were discontinued; the disposition of the rest is unknown.[22]

The Washington County court was opened on the twenty-second by Judge Addison with the same speech that he had delivered at Pittsburgh. Bradford's recommendation of submission had resulted in a decline in his popularity, and the pious, in discussing him, harked back to scripture with the words "Dagon is fallen." His inflammatory speech at Brownsville had placed him outside of the operation of the proposed amnesty but apparently he still hoped that signing would result in his inclusion. John Woods was present at the court and frequently in the company of Bradford. Brackenridge suspected, probably not without cause, that they were hatching trouble for him. The Washington Democratic Society also held a meeting at this time, and a young lawyer who had been appointed to draft resolutions relative to the outrages applied to Brackenridge for assistance. Brackenridge's draft condemned the disorders so strongly that at Bradford's motion action on the resolutions was postponed, and they subsequently died a natural death. After the adjournment of the court a meeting of the principal men of the county was held to consider conditions and pass resolutions in favor of law and order. Brackenridge, who was present, took the occasion to observe that the best method of assuring the government of the good intentions of the citizens was to reconvene the original Parkinson's Ferry meeting, pass the proper resolutions, and send delegates to the president. The suggestion was adopted and the meeting was called for October 2.[23]

The second Parkinson's Ferry meeting was brief. A considerable number of the original delegates attended and probably some others who had not served in the first meeting. David Bradford, as might have been expected, was prominent in the meeting and was instrumental in having his creature, John Canon, elected as chairman over the protests of the more conservative. Judge Addison, who had not been one of the original delegates, was made secretary. Resolutions were adopted promising submission to the laws and stating it as the opinion of the delegates that there was "a general disposition" to submit to all the laws. William Findley and David Redick were appointed, on Bradford's motion, as a committee to carry the resolutions to President Washington and to unfold to him the true state of mind in the Monongahela country toward the enforcement of federal authority.[24] The members then scattered to attend to their political fences, for the general elections of October 14 were in the offing.

The congressional seat of the district composed of Washington and Allegheny counties was being contested among Brackenridge, John Woods, Thomas Scott, and Daniel Hamilton. Hamilton, with the idea of strengthening his own candidacy by inducing Brackenridge to relinquish his, wrote to the latter asking whether or not he meant to stay in the race and pointing out that public sentiment had been strongly against him since the Brownsville meeting. Brackenridge answered that he was not thinking of the election now; he had more important matters in mind. As a matter of fact he was afraid that election at hands of the insurgents would put him in a bad light, but he had too much pride to withdraw from the contest. Hamilton, however, according to Brackenridge, took his reply as a withdrawal and rode over the country announcing that the lawyer was no longer running. At the same time, wrote Brackenridge a year later, Woods was going about representing Brackenridge to both sides as double-faced, and Major Craig was placing the horses from the government stables at the disposal of the Neville candidate for electioneering purposes.[25]

The outcome of this rivalry was a surprise. Scott was unpopular because he had leaned too much toward the excise. Brackenridge was accused of being double-faced, and McMillan and the Presbyterians distrusted him because he had resigned his license to preach and had learned to swear. Woods was a Neville satellite, and Hamilton was too much of a Jacobin. Three days before the election McMillan called a meeting of a few of his potent friends at Canonsburg and had Albert Gallatin announced as a candidate. Ballots were then printed and hastily distributed to the dozen or so election districts in the two counties, and Gallatin was swept into office. He himself did not know until the eve of the election that he was being run for this office, and in consequence he found himself elected to Congress and to the state legislature at the same time. In the election Brackenridge ran second, Scott third, and Woods and Hamilton trailed. Intransigent Mingo Creek gave Hamilton 132 votes, Woods 90, and Brackenridge only 24—apparently Woods stood better in that center of rebellion than did Brackenridge. Findley was reëlected for the Westmoreland-Fayette district. The other successful candidates were in the main moderates, or even federalistic: Washington County sent Stokely and Baird to the state Senate, and Presley Neville and Gallatin were among those elected to the state House of Representatives.[26]

The Monongahela country had put Tom the Tinker in his proper place, but it was too late. An army was already threading its way through the defiles of the mountains.

Chapter XII: *The Watermelon Army Marches*

DURING the summer of 1794 the Whiskey Insurrection shared the interest of Philadelphians with putrid hides from New Orleans and the plague in Baltimore. With the approach of fall, however, and the certainty that troops were going to be sent west the troubles in the Monongahela country sprang into an important place in the news. Rumors sped up and down the Atlantic seaboard. The *Boston Mercury* stated that the "Insurgent Club" of Pittsburgh had established an army and navy. Another paper quoted some "serious facts" to the effect that nine out of ten of the Pittsburgh insurgents were Irish and Scotch newcomers. A Philadelphia diarist wrote on September 16 that there had been a "great bustle in ye City yesterday, on acct. of a number of armed men who were coming down from the back country." It scarcely needs to be added that this was a false alarm.[1]

Hamilton had meanwhile published, under the name of Tully, a series of letters denouncing the insurgents and artfully attempting to show that anyone who critized the excise or prated of corruption in the administration was not only an enemy to the constitution but to all orderly government.[2] He had struck the point that the Federalists were to bring out again and again in their denunciations of the opposite party.

The Watermelon Army Marches

No matter how often the democrats proved that the attitude was unfair and extreme, the Federalists invariably wailed that any criticism of the administration would lead inevitably to violence and treason and that here in the West was the sad proof. Mere repetition often accomplishes what reason cannot, and it was not long before the dominant elements in the East were really convinced that a crisis was at hand. Even the leaders of the rising Jeffersonian party gave way, and Mifflin, Dallas, and McKean, outgeneraled by the superior tactics of Hamilton, found themselves reluctantly coöperating with him. The leader of the party, the redoubtable Thomas Jefferson himself, had retired from the cabinet before the outbreak of the crisis and had prudently declined to express publicly any firm opinion of the excise troubles in the West.

Those in the East who disagreed with the government's course were not disposed to make open trouble on behalf of the "yahoos" beyond the Alleghenies but they did object, particularly the citizens in the rural sections, to military service. Recollections of the hardships of the Revolution were too clear and resentment at speculators' profits was too keen to permit the government to raise troops without arousing the suspicion of the people concerning its motives. An "Old Soldier" spoke for this section of the populace in the columns of the *Independent Gazetteer*. He had served in the Continental army and had been paid in depreciated notes and certificates, which he had been forced to sell for three shillings to the pound to a man who had become a member of Congress. Now, he said, Mr. Steel brings "forward a motion on the floor of Congress, which was agreed by a great majority of the members, that the army had been lavishly paid by the rations they received. . . . A government capable of every species of violation cannot ensure to itself a second time success in arms, and the members of it a harvest in speculation. . . . there is a distrust of government for the payment of the militia, and also of the propriety of the cause. It is therefore my decided opinion that those gentlemen who reap the benefit of the late revolution by having become purchasers of Soldiers' notes at 2/6 in the pound ought to be enrolled in military form, and as they claim the revenue arising from the Excise Law, let them compel obedience to it— and not trouble An Old Soldier."[3]

The reluctance of the people to enroll in the militia led before long to a resort to the draft, and it was the Maryland and Pennsylvania riots against this measure that encouraged the people of the Monongahela country to refuse to sign the oath. The inspection officers of nearly every Pennsylvania county reported difficulty in filling the governor's requisition for troops and several of them stated that the people had specific objections to serving against their fellow citizens. Mifflin met the crisis by going on a tour of the counties to explain in person the nature and necessity of the service. The result, according to Dallas, was a resurgence of patriotism, the sudden springing up of "one common determination to defend the peace and order of society against the machinations of licentiousness and anarchy." Dallas probably spoke with an eye to political expediency; at least the draft remained in use. Another obstacle to the filling of the state's quota was the fact that because of the newness of the militia law details of procedure had not yet been worked out.[4]

Enlistments in New Jersey were hindered by propagandists. Governor Richard Howell, with amusing disregard for the fact that not many years before his state had been a hotbed of opposition to excise, issued a proclamation against these "strangers," intimating that of course no Jersey man would be "so lost to discernment and duty, as to harbor or countenance incendiaries who wish to reduce others to the level of their own crimes." Governor Howell added another gem to patriotic literature by writing the marching song of the New Jersey troops:

> To arms once more, our hero cries,
> Sedition lives and order dies;
> To peace and ease then bid adieu
> And dash to the mountains, Jersey Blue.
>
> Dash to the mountains, Jersey Blue,
> Jersey Blue, Jersey Blue,
> And dash to the mountains, Jersey Blue.
>
> .   .   .   .
>
> Should foul misrule and party rage
> With law and liberty engage,
> Push home your steel, you'll soon re-view
> Your native plains, brave Jersey Blue.[5]

Virginia, as has been seen, had trouble incident to the raising of troops in the Shenandoah Valley. There were also some slight disturbances in Surrey County, which quickly evaporated. An interesting incident occurred at Harrisonburgh while the troops were mobilizing there. The Presbyterian Synod of Virginia was meeting in the town at the time, and a minister named Moses Hoge presented for adoption an address to the people inculcating obedience to the laws. William Graham, another minister, a graduate of Princeton, opposed its adoption on the ground that the address was prejudging. The soldiers were enraged and, providing themselves with tar and feathers, went in search of Graham. He prudently "retired," and Hoge, the hero of the day, quieted the soldiers and preached them a sermon.[6]

Those opposed to military coercion resorted to the dissemination among the ignorant of palpable falsehoods—or perhaps the authors were only jesters. Rumors were spread that Congress was already extending the excise to all sorts of articles. Owners of plows had to pay a dollar; each wagon entering

Philadelphia was assessed a dollar; every new coat was taxed a shilling; the parents of new born male children at Pittsburgh had to pay a tax of fifteen shillings and those of female children ten shillings; and wheat, rye, and other grain were assessed at four pence a bushel—a man was found who claimed that he had actually paid that duty in Baltimore. One turbulent fellow in Winchester who in his enthusiasm "damned the Congress and cried 'God save king George'" was elegantly attired in tar and feathers and escorted from town.[7]

Some of the stilted invectives hurled at the insurgents merit a place in an anthology of humor. "A Volunteer" thus sounded a clarion call in the columns of the *Rights of Man*:

"The malignant vapours of a discordant nation have been borne across the Atlantic, to taint the clear atmosphere of Liberty—Already has its corrosive influence blighted a delightful part of your country, which now solicits your pruning hand, lest like ill weeds neglected in a beautiful field it over run and destroy the happy and more virtuous plants.

"The President of the United States has called upon you, through your Governor and Council, to turn out and suppress an insurrection, which, as a black hydra rising in the west, would wrap you in its poisonous web. . . . This country, which, from the walls of Quebec to its more southern boundary, has been purpled with the richest blood that ever fell from patriot veins, is now insulted and threatened by a deluded and vicious banditti. Can you bear this? Can you hear the voice of Washington, and not feel like the soldiers of Gideon? No. Go then—and if you find the mountains and fields covered with them—march—At your approach—at the approach of your invincible and courageous virtue, their weapons, as if by celestial shock, will drop from their hands. Oh! let me then plead this much for them—Remember that mercy and forgiveness, are divine and holy attributes of your country."[8]

The Watermelon Army Marches

The troops of Virginia, about 3,300 in number, under Governor Henry Lee were to meet at Cumberland with the 2,350 militiamen from Maryland under Governor Thomas S. Lee. Governor Howell of New Jersey with 2,100 men was to march to Carlisle where 5,200 troops under Pennsylvania's Governor Mifflin were gathering. The plan was that the troops in the north should constitute the right wing of the army, and march along Forbes's Road, and those at Cumberland should constitute the left wing and travel by Braddock's Road. Of the entire 12,950 men, 11,000 were infantry, 1,500 cavalry, and 450 artillery.[9]

The New Jersey troops on their way to Carlisle were involved in the killing of a man at Meyerstown. An Irishman named Boyd who was in his cups indulged in "indecent and seditious expressions" to some officers who had stopped in the tavern where he was drinking. His arrest was finally ordered and in the ensuing struggle he was stabbed with a bayonet and died within half an hour. The townsmen were naturally indignant, and one of them sent a message to the country people, apparently to summon help in resisting. He was thereupon taken into custody. As the troops were without ammunition, flankers were thrown out prepared to charge with fixed bayonets in case of attack, but fortunately the occasion for such action did not arise.[10]

Carlisle, it will be remembered, had been in the control of the Whiskey Boys during the middle of September and now its citizens in general were not disposed to regard benignly the gathering of the army. In fact they were distinctly inhospitable. A Major Gould of the New Jersey troops fell ill and when chicken soup was recommended for nourishment the major gave his servant a dollar and sent him out to buy a chicken. Wherever the servant tried to buy one the people would ask for whom he wanted it and when told that it was for a sick officer would reply that they had none for him, when at the moment chickens in great numbers were plainly visible all about. Upon his return the lady with whom the major was quartered sent out her maid and easily bought two chickens for a quarter.[11]

The army, as is so often the case with armies, was divided in spirit between the crusader and the holiday maker. Those on the scene on September 28 were regaled with a fervent sermon from the lips of a Carlisle minister, the Reverend Robert Davidson, who took as his text "Righteousness exalteth a nation: but sin is a reproach to any people." The insurgents by their rebellion, said he, had sinned and the forces of righteousness were now arrayed against them. His parting shot was reminiscent of Luther during the peasant revolt. "But if they will *resist,* and involve themselves in the *guilt* of rebellion, they deserve not to be pitied nor spared." Mifflin's arrival on October 2 was signalized by the marshaling of cavalry and the bellowing of artillery. Mifflin, as was the custom, responded with a "most flaming speech."[12]

The holiday spirit found a welcome vent in man hunts. One of these expeditions in search of "Pole gentry" resulted in the capture of a young man who was so ill he could not stand. He was put under guard of a single trooper while the others went to search a barn. The prisoner attempted to go into the house, but the guard cocked his pistol and ordered him to stop, telling him that he could sit or lie down if he could not stand. The boy was in the act of lying down when the trooper's pistol went off and wounded him mortally in the groin. Judge Yeates, at the request of Washington, later made an investigation of both the Meyerstown and Carlisle deaths. The first was classed as justifiable and the latter as an accident, and the perpetrators of both were released on bail for small sums, and were probably never brought to trial.[13]

The Watermelon Army Marches

The visit of Washington to Carlisle was the high spot during the time of mobilization. He arrived on the fourth of October and was received by an escort of New Jersey and Philadelphia cavalry headed by a dozen generals. As he passed through the town he was greeted by salutes and the ringing of bells, though the people who filled the streets looked on in silence. Upon his emergence into the camp beyond the town he found the Pennsylvania troops drawn up in martial array. The president rode down the line with his hat in his hand "bowing in the most respectful and affectionate manner to the officers." A Pennsylvania soldier taxed his vocabulary and imagination in describing the scene for the benefit of friends back home:

"When the sun occasionally broke through the fleecy and obstructing clouds the field in one part glittered with a forest of muskets and death pointed bayonets, while in another part streams of lightning flashed from the drawn blades of the gorgeous cavalry. Amidst all this reflected blaze of armoury, THE MAN OF THE PEOPLE, with a mein intrepid as that of Hector, yet graceful as that of Paris, moved slowly onward with his attending officers, nor once turned his eagle eye from the dazzling effulgence of the steel clad band. As the Heroic Sage advanced on his light moving steed along the line, which was mute with admiration and respect, our standards involuntarily bowed their heads, while their flags chaunted to the passing gale, in unison with the trumpets clangor, and the wild music of the martial field—the scene was augustly picturesque and inspiring. My imagination caught fire, and I thought myself a second Homer, born to sing the praises of the American patriot and hero. Thus transported, I beheld as he retired, fifteen blazing suns encircle his elevated brows: in the centre sat Justice, with her sword and balance, giving way to meek-eyed Mercy, with extended arm."[14]

That night the Carlisle courthouse was illuminated in honor

of Washington, who had taken up his lodging in the town at the home of Colonel Ephraim Blaine. Dallas, who attended a dinner given two days later by the president for Howell and Mifflin and their official families, reported him in "excellent humor, free and full of conversation."[15]

On October 8 there occurred an amusing incident that might well have had a serious sequel. Colonel Gardner's regiment of New Jersey troops was disaffected because of the irregularity of its supply of provisions, and the men announced an indignation meeting for the evening. Officers were hastily summoned to their posts, the dragoons were ordered to hold themselves ready for instant duty, and a troop was stationed on the road to intercept deserters. In the midst of the confusion Governor Mifflin, who had been drinking heavily, ordered out some Philadelphia light-horsemen with instructions to fire on any parties of men. There was a clash with the Jerseymen, and a battle was narrowly avoided. In the end Mifflin was obliged to explain publicly that the reason for his action was that he had been intoxicated and to ask pardon of certain officers.[16]

It was during Washington's sojourn at Carlisle, probably on October 9, that Findley and Redick appeared as commissioners on behalf of the Parkinson's Ferry meeting. No sooner had they reached Carlisle than they were warned by a friend that news of their coming had preceded them and that they were in great danger of injury from the soldiers. Their first interview with the president, about seven o'clock in the morning, was very brief as it was only for the purpose of handing in their papers and arranging for a longer conference. A circumstantial rumor quickly spread that they had been given short shrift and that Washington had refused to see them again. At ten o'clock they returned and conferred with Washington and Hamilton. The commissioners strove to convince their audience that order had been restored and that there was no use of sending troops West. Washington and Hamilton replied with moderation but firmness that the evidences of submission were not convincing and that the army must go on. The next day Washington stopped at the commissioners' lodging and asked them to renew the conference that evening. Findley and Redick were assured that a spirit of revenge in the army would not be tolerated and that any attempt to harm the people would be severely punished. During this interview a general officer, walking with others beneath the window, railed at Washington for conversing with the commissioners and asserted that the president "never would recover the popularity that he lost by countenancing insurgents."[17]

Findley and Redick began their return home in anything but confident spirits. Washington left on the same day, October 11, for Williamsport, Maryland, to visit the troops assembled there. From there he went on to Fort Cumberland, where he arrived on the sixteenth and where the scene at Carlisle was repeated with the troops drawn up to receive him. Washington had five nephews among the troops at this place and before his departure he took occasion to deliver a lecture to Major George Lewis, the eldest of them, upon his duty in setting an example to the rest. At Bedford he received another ovation and reviewed the troops that had arrived from Carlisle. On October 20, before setting out for the East, he placed the army under the command of Governor Henry Lee and gave him instructions for his guidance. Washington's return to Philadelphia was uneventful save that his coach hung for a while on the rocks in the middle of the Susquehanna River. That evening at Wright's Ferry he wrote to Hamilton expressing the hope that the latter would "be enabled by *Hook* or by *Crook* to send B[radford] and H[usband] together with a certain Mr. Guthrie to Philadelphia for their Winter Quarters." On the thirty-first, three days after his arrival in Philadelphia,

Washington wrote that Husband and three other prisoners had been safely lodged in the jail.[18]

In a letter to John Jay Washington gave a glowing account of the enthusiasm that pervaded the army in the sacred cause of liberty: "The spirit, which blazed out on this occasion, as soon as the object was fully understood, and the lenient measures of the government were made known to the people, deserves to be communicated. There are instances of general officers going at the head of a single troop, and of light companies; of field-officers, when they came to the places of rendezvous, and found no command for them in that grade, turning into the ranks and proceeding as private soldiers, under their own captains; and of numbers possessing the first fortunes in the country, standing in the ranks as private men, and marching day by day with their knapsacks and haversacks at their backs, sleeping on straw with a single blanket in a soldier's tent, during the frosty nights, which we have had, by way of example to others—nay more, many young Quakers, not discouraged by the elders, of the first families, character, and property, having turned into the ranks and are marching with the troops."[19]

Henry Lee traveled with the left wing of the army, composed of Maryland and Virginia troops. The last week of October was consumed in the march from Cumberland to Uniontown, a week of almost continual rain. One of the men grandiloquently described the crossing of the mountains thus: "No expedition during the last war, nor even that of Hannibal's passage over the Alps, could equal the almost insuperable hardships we have suffered." The Youghiogheny was so swollen by the rains that it was crossed in boats with great difficulty. By the time the troops reached Uniontown the surgeon general found it necessary to establish a hospital for the 116 sick men who could not go on.[20]

The Watermelon Army Marches

The right wing had begun the march from Carlisle while Washington was still there; and, after a week of marching, it arrived at Bedford on about October 17. There the army stopped until the twenty-second, recuperating from the exertions of the march from Carlisle and preparing for the difficulties ahead. Many took the occasion to catch up in their correspondence, and the illiterate paid twopence a letter to those willing to be their amanuenses. The cavalry amused itself by bringing in the four prisoners, the ones that were later noted by Washington as having arrived at Philadelphia.

It was already apparent to some that the opposition in the West had collapsed and that it was useless for the entire army to go on. One writer gave it as his opinion that there was "too much parade in this business" and hinted darkly that it was all for the pleasure, profit, and glory of the high in station. Another correspondent, however, struck the opposite note as the army prepared to go on: "Anarchy trembles, and order triumphs—consternation rides post-haste throughout the whole territory of sedition. The martial appearance, the health, the spirits and the good order of our military, exceed the most sanguine expectations of the warmest friends to order and good government. A spirit of fraternal harmony breathes throughout our whole line. Horse and Foot, Jerseyans and Pennsylvanians, regard each other in all their transactions as brethren embarked in a common cause, and appear determined to coöperate, on every emergency, for the noblest of objects, the public good."[21]

The right wing was scarcely out of Bedford before heavy rains set in. The wagon trains were beset by almost insuperable difficulties: roads muddy, rocky, and, on the mountains, dangerous; wagons breaking down; horses lame, sick, and foundering, with the consequent necessity of impressing more from the reluctant inhabitants. The troops often arrived at the designated camping grounds and waited for hours in the cold rain while the wagonmen with the food, tents, and baggage struggled in the mud miles behind. Fortunate indeed were the soldiers if they did not have to retire supperless to a mud bed and spend the night with the rain beating upon their defenseless forms. If they did receive their rations they might be hurried into line and marched on before they could cook their meals. The beef was bad, there was no way to bake bread most of the time, the whiskey was weak, and the straw for bedding was insufficient or soaked. The officers who could slept in taverns or private houses, though these were often so rickety and poorly constructed that they were no better than tents. The witty Judge Peters, who accompanied the army to deal with recalcitrant Whiskey Boys, remarked that it was the most hospitable country that he had ever traveled through, for all the inhabitants kept open house.[22]

The confirmed patrioteers in the ranks asserted that there were no complaints at the hardships—a unique army, if the statement were true, but it was not borne out by unanimous testimony. One idyllic account that has come down features whiskey so prominently that the writer should have been ashamed to be marching to help the excisemen hamper the westerners' use of that tipple:

"No sooner does the drum beat in the morning, than up I start, and away to my canteen, where a precious draft of new distilled whiskey animates and revives me. This being done, away to fire, where in ten minutes you will hear more genuine wit than Philadelphia will afford in a month. When we halt at night, our tents being pitched, we sit down on the straw, cover ourselves over with blankets, and push about the canteen so briskly, that at length we are obliged to lie down: A sound sleep then enables us to endure a repetition of fatigue—and so on. I am cook to our mess, and am pretty famous for my beef steaks and pancakes—the latter we are obliged to make as we cannot draw bread—flour only being given, and for the making of which the following is a recipe.—Take of flour 1 lb. of water 1 gill, or half and a little more—(let the water be the CLEANEST you can procure, otherwise your cakes will be gritty)—mix these well into a sort of dough; then fill a frying pan with the same, and over a gentle fire let it bake: when one side is sufficiently done, turn your cake and do the other side. N. B. Don't make this too public."[23]

Thievery and wanton destruction, those inevitable accompaniments of armies, were problems from the first. In the left wing fifty men found pilfering were dismissed "with infamy." A man who had beaten a farmer who detected him in the act of stealing honey was given one hundred lashes. General Daniel Morgan, who had become commander of the Virginia troops upon Lee's promotion, made it a point to pay the citizens immediately for any damage done, and in cases where Whiskey Boys who unwisely expressed their sentiments were in danger from the soldiers he would confine them until they could safely be allowed to depart. The right wing was even more disorderly than the left. There was complaint at Strasburg that the men had burned down the fences and that when they were not watched by their officers they did not leave a plate, spoon, knife, or glass to the people. Near Berlin Governor Howell was so scandalized by the stealing of farmers' fowls that he ordered the officers to examine the messes and confine the men who had been guilty of marauding. The soldiers were given to violence and disorders and discipline was never too strong. A severe example was made (in what way is not clear) of two men for disobedience and mutiny after the wing reached Westmoreland County. The danger of mutiny in the regiment was so serious that a loyal brigade was drawn up while the sentence was being executed.[24]

The camps resounded with threats of a holocaust of hanging, shooting, and bayonetting as soon as the army reached the West. Even those in the army itself who reasoned that they had not been sent to punish but merely to aid the judiciary were called Whiskey Boys and threatened with the same treatment. All this martial patrioteering amongst militia unable to march in a straight line and not uniformed except for some of the *élite* corps has a ridiculous aspect at a later date, but it did not appear ridiculous to the insurgents. There was a real menace in putting deadly weapons into the hands of irresponsible boys from eastern counting houses and farms and in whipping their passions into white heat. The reports concerning the inflammatory spirit of the army brought back to the Monongahela country by Findley and Redick and confirmed by every eastern breeze struck terror into the breasts of the westerners. Experience with the armies of the Revolution was a powerful factor in promoting submission on the part of the insurgents. Everyone was familiar with the depredations that had accompanied that war; and, as the reports of outrages along the line of march rolled westward gathering horrors through the specious mouth of rumor, there was engendered in some quarters a feeling akin to despair.

The third Parkinson's Ferry meeting, which convened on October 24 to hear the report of Findley and Redick, was completely controlled by the friends of order. The radicals had either fled the country or had been silenced by the approach of the army. The meeting, with Edgar and Gallatin as chairman and secretary respectively, could do nothing more than put forth new assertions that civil authority had been reëstablished and send Findley, Redick, Douglas, and Morton to see the president. Washington was already on his way back to Philadelphia but the commissioners did see Alexander Hamilton at Bonnet's camp. After listening to them, he suggested that "for the sake of decorum" they interview Henry Lee. The four then set out for Uniontown, where Lee was quartered, followed closely by Hamilton. Lee listened to their assurances politely, waited until the next day, and then handed them a written address to the people. The gist of the address was that the inhabitants of the region had in general been involved in the treason, that it was only the approach of the army that had occasioned the change of sentiment, and that the four commissioners themselves had stated these facts to him.

Imagine the dismay with which the commissioners heard this accusation and the haste with which they endeavored, though unsuccessfully, to set the matter right. Findley hinted later that the address was not the work of Lee at all, but of the astute Hamilton. The mission was completely unsuccessful. Lee continued to regard himself as the head of a conquering army in a rebellious province, and Hamilton presently began actively to make political capital of the situation. Hamilton, so said Findley, had constituted himself in fact commander of the army. He occupied a tent finer and more striking than that of Governor Lee, and once undertook to write a severe reprimand to Mifflin. At the same time he was credited with preserving discipline and regulating the service of supply so far as it was regulated.[25]

The two wings of the army, having crossed the mountains, began to converge upon the Youghiogheny River near Budd's Ferry (upstream from the site of West Newton). The right wing encamped east of the river for a time; part of the Pennsylvanians then marched north and encamped on the Allegheny about five miles out of Pittsburgh. The remainder of the Pennsylvania troops and those of New Jersey crossed the Youghiogheny and the Monongahela into Washington County. The left wing marched from Uniontown to a point between Budd's Ferry and Parkinson's Ferry, and for several days during the first part of November Henry Lee was stationed at the home of Major Powers in this vicinity. Several camps were occupied by the troops in addition to those mentioned. One was at the mouth of Mingo Creek and another at Perry's Ferry on the west bank of the Monongahela above Elizabeth. A detachment was stationed at Washington, tradition says on the Washington College campus.[26]

It will be remembered that Brackenridge was being made the subject of a whispering campaign by the members of the Neville connection left in the West. David Bradford, in answer to an inquiry by Major Craig, had written that Brackenridge had tried to stir him up against the major. Bradford also added some other incidents so twisted in the telling that they were likely to be very damaging to the lawyer. The two Nevilles, meanwhile, so said Brackenridge, were painting him as "the damnedest rascal that ever was on God Almighty's earth," and were accusing him of having been cognizant that Bower Hill was to be burned. The letter to Tench Coxe was being pointed to as evidence of his treason. Redick reported to Brackenridge upon his return from Carlisle that the army was accusing him of being the arch traitor and that he would be the first object of vengeance. When the commissioners had mentioned to Washington that Brackenridge had not been engaged in the insurrection, he was silent, though others did not hesitate to speak strongly. Brackenridge had been writing a letter to the president when Redick called, but now he laid it aside, for he felt that no matter what he said it would be misconstrued.

As the army advanced there was great interest exhibited in its ranks as to whether Brackenridge would wait to take his medicine. In his anxiety to ward off an unmerited destruction the lawyer followed what was probably the unwise course of publishing handbills in his own defense and sending them to the army to be distributed through the commanders. Redick took them with him upon his second mission. Howell threw them instantly into the fire, and Mifflin and Lee gave feeble assurances that the lawyer would be safe. Redick thereupon took occasion to pass out some of the handbills privately to the rank and file, a measure that only put Brackenridge in an even worse position, laying him open to the charge of impertinently trying to interfere in the conduct of the army.

Brackenridge now began to consider the advisability of flying to the Indians for a month or two until the danger had blown over, and General Wilkins, when he was consulted, approved of the plan and promised to send for a guide the next morning. That night the lawyer tossed on his bed thinking of what course to pursue. "People would always talk more than they would do," he reflected; but there was the danger that this "strain of talking . . . might lead some inconsiderate and unprincipled men, to perpetrate what they heard spoken of." Suddenly he sprang from his couch exclaiming that if he was to be assassinated it should be in his own house. During the next day or two he put his papers in order and wrote a short sketch of his conduct during the insurrection. This last was directed to James Ross with the request that he would make it public in case Brackenridge was assassinated.

The sketch was no sooner written than Josiah Tannehill, an assistant burgess of Pittsburgh, came to him with a bit of interesting news:

"Woods has discovered—"

"What?" Brackenridge cut him short, "The longitude?"

"No," answered Tannehill, "but that you are not within the amnesty. You did not sign upon the day."

"Is that all?" answered Brackenridge. "That will not do me any harm."

The more he thought about it the more Brackenridge felt that this discovery would change the talk from shooting to legal hanging; and so it was. The Nevilles, still with the army, began the talk of having Brackenridge dealt with by the judiciary. When a group of people, alarmed for their safety, solicited the favor of the old general he answered them indulgently, "Children," said he, "it is not you we want; it is some of the 'big fish,' Brackenridge, Gallatin, and Findley." Brackenridge, even in the midst of his apprehension, found time to smile wryly at thus being classed as engaged in an intrigue with a man with whom he had scarcely ever spoken and with an ancient enemy. Anxious to avoid the indignity of arrest he wrote Judge Peters and offered to appear before the court upon a moment's notice and at the same time prepared a note for the *Gazette* in which he challenged anyone to produce against him any proof of treason. Before sending these missives away he showed them to James Ross, who was in Pittsburgh on his way to the army. Ross advised him that the true course was neither to court prosecution nor to fear it. He offered, moreover, to apprise Judge Peters of Brackenridge's intention to await a full investigation, and to pledge his own honor to the judge that the Pittsburgher would not leave town nor avoid the issue. On this advice Brackenridge laid aside the letter and the note and determined to adopt the dignified course—to consider the situation a great misfortune but at the same time "to bear it with modesty and firmness."[27]

Brackenridge could not, however, avoid reflecting bitterly upon the viciousness of the Nevilles toward him after he had risked so much to defend them, particularly Presley, from the wrath of the insurgents up to the time of the march on Pittsburgh. As usual, when in a tight situation, the lawyer became whimsical and bethought him of a parallel case from the "Negaristan."

"Two travellers passing by a pool, on the side of the road, one of them, missing a foot, fell in. The surface of the pool was some feet beneath the level of the bank, and of itself deep; laying hold of the bank, he struggled to get up, but it was steep, and he could not. His companion, extending himself on his breast, and reclining over the bank of the pool, and reaching down his hands, got hold of the hair of the other, and with some difficulty, extracted him from the pool. But in dragging him against the bank, by some means an eye was injured, so as to lose the sight of it. He conceived himself intitled to damages against his companion, who had thus, without his interference and application, dragged him out. He claimed the sum of 10,000 dinas. The cause came before the cadi, who was puzzled, and laid it before the califf, who was puzzled, and took the opinion of a famous lawyer, Ala Joseph.

"The decision recommended by Ala Joseph was, that the injured man should have his election of two things; either to go back to the pool, from which he had been rescued, and take his chance of getting out, or be satisfied with the act of his companion, and the consequence of it, even though an application for assistance had not been made by him, and his consent to be dragged up formally obtained."[28]

Chapter XIII: *The Watermelon Army among the White Indians*

THE first of the troops to enter Pittsburgh was a detachment of Philadelphia cavalry acting as the escort of the exiled General Gibson. Brackenridge, who was at his window when the cavalry passed his house, saw Gibson look up and laugh, and the sensitive lawyer took the action to mean, "there lives a fellow that is to be hanged." The next to arrive were several squadrons of horse accompanying General Morgan and Presley Neville. They appeared on the south bank of the Mononga-hela, forded the river, and approached Fort Fayette with flying colors and sounding bugles. The garrison replied with a salute of artillery. Brackenridge's house was an immediate center of attention—dragoons occasionally came and went; two of them even entered the kitchen and from there peered into the ad-joining rooms. That evening, so it was reported to Bracken-ridge, General Morgan, walking with his staff near the house, was heard to exclaim, "Hang the rascal, hang him."

At about eleven o'clock that night a group of soldiers ac-tually undertook to assassinate Brackenridge. One of their officers who had unsuccessfully remonstrated with them ran to Presley Neville's home and routed out Morgan and Neville. They rushed out hatless and met the soldiers twenty yards from the lawyer's door and by a mixture of authority and persuasion succeeded in turning them back, telling them that their intended victim would be tried in good time and that the law must take its course. The crisis passed so quickly that Brackenridge himself knew nothing of it for two or three days.[1]

The federal judge, Richard Peters, the federal attorney, William Rawle, and Marshal Lenox had accompanied the army. Hamilton, Peters, and Rawle now began the process of making preliminary investigations, and Parkinson's Ferry seems to have been the seat of their activities. General Neville and John Woods were active in this work, marshaling witnesses and testimony, apparently with the main object of snaring Brackenridge. There was no dearth of witnesses willing to testify against him. Some persons friendly to him, who came to him for legal advice on how to extricate themselves from their embarrassments, were told to join in the cry against him to save themselves. "I directed them," said Brackenridge, "to contrive to let my brother of the bar hear them curse me, and say they had voted against me at the election; this would be carried to the ear of my adversaries, and they would be represented as friends of government. They did so; and it had the effect."

Brackenridge, whose nerves were none too strong, was almost prostrated by the suspense. A seasonable incident, however, had, unknown to him, weakened the case against him. The most damaging bit of evidence was a letter he had written to Bradford, which had been picked up in a tavern. It concerned certain papers that Brackenridge had lost and asked that duplicates be sent in order to enable "the business" to go on. Alexander Hamilton laid the letter before James Ross.

"What do you make of that?" he said. "You have averred, as your opinion, that Brackenridge has had no correspondence with Bradford; look at that, is it not the hand-writing of Brackenridge?"

The senator looked the letter over carefully while the examiners waited. Brackenridge's crabbed handwriting was unmistakable.

"It is the hand-writing," answered Ross finally, and there is only this small matter observable in the case, that it is addressed to William Bradford, attorney general of the United States, not to David Bradford."

One could have heard a pin drop in the room; Neville and Woods stood motionless and speechless. Hamilton was the first to break the silence.

"Gentlemen," he said acidulously, "you are too fast; this will not do."

The testimony that Ross then proceeded to give made it doubtful whether the examiners would be justified in holding Brackenridge for trial, and the case was carried over for further testimony.[2]

An inquiry made afterwards among the officers of the militia resulted in the information that two thousand men had fled from the Monongahela country upon the approach of the army. The terror among some of those remaining was ludicrous as well as pitiful. Alexander Fulton in a petition to Washington asserted that he had been forced to act as brigade major on the march to Bower Hill "having in my youth, under the greatest General in the world (whose name it would be deemed improper here to mention) acquired some knowledge of tactics, and gained in a small circle some military fame." John Baldwin abjectly apologized to General Neville for having taken part in the attack and offered to pay his proportion of the loss "with out having my name Cauld in A public Cort to under goe the rede Cule of a Lawyer, or to be an object of Contempt for the Publick to gase uppon . . . as the Law of Conviction has taken place in my one brest to gide mee to do right."[3]

David Bradford, the man who had wanted to be the Washington of the West, was one of those who fled. It had become apparent that his inflammatory speech at Brownsville had excepted him from the provisions of the amnesty and that it was dangerous for him to stay and stand trial, so he rode out of Washington a few days before the entrance of the troops. A flatboat had been waiting for him at the mouth of Grave Creek; but, as he was pursued by a man whom he had forced to release a slave illegally held, he started down river in a canoe. Near the mouth of Sandy Creek he took refuge on a coal boat belonging to some army contractors about two hours before a party of four soldiers from Gallipolis overtook him. The soldiers boarded the boat and had actually laid hands on Bradford when a young man, himself a fugitive, seized a rifle and forced them to withdraw without their victim. Bradford was pursued as far as Redbank by a Captain Jolly, but he succeeded in escaping to Spanish territory.[4]

Governor Henry Lee had no sooner descended from the Laurel Hill than he issued a proclamation severely lecturing the people of the Monongahela country. He followed it a few days later with a similar one, which in addition directed that the people should take a new oath of allegiance before the magistrates. How George III, if he came across these proclamations in a lucid interval, must have laughed at the irony of the situation. But then he seems never to have had his convictions troubled by that egregious thorn in the flesh, a sense of humor. The local justices of the peace made hay by charging a fee for administering the oaths, much to the "surprise and mortification" of Lee at this violation of the "spirit of affection and kindness" that he was so anxious to diffuse among the misguided children of the West.[5]

By the ninth of November the judicial authorities felt they were ready to act. Fearing another exodus from the country if they went about making arrests in haphazard fashion, they

planned a sudden and concerted movement. General Lee
issued the orders from his headquarters at Parkinson's Ferry
and sent lists of suspects and witnesses to army officers in the
various sections where the arrests were to be made. The time
was set for the early morning of the thirteenth.

The list of eighteen sent to General Irvine, in command of
the Pennsylvania troops near Pittsburgh, made no distinction
between suspects and witnesses, so that all received the same
treatment. Two, however, were not arrested, and Brackenridge's jaundiced eyes saw in these omissions proof of prejudice and favoritism. Those taken were dragged out of their
beds at two o'clock in the morning; some were not even given
time to dress completely and were obliged to start out with
their shoes in their hands. They were driven at a trot before
a troop of horse through the mud seven miles out of Pittsburgh,
then back several miles toward town, and were finally thrust
into an open pen. Here they were obliged to stay in the snow
and rain, subject to the jeers and insults of the guards, and
driven from the fire by bayonets when they attempted to approach it. The next day they were impounded in a "waste
house" where they remained five days; they were then taken to
a chilly guardhouse in Fort Fayette. Ten days after the arrest
the prisoners were brought before the judge, the evidence
against them was found to be insufficient, and they were released. It was not until then that General Irvine discovered
that the prisoners were not all traitors, that some of them were
only witnesses, and that all but two had signed the amnesty in
good faith. Among those imprisoned were George Robinson,
the chief burgess, Andrew Watson, the tavern-keeper, and
William H. Beaumont, a prominent merchant. Robinson and
Beaumont were both incapacitated for some months as a result
of exposure during their imprisonment.[6]

The night of the arrests came to be known in the Mononga-

hela country as "the dismal night" or "the dreadful night."
Washington County had even more ground for complaint than
Pittsburgh. A troop in the southern part of the county seized
several prisoners and forced them to trot on foot over muddy
roads and through the swollen waters of Chartiers. At night
they were quartered in a wet stable, and their food, consisting
of dough and raw meat, was thrown into a manger. The Mingo
Creek settlement suffered the most. Here General "Blackbeard" White of New Jersey was in command of a detachment
of cavalry that dragged about forty suspects from their beds
and imprisoned them in the cellar of the Buck Tavern, owned
by Benjamin Parkinson and operated by a man named Stock-
dale, eight and one-half miles west of Parkinson's Ferry. The
building was new, the cellar floor was muddy, and the log walls
were undaubed. General White was on hand to receive the
prisoners as they arrived; he insulted and abused them and
tied them together by twos, back to back. The guards were
allowed a fire, but in spite of the inclemency of the weather
the prisoners were not permitted to approach it nor were they
given any food. One man who had a dying child went to
General White and offered to give bail in case there was any
charge against him. He was, however, thrown into the cellar
with the others, and it was only with the greatest difficulty that
he obtained liberty to attend the child's funeral.

A Captain Robert Porter, hearing that a certain Pollock was
making charges against him, gave himself up to the commandant at the mouth of Mingo Creek and asked for an exami-
nation. When Pollock appeared he was so drunk he could
hardly stand and gave such evidences of spite against Porter
that he was ordered out of the camp. Porter, however, was held
on one excuse or another and was finally sent on to Pittsburgh.
The prisoners taken in the Mingo settlement were kept in the
cellar from one to two days and were then haled forth and

driven twelve miles to Washington. On the way one man fell into convulsions, and White ordered him to be tied to a horse's tail and dragged along. A fellow prisoner, however, who had a horse, dismounted and let the man ride. In fact it was said that the troopers themselves did not always share White's attitude and that some of them gave up their horses to exhausted prisoners and plodded knee-deep through mud and water on that weary march to Washington.[7]

James Carnahan, who was a student at Canonsburg Academy, has described the march of some cavalry and prisoners on the way through Canonsburg to Pittsburgh. The column was made up of alternate couples of cavalrymen and prisoners and extended perhaps half a mile. The troopers, recruited from the *élite* of Philadelphia, all in the prime of life, were uniformed in blue; they were mounted on perfectly matched bays and their accoutrements glittered with silver. The prisoners were of all ages and physical conditions, poorly and variously dressed, and mounted on all sorts of horses with all sorts of equipment.[8]

The arrests went on during the days succeeding the thirteenth of November. An old resident in the Chartiers Valley related in later years that on one Sunday morning when she was on her way to church with her father, the Reverend Matthew Henderson of the Associate congregation of Chartiers, they met a file of soldiers with a horse hauling a still on a jumper made of hickory poles. In the midst of the soldiers was one of Henderson's elders, the owner of the still, being taken prisoner to Pittsburgh. "Ah, Meester Henderson," cried the unfortunate elder, "ain't this terrible?" An army lieutenant visited his uncle near Pittsburgh and at a corn husking took occasion to refer to the people in general as "rebels." An old man rebuked him and was answered insolently by the lieutenant. A young man interposed and was restrained with diffi-

culty from thrashing the officer. As a result the two countrymen were arrested, and, though the friends of the young man
got him released, the old man was taken to Philadelphia and
held in prison for six months.[9]

David Hamilton of the Mingo Creek settlement had his still
seized by collectors under Robert Johnson on November 14.
The wily Hamilton, assuming a semblance of good-fellowship
and pleading the inclemency of the weather, persuaded the
men to remain over night and plied them with Jamaica ginger
and whiskey. The excisemen finally dropped into a drunken
stupor, and Hamilton's friends carried the still to a safe hiding
place. As to what happened to Hamilton for this frustration of
justice, tradition saith not. Perhaps Johnson was too embarrassed to be in a situation to do anything about it. After this
episode the section where Hamilton lived was called Ginger
Hill, an appellation that it bears to this day. Among the other
prominent men of the settlement who had their stills seized at
the same time were Benjamin Parkinson, John Hamilton,
and John Baldwin.[10]

Colonel John Hamilton, the sheriff of Washington County,
seems to have served as a scapegoat. It is true that he had attended every insurgent gathering, but he probably did so only
from a desire to promote moderation. It was intimated that the
secretary of the treasury had decided to make an example of the
sheriff because he had no family to mourn his loss. Colonel
Hamilton, hearing that he was slated to be taken into custody,
voluntarily went to Judge Peters and requested an examina-
tion. Peters answered that he was too busy at the moment but
would call on him presently. Hamilton waited, soon to find
himself put politely but firmly under arrest. Meanwhile every
effort was made to incriminate him, and John Baldwin, David
Hamilton, and others, when they failed to testify against him,
were told that they had thus forfeited the benefit of the amnesty

and were threatened with dire punishment. On the third day after his arrest John Hamilton was sent under escort to Washington and from there a week or so later to Pittsburgh and thence to Philadelphia without once having had an opportunity for a hearing.[11]

Major Powers, with whom Governor Henry Lee had made his headquarters near Budd's Ferry, was asked to wait upon Secretary Hamilton at Washington. There Powers was examined as to the treasonable conduct of certain persons, among them Gallatin, but he could say nothing incriminating them. Hamilton complained of the difficulty of getting information and advised the major to retire for an hour to reflect; in order to aid his memory he had him placed in a room with other prisoners under guard. After some time Powers was brought out and asked if he had recollected anything further. He answered that he had not. Hamilton then proceeded to upbraid him harshly for thus sheltering treason and remanded him to prison. He was soon taken to Pittsburgh, where he was held until after the secretary had left the country. Peters then let him go for lack of charges against him.[12]

Peters seems to have been a humane man anxious to temper the violence of the army and to deal justly with the westerners. It may be that circumstances forced him to send more prisoners to Philadelphia than he wished to, and one may hold the charitable suspicion that he consistently sent men whom it would be impossible to convict—a method rather hard on the victims, but nevertheless the lesser of two evils. Most of those accused of small offenses were handed over to the state courts or sent to Lee to be reprimanded, warned, and dismissed. Brackenridge wrote that "it was no uncommon thing for girls, with pads, to save their lovers, by passing for married and pregnant women, with two or three children at home, calling for bread. Judge Peters could not be supposed to be a midwife, nor could the writ *de ventre inspiciendo* issue, but from the court. It was therefore necessary to admit the fact."[18]

From Washington Hamilton went on about November 16 to Pittsburgh to continue the investigations. General Lee had meanwhile gone to Pittsburgh and established his headquarters at the Brackenridge house, one of the most spacious in the town. The family during his presence was crowded into one room. Brackenridge, continually apprehensive because of the cloud that hung over him, received Lee with marked restraint, though they had known each other well at Princeton, where the laywer, in fact, had been a sort of tutor to the general. Brackenridge intended to keep himself secluded, but the next day on Lee's insistence he dined at the general's table. It may well be imagined that Brackenridge felt the absurdity of his position—that of a suspected insurgent liable at any moment to be arrested.

The next morning the lawyer was subpoenaed to appear before Judge Peters. When he presented himself he was referred to Secretary Hamilton. The latter received him politely, but the apprehensive Brackenridge conceived the secretary's countenace to express a struggle between humanity and a sense of justice. Hamilton asked some general questions to which Brackenridge soon put an end by proposing to give a narrative of events from the beginning. This plan was agreed to, and Brackenridge proceeded while the secretary wrote down his statement. The account had reached the point where, after the burning of Bower Hill, the people had forced Bradford and Marshall to come forward and support what had been done under pain of receiving like treatment, when Hamilton laid down his pen and addressed the witness:

"Mr. Brackenridge," said he, "I observe one leading trait in your account, a disposition to excuse the principal actors; and before we go further, I must be candid, and inform you of the delicate situation in which you stand; *you are not within the amnesty; you have not signed upon the day;* a thing we did not know until we came . . . into the western country; and though the government may not be disposed to proceed rigorously, yet it has you in its power; and it will depend upon the candour of your account, what your fate will be."

Brackenridge answered to the point. *"I am not within the amnesty,"* he said, "and am sensible of the extent of the power of the government; but were the narrative to begin again, I would not change a single word."

The recital proceeded, and Brackenridge told of the visit of Black and David Hamilton to Pittsburgh and of Presley Neville's request that Brackenridge go to the Mingo meeting. At that point the hearing was adjourned for dinner, Brackenridge, now in the predicament that he had dreaded, could not bear to dine with Lee and refused to attend though urged by several messages. As Hamilton entered the room where he was to meet Brackenridge that afternoon he greeted the Pittsburgher with the words: "Mr. Brackenridge, your conduct has been horribly misrepresented." The latter conjectured from this remark that at dinner Presley Neville had acknowledged, under Hamilton's questioning, that he had urged Brackenridge to attend the Mingo meeting.

When the hearing was resumed and Brackenridge continued his narrative with regard to the Mingo meeting, Hamilton appeared increasingly dissatisfied. "Mr. Brackenridge," he said finally, "you must know we have testimony extremely unfavorable to you, of speeches made at this meeting; in particular your ridiculing of the executive." Brackenridge saw that his pleasantries at the expense of Knox in regard to the Presque Isle situation made with a view to encourage the hope of an amnesty, had been misunderstood, and he suggested that the five witnesses who had accompanied him to Mingo be examined as to the tenor of his remarks. When he came to the account of the course followed by the Pittsburgh town meeting before the muster at Braddock's Field at which he had moved that the town militia march out and affect to join the militia, he saw that the secretary ceased his writing and sank into deep reflection. Brackenridge proceeded to drive the point home. "Was it any more," he said, "than what Richard the second did, when a mob of 100,000 men assembled on Blackheath? The young prince addressed them, put himself at their head, and said, 'What do you want, gentlemen? I will lead you on.'"

The narrative was resumed, but presently Hamilton dismissed Brackenridge with the request that he return at nine o'clock the following day. The next morning General Lee made his apologies to Mrs. Brackenridge, saying that "for the sake of retirement" he was withdrawing with part of his staff to a less central part of the town. As a matter of fact he had been embarrassed by the refusal of certain men to enter the house of the hated Brackenridge. At nine o'clock Brackenridge again appeared before Secretary Hamilton. As he spoke the secretary's face began to brighten, and at the conclusion he emphatically declared his satisfaction. The Pittsburgher thus relates Hamilton's words:

"Mr. Brackenridge, in the course of yesterday I had uneasy feelings, I was concerned for you as for a man of talents; my impressions were unfavorable; you may have observed it. I now think it my duty to inform you that not a single one remains. Had we listened to some people, I do not know what we might have done. There is a side to your account; your conduct had been horribly misrepresented, owing to misconception. I will announce you in this point of view to Governor Lee, who represents the executive. You are in no personal danger. You will not be troubled even by a simple inquisition by the judge; what may be due to yourself with the public, is another question."

The news of this acquittal brought different reactions. Governor Howell called and apologized handsomely for having destroyed Brackenridge's handbills, not, however, for his allegation as to the impropriety of addressing the army. John Woods "expostulated very warmly with the judiciary, for the astonishing defect of official duty" in not sending Brackenridge in irons to Philadelphia. Presley Neville, so asserted Brackenridge, having failed in the public prosecution, resumed the campaign of drumming up private resentment. General Neville, when he heard of the acquittal, exploded with wrath, and Brackenridge was diverted with what he was reported to have said: "The most artful fellow that ever was on God Almighty's earth; he has deceived Ross, he has put his finger in Bradford's eye, in Yates' eye, and now he has put his finger in Hamilton's eye too; I would not wonder if he is made attorney for the states, on the west of the Allegheny mountains."[14]

Brackenridge's exoneration did not restore him to the good graces of society, even outside the Neville connection. The presence of the troops had occasioned a number of social events such as always occur when an army is close to a town. In fact the social life of the army of occupation in Pittsburgh was probably an agreeable surprise to many of the officers. One easterner with the army, who "vainly anticipated a Country awkward Society," expatiated upon the accomplishments of those he met. He told of one evening, which doubtless was much like others, passed "agreeably in Company with a great number of Gentlemen of and belonging to different Volunteer Corps, in singing and Drinking of Brandy, &c."[15] Governor Lee gave a dinner to the gentlemen of the town, to which Brackenridge was not invited, but the lawyer was later complimented by a special invitation from the governor to a private conference. The Pittsburghers proposed to return Lee's courtesy by giving him a dinner, but Brackenridge did not feel free to take part, and Prothonotary Brison, who was manager of a ball to be given after the dinner, refused to send Mrs. Brackenridge an invitation. She protested to her husband with unconcealed indignation.

"What," he exclaimed, "you are hurt at this? You insult me, because it is on my account you suffer the indignity. Did you not read to me, the other evening, the life of Phocion?—after having rendered services to the state, and accused of treason by the arts of malignant individuals, and acquitted by the people; suppose his adversaries to have taken their revenge, by getting a master of ceremonies to exclude his wife from a ball; would you not think it more honourable to be the wife of Phocion, under these circumstances, than of a common Athenian, though you had received a card, and been called upon to lead down the first dance?" In his account of the conversation Brackenridge added quaintly, "by this address to the pride of the human mind, I had a philosopheress in a moment, perfectly reconciled with the circumstances."[16]

The army did not stay long in the Monongahela country, but, somewhat like the King of France and his twice ten thousand men, marched to the west and then marched east again. By November 19, not even three weeks after its arrival, the army had begun its return. The campaign had been arduous, chiefly because of the season of the year in which it had been undertaken, but the health of the men had been good—probably not more than a score died of disease and, of course, none by violence.[17] Great was the glorification as the troops began to reach home. The *Pennsylvania Gazette* of December 17 thus painted the scene in Philadelphia:

"Wednesday last returned from the western expedition, MACPHERSON's volunteer battalion of blues, headed by their friend Gen. Frelinghuysen; who commanded the legion. At

Broad street, they were received under a discharge of artillery, by a detachment which went out for that purpose—from
Schuylkill they were escorted into the city by Captains Dunlap,
Singer, and M'Connell's Horse, in full uniform—their companions in the late truly glorious, successful, and bloodless expedition. The concourse of citizens which shouted a welcome
to their return was immense—every eye beamed gratitude and
pleasure.

"As they passed the President's house, who was at the door,
the band played; the Father of his country expressed, in his
countenance, more than can be described.

"The colours of the shipping in the harbour were displayed,
and the bells of Christ Church rang a joyful peal upon the
occasion.

"And on Saturday last the city cavalry, four companies of
artillery, Macpherson's volunteer blues, that part of Colonel
Gurney's regiment then in the city, and the officers of the first
division of the militia of Pennsylvania, repaired, agreeable to
appointment, to the Middle ferry, where they met the remainder of the troops belonging to the city, on their return
from the western expedition. They were welcomed with shouts
of pleasure and approbation, by their brothers in arms, and a
great concourse of other citizens, a detachment of the artillery
fired a federal salute—the bells rang a joyful peal—and universal congratulations closed the scene."

General Lee remained behind to put the finishing touches
to the pacification. The justices of the peace were thanked for
their coöperation in administering the new oaths of allegiance
and were warned that the books should be closed on the last
day of December. The collectors' offices, of course, were re-
established, and "all distillers required forthwith to enter their
stills." A general pardon was issued on the twenty-ninth of
November to all save those at the moment entangled in legal

processes, those who had fled from the region, and twenty-eight Pennsylvanians and five Virginians "the atrocity of whose conduct" made them marks for judicial vengeance. John Mitchell and William Bradford, the two mail robbers, Benjamin Parkinson, John Holcroft, Daniel Hamilton, David Bradford, Alexander Fulton, William Miller, and, of all people, Edward Cook, were among the recalcitrants named. It would be difficult indeed to prove that the signing of the oath on September 11 and a law-abiding life after that date had earned the promised amnesty in every case.[18]

General Morgan remained behind during the winter with 1500 men to see that the fear of God did not evaporate from western breasts before spring. The camp was established on Bently's farm at Perry's Ferry. Strangely enough four battalions of Morgan's men were recruited in the West from the very elements that had been most violent during the late disturbances, and these men were amongst the most troublesome in abusing and insulting the people. Morgan's orders were that the inhabitants and their property were not to be injured, but the influence of the general is to be doubted since it was alleged that he had scarcely entered the country before he had set an example by knocking down and abusing an innkeeper who was said to have overcharged a soldier for a quart of whiskey.

The camp was only fourteen miles from Pittsburgh so that the officers were frequently in town, and their conduct was such as to make them public nuisances. They roistered in the taverns, roved the streets at late hours, and slaughtered domestic animals; once there was a clash between a party of them and some wagoners in which one of the latter was cut about the head and lost a finger. Brackenridge was retained by the injured freighter to bring action against an officer named McDermot, but a compromise was effected and the injured man was compensated. McDermot and some others were involved in another outrage against a certain Bayard, perhaps Colonel Stephen Bayard of Elizabeth. They demanded food from him but were refused on the ground that his wife was sick. Finally after he had been threatened he complied and found something for them. After the soldiers had eaten and drunk they imprisoned Bayard in his chamber and "made strokes at him with their swords—threw his bedding on the floor, danced up on it—broke his tables and chairs, and other furniture." Brackenridge was retained in this case also, and upon his advice Bayard made out a bill for damages, went to camp, and demanded and received payment.

Brackenridge's prominence in prosecuting these and other cases of outrage did nothing to endear him to the troops. Morgan had been absent in Virginia during some of these occurrences and upon his return he issued general orders bearing upon the situation in which he declared that he could not "avoid a suspicion, that some evil disposed professional character, and who is an enemy to the happiness of this country, has been busy in fomenting differences, and urging prosecutions of a vexatious kind, which otherwise, from the favorable opinion of the people in general, would not have existed." The orders appeared in the Philadelphia papers while Brackenridge was in that city on business, and he replied by a public defense of his conduct, in which, with the amazing intemperateness sometimes characteristic of him, he labeled the offending officers "unprincipled, wanton, marauding pandours." It can be easily seen what a stir this reply made. Colonel Presley Neville enclosed a copy of it to a Colonel Stephenson, a famous duelist, then with Morgan, as a broad hint to him of the kind of action needed. The lawyer had provoked a whirlwind but he did not hesitate to face it. As soon as possible he hastened back to Pittsburgh, but in the meantime dissensions had split the ranks of the avengers. McDermot had had the fight knocked out of him by a fellow officer; Stephenson had been put under arrest for a number of offenses as well as to keep him from killing Randolph, another of the fire eaters; and Simeson, a fourth paladin, seeing writ after writ served in the camp with no recourse possible, decided to resign and take up the study of law at Washington, Pennsylvania.[19]

A number of the men excepted from the general pardon surrendered themselves during the winter. Morgan released them on parole in consideration of their promise to appear before the federal court at Philadelphia, and it was said that only two failed to show up. It is doubtful if any of them were prosecuted, with the exception of John Mitchell. He gave himself up, confessing that he was one of the mail robbers, but Morgan, struck with his "simplicity," affected disbelief of his assertion. Mitchell, however, insisted upon his guilt; Morgan, therefore, hoping that he would have sense enough to escape, gave him a pass and sent him to Philadelphia alone. He did not fail, however, to appear in time to stand trial, and he was one of the two sentenced to death.[20]

The prisoners reserved for trial in Philadelphia were started toward that place on November 25. Ensign McCleary, with forty soldiers of the garrison, was in charge. There were seventeen men, nine from Washington County, six from Allegheny, and one each from Fayette County and Ohio County, Virginia. Colonel John Hamilton and the Reverend John Corbley were the best known of the prisoners. At Greensburg three more were added to the group, and General "Blackbeard" White took charge of them with the assistance of a troop of New Jersey cavalry under Major James Dunham. The prisoners marched on foot, each one between two troopers. General White ordered the guards to keep their swords always drawn and announced that in case of an attempted rescue the prisoners' heads were to be cut off and taken to Philadelphia.

On the twenty-fifth of December, after a weary march of just a month through mud and snow, the procession entered Philadelphia. The city had been notified of the impending entry, and the population turned out to the number of perhaps twenty thousand to see this mockery of a Roman triumph. The prisoners were drawn up in front of the Black Horse Tavern at half past eleven in the morning and presented with slips of paper to wear as cockades to distinguish them from the crowd. Major Dunham protested against this gratuitous insult but White overrode his remonstrance. The line of march was by a circuitous route through the city so that every thrill seeker might have a glimpse of the hairy "yahoos" from over the mountains. If the prisoners had ever shown defiance there was very little of that spirit left; Presley Neville, who was then in Philadelphia to attend the sessions of the legislature, wrote that the prisoners "wore the appearance of wretchedness" and that he "could not help being sorry for them, although so well acquainted with their conduct." When the exhibition was over the prisoners were shunted into a new jail, there to languish for periods extending up to six months.[21] Not a one of these twenty men led like Parthian captives through the jeering crowds of the capital city was found guilty!

Chapter XIV: *The Aftermath*

THE early American inclination for passing resolutions must have reached its finest flower during the winter of 1794-95. A pæan of thanksgiving rose from the ranks of a grateful people upon their miraculous delivery from the maws of Findley, Brackenridge, and Gallatin, those ravening wolves from *ultima Thule*. Washington, the Joshua of law and order, found himself once more treading the pinnacle of popularity from which the Democratic societies had almost cast him, receiving the encomiums not only of the people but of all sorts of organizations from Democratic societies to state legislatures. On New Year's Day, 1795, the gravely exultant president issued a proclamation setting February 19 as a day of thanksgiving for "the seasonable controul which has been given to a spirit of disorder in the suppression of the late insurrection."[1]

Only the hardiest of democratic rogues dared at first to lift their dissident voices above the symphony of popular approval. Benjamin Franklin Bache, the sturdily Jacobin editor of the Philadelphia *Aurora,* was of this number. It was queer, he remarked impertinently in the issue of November 10, 1794, that fifteen [?] thousand men had been called out against unembodied insurgents, when in Massachusetts, a few years before, two thousand troops had been sufficient to put down eight thousand embodied men. Washington, himself, however, a few days later threw a bone of discord to the political dogs. On the twentieth of November he addressed Congress in a message that expressed pious horror at the insurrection and cast the onus squarely upon "certain self-created societies." The leaders of the eastern and southern Democratic societies had months before this foreseen a day of reckoning and hastened to place their organizations on record as opposed to resistance to the laws by force, but their canniness did not save them from the wrath of the Federalists.[2]

It did not matter now that many of the societies' members, particularly those of Baltimore, had marched west with the army—they had kindled the blaze, and the tardy merit of having helped to quench it was no palliation. The societies for their part fought back viciously. Were they abettors of treason for having supposed that governments could do wrong? If that were true, what of the glorious example set by the men of '75? Bache was still wielding the cudgel for the societies: "We have been accused of wearing the masque of conspirators.—As well might we say . . . that the pretended friends of law and order had secretly fomented the insurrection that they might borrow another argument against republicanism and be furnished with a stronger evidence in favour of a standing army. . . . All governments are more or less combinations against the people . . . and as rulers have no more virtue than the ruled. . . . the power of government can only be kept within its constituted limits by the display of a power equal to itself, the collected sentiment of the people." The abuse was largely leveled against the Pennsylvania Democratic Society, but that society pointed out that it had not said anything that had not also been said by a respectable minority in the House of Representatives. In the latter place it had even been predicted that the excise would create dangerous uneasiness in some part of the country, and the Pennsylvania society had never gone that far in its statements.[3]

Washington's message found a ready echo in the Senate, and a resolution was passed approving its sentiment, but there was a rebellion in the House, where the majority refused to adopt a reply specifically using the phrase "self-created societies." The struggle lasted for a week while curiosity stood "a tiptoe on all our Post Roads," to quote one of the House members. Giles of Virginia pointed out that there was scarcely a citizen who did not belong to a self-created society: Methodists, Friends, philosophical, or—boldly tweaking the lion's tail—even the Society of the Cincinnati. The House, he pointed out, was no place to argue the merits or demerits of the Democratic societies. Did the members "imagine that their censure, like the wand of a magician, would lay a spell on these people?" It had been "alleged, as the very worst trait in the character of Democratic societies, that they began their business after dinner, bolted their doors, and voted in the dark. This was a very alarming and detestable species of conduct! But Mr. Chairman," and Giles pointed up to the room above where the notoriously exclusive Senate sat, "is there no other place where people bolt their doors and vote in the dark?"

McDowell of North Carolina, striking an I-told-you-so attitude, cried, "your wanton laws, begotten in darkness, first raised insurrection." The Federalists scurried for Washington's coat tails as a family of chicks caught in the hail scramble under their mother's wings. "Gentlemen, gentlemen, softly, if you please!" they said in effect. "If we do not support the president, will not our silence be interpreted as criticism of that great and good man?" And so successful were these tactics that more than one critic felt forced to deliver "an elegant panegyric on the character and conduct of the President" before launching into his speech of dissent with the address. In the end, however, the address was sent to the president emasculated of the odious phrase. Doubtless there was great rejoicing on all the post roads.[4]

Madison, a month after the close of the polemic battle, wrote to Monroe characterizing Washington's attack upon the Democratic societies as "perhaps the greatest error of his political life." The game of the Federalists, he continued, was to fasten the odium of the insurrection upon the societies, thus throwing them into disrepute, and at the same time to draw the president into the aristocratic party. Only the speedy collapse of the western resistance had weakened the assertions that a standing army was essential to the continuance and the strength of the federal government.[5]

The lightning struck first in the Pennsylvania legislature when on December 16 a motion was introduced in the House to deprive the members from the four western counties of their seats on the ground that they had been elected at a time when "a majority of the inhabitants" of those counties had been in a "state of insurrection." A similar resolution was introduced in the Senate two days later. In spite of the efforts of Gallatin and his colleagues the Senate on January 3 and the House on January 9 declared the election in the West void. The unseated members departed at once for home, where they were promptly reëlected by their constituents, with the exception of one who refused to run again. They resumed their seats about the middle of February.[6]

The trials of the insurgents dragged on during most of the spring, summer, and fall of 1795. The difficulties of bringing jurors and witnesses from the West were great and hampered the proceedings at every step. Some of the prisoners brought east by the cavalry in December were admitted to bail at various times. The grand jury by the end of May had found more than thirty bills for treason, fourteen of them, it was said, against men still held in jail. These arraignments for treason stirred up a great deal of controversy as to the exact nature of the western opposition to government—in other words as to whether or not it was levying war within the meaning of the Constitution. The adherents of the view that the opposition constituted treason had the advantage in the courts, and most of the accused escaped only because there was a lack of evidence against them. Brackenridge upheld the opinion that the westerners were involved only in riot, and later events seem to show the justice of his contention. If every subsequent riot paralleling the Whiskey Insurrection in nature or rivaling it in size had been construed as treason and so treated, liberty would have become as constrained in the United States as it was under the Sennacheribs.[7]

The trials, with two exceptions, were to no purpose, and the prisoners were acquitted for lack of proof; for the witnesses apparently were unwilling to say anything to the damage of their neighbors. On July 10 Washington issued a proclamation pardoning all those who were not under indictment or sentence, and on August 26 Mifflin followed with a similar proclamation for the state. In the middle of August District Attorney Rawle not only complained that witnesses and juries were unwilling to do their duties but that there were some conflicts of jurisdiction. The last of the trials ended about the first of November with the acquittal of Edward Wright and James Stewart, the latter a member of the band that had entered Philadelphia on Christmas Day of 1794. Poor old Harmon Husband fell ill in prison and died soon after his release, one of the many uncouth martyrs whose graves have marked the advance of American democracy.

The first of the two men to be found guilty was Philip Weigel, an ignorant German from Westmoreland County, who had been involved in one of the riots in Fayette County, probably the one in which Wells's house was burned. Mitchell, the mail robber, was poorly defended, for his lawyer rejected western jurymen and chose Quakers under the belief that they would bring in a verdict of not guilty. In this he was badly mistaken for the Quakers showed no patience with treason. Brackenridge, who was observing with interest, remarked to Gallatin that Quakers or Episcopalians were best in common cases such as murder or rape, but in every case of rebellion or treason give him a jury of Presbyterians by all means. It was so obvious that Weigel was insane and Mitchell a simpleton that the philanthropists of Philadelphia interested themselves in the case, sent several petitions to the president, and finally obtained pardons for both.[8]

The Whiskey Insurrection failed utterly in fulfilling the diverse economic and political purposes that had animated the people. The small distiller was doomed, not by the excise but by irresistible economic forces, and he rapidly gave way to the larger *entrepreneur*. In fact the federal excise itself was repealed in 1802 after Jefferson took office as president. The distillers meanwhile became more cautious in their evasion of the law when they did not choose to pay. They took care to be trading down the river at registration time and upon their return hired better lawyers the more effectually to entangle their cases in the mazes of the law; or perhaps they simply compounded with the collectors.[9]

The cleavage in western politics did not immediately become evident after the insurrection, and when it did come it may have been as much the result of the general democratic movement as of antipathies resulting from the events of 1794. The church had never taken the popular side and now it exercised a powerful influence in forcing its members to accede to the existing state of affairs. As late as June, 1795, the Presbyterians were refusing church privileges to those who had not given satisfactory evidences of repentance. It is probable that the craze for emigration noted by travelers was in part the result of dissatisfaction with the outcome of the insurrection, and of the two thousand men who had been temporarily exiled, many may have decided to make their permanent homes farther west. David Bradford, for one, obtained a Spanish land grant near Natchez and though he was pardoned in 1799, probably returned to Pennsylvania but once, and then only for a brief time in 1801 to dispose of his property.[10]

The land abandoned by the natives was taken up in some part by men who had had their first introduction to the West as soldiers in the army sent out to suppress the insurrection. There may have been a temporary lull in the economic development of the region, as Brackenridge stated, but it could not have been so serious as he claimed at the moment.[11] The presence of the army increased the demand for the very products in which the West specialized and put thousands of dollars of new specie into circulation. Commerce and industry, if the scanty records of the time are reliable, barely paused in their onward stride. Iron furnaces and forges increased in number; Craig and O'Hara erected a glass factory; Jacob Roman began the first manufacture of nails by machinery in 1795; wagonmakers set up their shops; spinners, weavers, ropemakers, hat makers, and all the assorted artificers and professional men necessary to make a civilization pitched upon Pittsburgh as the proper place in which to settle. Craig and O'Hara began importing salt in ever increasing quantities from New York state, flatboats loaded with foodstuffs and fabricated articles weighed anchor in greater numbers each year, and keelboats plied busily from port to port. Western Pennsylvania by 1800 was fairly launched upon the course that was eventually to make it the "workshop of the world."

The Whiskey Insurrection played an important part in

strengthening the grip of the Federalists upon the national administration. In the first place, by the end of the summer of 1795, they were able to oust the last of their opponents from Washington's cabinet and replace him with a Hamiltonian; in the second place the popular reaction against the insurrection was an important factor in making it possible for them to so manipulate public opinion as to perpetuate the party in office several years beyond what might have been possible otherwise. When Jefferson had resigned from the office of secretary of state at the close of 1793, Edmund Randolph of Virginia had succeeded him. The best proof that Randolph performed his duties honestly lies in the fact that both the French and British ministers were dissatisfied with his lenience to the other side. Jean Antoine Joseph Fauchet, the French minister, was angered because Randolph reined him up for illegally using American passports, and James Hammond, the British minister, sought to bring about Randolph's removal because he stood out against British domination, particularly against the adoption of the Jay Treaty. By the latter action, Randolph, though he was not consistently coöperative with either party, had placed himself in alliance with the rapidly solidifying Democratic-Republican Party. Oliver Wolcott and Timothy Pickering, the most partisan of the three Federalist cabinet officers and secretly under Hammond's thumb, eagerly seized the first opportunity to get rid of the only fly remaining in the party ointment.

It happened that on October 31, 1794, Fauchet sent home dispatch Number 10 by the corvette "Jean Bart." On the way the "Jean Bart" captured a British merchant ship and brought the captain on board as a captive, but in the channel was herself overhauled by a British man-of-war, the "Cerberus." The French captain immediately ran for the ship's papers, including Fauchet's dispatch, and tossed them overboard, but the captain of the British merchant vessel leaped into the water and held them until he was picked up by a boat from the "Cerberus." Dispatch Number 10 was sent to Lord Grenville, who immediately saw an opportunity to force the dismissal of Randolph by the threat of publicly tarring the administration with the accusation of venality. The dispatch was therefore sent on to Hammond and by him given to Pickering on July 28, 1795.

It had been given to Pickering rather than to Randolph for the simple reason that it contained a direct charge that the latter had sought a bribe from Fauchet. It analyzed the political state of the country, described the genesis of the Democratic societies as a protest against the stock-jobbery of the federal officials, and accused the government of having stirred up the western insurrection with the aid of the English in order to avert the impending general storm. The crisis, said the dispatch, had found prominent politicians such as Randolph, Mifflin, and Dallas teetering between the parties, and it was during this crisis that Randolph had come to Fauchet with the proposition that the insurrection, which was only playing into Federalist hands, could be averted if the French minister would "loan" enough money to four prominent democrats to save them from the oppression of English merchants who held over them the threat of debtors' prisons. "Thus," exclaimed Fauchet, dramatically, "with some thousands of dollars the Republic could have decided on civil war or on peace! Thus the consciences of the pretended patriots of America have already their price!"

The opportunity to ruin Randolph politically and perhaps the Democratic-Republican Party was too good for Pickering and Wolcott to let slip, in spite of the unimpeachable record for probity hitherto borne by the secretarial victim. William Bradford, to his credit, did not seek Randolph's disgrace but suggested his transfer to the Supreme Court, thus tacitly avowing his disbelief in the accusation. Randolph, by a false pretext, was prevailed upon to urge Washington's immediate return from Mount Vernon. As soon as practicable after the president's arrival on August 11 the dispatch was presented to him, but until the nineteenth Washington treated his secretary of state with every accustomed mark of confidence. He was closeted with him daily on affairs of state, went to his home, and repeatedly entertained him at dinner. On the nineteenth the blow fell. The president, in the presence of Pickering and Wolcott (Bradford was on his deathbed), handed Randolph the dispatch and coldly asked if he had any explanation. The accusation made by Fauchet, Randolph asserted, was an utter surprise to him, but it did not take him long to realize that he had been prejudged and that nothing he could say or do would change the verdict. Immediately upon his return home he wrote his resignation and then set out to obtain the proofs of his innocence.

Hammond had sailed for England a few days before the nineteenth, and Fauchet, who had been recalled to France, was awaiting an opportunity to sail from Newport, Rhode Island. Randolph reached Newport just in time to see Fauchet before he sailed and obtain from him a promise to furnish a written explanation of the bribery charges in Dispatch Number 10. Fauchet's explanation was that Randolph had suggested that some flour contractors employed by Fauchet be used to spy on Hammond and his agents who were fomenting the western insurrection, and that civil war be averted by disclosing to the nation that civil war was just what England desired.

It must be admitted that the explanation is halting. It is possible that Fauchet, not thoroughly conversant with English and dependent upon Randolph's English or imperfect French, really misunderstood the import of the conversation and upon reflection decided that he had been mistaken. It is more probable, however, that Fauchet, in pique at Randolph's refusal to wink at his trespasses, had deliberately borne false witness against him and now was tardily trying to patch up the story since it was playing into British hands. In fact the vital passages in his dispatches were such tissues of unintelligible absurdities that, in the face of Randolph's reputation, it is difficult to credit them. Randolph's "precious confessions" to which the Frenchman alluded were common knowledge, and no one connected with the government believed that Fauchet, impecunious and almost in disgrace with his superiors, had any gold to offer to traitors. The whole transaction, as Conway, Randolph's biographer, asserted, may have been a British finesse with Federalist connivance to force Washington to get rid of the overly patriotic Randolph and accept the Jay Treaty, or be penalized by having the dispatch published and his already divided administration disgraced. In the dilemma Washington chose to sign the treaty and toss Randolph to the British lion and the Federalist vultures. At any rate Randolph was now definitely off the political stage and the Federalists held absolute control of the executive arm of the government.[12]

There is no proof that the Federalists actually intended to stir up an insurrection in the West in order to justify their preachments as to the necessity of a standing army, nor is it likely to be demonstrated by our present knowledge that they planned by crushing the local insurrection to prevent more serious risings. Circumstances and unofficial utterances, however, strengthen the suspicion that both outcomes were welcomed. If Hamilton was actually trying to pacify the West the circumstances surrounding the issuance of the processes served in July, 1794, certainly showed political ineptitude; an accusation not lightly to be made against him. The rumors of activity by British agents in the Monongahela country may or may not have been founded on fact.

Whether or not the Federalists stirred up the insurrection it proved a godsend for them and they skillfully took advantage of it. True, the Republicans, insofar as partisans could be distinguished, kept their Congressional strength in the ensuing elections. However, the Democratic societies found themselves maneuvered into a vulnerable position because of the activities of their brethren in the West, and the Federalists plucked incessantly on that string.

The danger that the people might tire of listening to a harp with one string was averted by Randolph. His resignation not only cleared the president's council board of Democrats but added another string to the Federalist harp. Who would dare now to accuse them of Pharisaism toward the common people and of manipulation in politics in the face of this blighting display of corruption in the ranks of the opposition? This was the capsheaf in the Federalists' characterization of the Democrats; they lost no opportunity to belittle their opponents and went to ludicrous lengths to exalt themselves and their great leader as exemplars of all the virtues of patriotism. Only from such meretriciousness as was evidenced in the case of Randolph, said they, could spring any opposition to that faithful band of men who like a sacred priesthood nobly disregarded self-interest to spend their lives tending the fires upon the federal altar under the leadership of that sum of righteousness, the great hero, statesman, and warrior, His Excellency, the President of the United States. Thus hiding behind the skirts of Washington the Federalists once more won the Presidency in the election of 1796. The Alien and Sedition Acts, however, were not far in the future, and it was they that were to render top-heavy the dam that had been built to restrain the radicals and that was to tumble before the Jeffersonian revolution.

The Whiskey Insurrection was one of the signposts that

marked the cleavage amidst the people, particularly between the agrarians and the rising industrial and mercantile class. Probably the thinking members of both sides did not fail to note this. The anger of the dominant elements against the West showed the hollowness of their tirades in favor of Liberty— at least from the equalitarian standpoint—and laid them open to the accusation of having wanted independence so that they could rule without British interference. Confronted with such charges the Federalists, with the wisdom of the children of this world, ignored them and consistently stuck to their tale of treason, ingratitude, and injured innocence.

Perhaps John Adams was right in saying that only the death of Hutchinson and Sergeant from the yellow fever plague in 1793 prevented a revolution in the United States. The Whiskey Insurrection at least was abortive, and the Jeffersonian revolution when it came was not as complete as the Democratic societies might have advocated in 1793. The westerner of the seventeen-nineties saw more or less clearly that it was the economy of the frontier individualist that was being undermined. With the limited vision incident to any decade he thought he had his back to the wall making his last stand against plutocratic individualism. As a matter of fact Armageddon, that mythical struggle that is always coming but never arrives, was as far in the future as ever. There was too much cheap land farther west to make it worth while to stand and fight to the bitter end. The eastern army as it crossed the mountains marveled at the quietude of the Monongahelans and with the contempt of the city "slicker" for the "sticks" dubbed them poltroons because they did not afford more opportunity for blood-letting.

Brackenridge with his usual clarity of vision pleaded not only for the West of his day but for the ever changing West of the future: "I have seen the waves, when they were calm, and

I have wondered that they ever could be wrought into a storm to shipwreck navies. Let my fellow citizens on the east of the mountain, be as happy as I am, that they met with no resistance. The rage of the forest would have been more awful than its solitude. Be not offended, that I am partial to the spirit of these people; they are yourselves; you have them for your compatriots against a common foe; and I will pledge myself, they will not disgrace you in any enterprise it may be necessary to undertake, for the glory of our republic, however daring and hazardous it may be."[18]

NOTES

Notes to Chapter I

The Monongahela Pioneers

1. H. M. Brackenridge, *Recollections*, 60 n.

2. H. H. Brackenridge, *Gazette Publications*, 93-107, 228-235; Israel D. Rupp, *History of the Counties of Berks and Lebanon*, 114 (Lancaster, Pa., 1844).

3. Max Farrand, *Records of the Federal Convention of 1787*, 1:583 (New Haven, 1911). It is only fair to say that the "gentlemen" of the West favored the popular program of expansion and public improvements, even though many of them hated and feared democracy.

4. H. H. Brackenridge, *Incidents of the Insurrection*, 1:113; 2:9.

5. Accounts of the Moravian massacre are in Consul W. Butterfield, ed., *Washington-Irvine Correspondence*, 99-102, 236-244 (Madison, Wis., 1882), and in Crumrine, *Washington County*, 102-110.

6. Butterfield, *Washington-Irvine Correspondence*, 232.

7. *Pennsylvania Archives*, first series, 8:713-715; 9:572, 637, 661-663, 666, 729; 10:40-44, 163-165. An account of the controversy over the proposed erection of a new state is in Crumrine, *Washington County*, 185-188, 231-235.

8. H. H. Brackenridge, *Gazette Publications*, 28.

9. Charles Beatty, *The Journal of a Two Months Tour in America*, 18 (London, 1768).

10. Accounts of this incident, differing somewhat, are in Eaton, "Ecclesiastical History," in *Centenary Memorial of . . . Presbyterianism*, 220, and in McCook, *The Latimers*, 101-106.

11. *Notes and Queries*, first-second series, 1:435.

12. James B. Finley, *Autobiography*, 15 (Cincinnati, 1867); John Pope, *A Tour through the Southern and Western Territories of the United States*, 25 (New York, 1888).

13. H. H. Brackenridge, *Gazette Publications*, 243. The Scotch-Pennsylvania lawyer, Alexander Addison, found himself handicapped in his law practice by his broad Scots dialect.

14. *Pittsburgh Gazette*, September 16, 23, 1793; October 11, 1794.

15. Ward, "Insurrection," in Historical Society of Pennsylvania, *Memoirs*, 6:120-125.

16. H. H. Brackenridge, *Modern Chivalry*, 1:247-254, 265-274.

17. *Pennsylvania Archives*, second series, 4:442; H. M. Brackenridge, *Western Insurrection*, 17; *Review of the Revenue System*, 61; *Pittsburgh Gazette*, November 15, 1794.

18. *Pennsylvania Archives*, first series, 11:671.

19. Albert, *Westmoreland County*, 171.

20. Smith, *Old Redstone*, 252.

Notes to Chapter II

"Gentlemen of Respectability"—and Others

1. *Pittsburgh Gazette*, May 31, June 14, 1794.

2. Pope, *Tour*, 17 (*see* chap. 1, note 12).

3. H. H. Brackenridge, *Gazette Publications*, 7.

4. Unless otherwise stated this description of Pittsburgh is taken from Craig, *Pittsburgh*, 279-284; H. H. Brackenridge, *Gazette Publications*, 7-19; and H. M. Brackenridge, *Recollections*, 59-68.

5. Collot, *Journey in North America*, 1:141.

6. H. M. Brackenridge, *Recollections*, 62.

7. H. H. Brackenridge, *Gazette Publications*, 18.

8. These and other facts of Brackenridge's career are set forth in Newlin, *Brackenridge*.

9. Samuel B. Harding, "Party Struggles over the First Pennsylvania Constitution," in American Historical Association, *Report*, 1894, p. 371-402.

10. Newlin, *Brackenridge*, 49, citing the *United States Magazine* (1779).

11. H. H. Brackenridge, *Gazette Publications*, 169-187; H. M. Brackenridge, "Biographical Notice of H. H. Brackenridge," in H. H. Brackenridge, *Modern Chivalry*, 2:154 (Philadelphia, c1845).

12. John S. Bassett, "The Regulators of North Carolina," in American Historical Association, *Report*, 1894, p. 141-212.

13. H. H. Brackenridge, *Incidents of the Insurrection*, 1:95.

Johann D. Schoepf had a somewhat similar experience with Husband. See his *Travels in the Confederation, 1783-1784*, 1:292-297 (Philadelphia, 1911).

14. Newlin, *Brackenridge*, 61.

15. Findley, "Autobiographical Letter," in *Pennsylvania Magazine*, 5:440-450.

16. Newlin, *Brackenridge*, 78.

17. H. H. Brackenridge, *Incidents of the Insurrection*, 3:13.

18. Newlin, *Brackenridge*, 87-106.

19. The quotation is from "The Modern Chevalier," in *Gazette Publications*, 330, a metrical forerunner of *Modern Chivalry*.

20. H. M. Brackenridge, *Recollections*, 10, 43-54, 69, 111.

21. The account is a consolidation of two versions, one in Wilson, *Pittsburg*, 389, and the other in Pope, *Tour*, 14-16.

22. Felton, *General John Neville*, 1-24 and appendix G.

23. H. M. Brackenridge, *Western Insurrection*, 31-36; H. H. Brackenridge, *Incidents of the Insurrection*, 1:16; 3:142-145; Craig, *Pittsburgh*, 229-231.

24. H. H. Brackenridge, *Incidents of the Insurrection*, 1:16; 3:142-145; H. M. Brackenridge, *Western Insurrection*, 33.

25. Craig, *Pittsburgh*, 231.

26. Craig, *Isaac Craig*, passim; H. H. Brackenridge, *Incidents of the Insurrection*, 2:39 n. 1; Turnbull, *William Turnbull*, 15, 23-25.

27. H. H. Brackenridge, *Incidents of the Insurrection*, 2:39 n. 2.

28. H. M. Brackenridge, *Western Insurrection*, 179; Craig, *Exposure of . . . Misstatements in H. M. Brackenridge's History of the Whiskey Insurrection*, 56; H. H. Brackenridge, *Incidents of the Insurrection*, 1:57; 3:143. Kirkpatrick was involved in a suit with Eve in 1799. See Jasper Yeates, ed., *Reports of Cases Adjudged in the Supreme Court of Pennsylvania*, 2:444 (Philadelphia, 1817-19).

29. H. H. Brackenridge, *Gazette Publications*, 20.

30. Junkin, "John McMillan," in *Centenary Memorial of . . . Presbyterianism*, 33.

31. Crumrine, *Washington County*, 489, citing the *American Museum* (March, 1792); Creigh, *Washington County*, 136.

32. Creigh, *Washington County*, 130.

33. Brownson, *James Ross*, passim.

34. Material on Addison may be found in Crumrine, *Courts of Justice*, 40-46, and *Washington County*, 243; H. M. Brackenridge, *Recollections*, 100; Addison, *Reports of Cases*, passim.

35. Crumrine, *Courts of Justice*, 263 n. 2, and *Washington County*, 483.

36. The succeeding facts are drawn largely from Ferguson, "Gallatin," in *Western Pennsylvania Historical Magazine*, 16:183-195, and from Adams, *Gallatin*, 77-119.

37. Adams, *Gallatin*, 118.

Notes to Chapter III
Mr. Hamilton's Excise

1. *Colonial Records of Pennsylvania*, 1:108-111; 4:685-687; 6:241; 7:58, 177, 181, 184; *Pennsylvania Archives,* first series, 4:633, 634; "Letter from a Citizen of Philadelphia to an Inhabitant of Pittsburgh" (Coxe to Brackenridge?), in the *Pittsburgh Gazette,* September 20, 1794. Pennsylvania, *Statutes at Large,* gives the texts of the excise laws; they can be found by consulting the index of each volume.

2. William Findley asserted that he had never heard of an exciseman visiting distillers before the Revolution, and he judged from this that the excisemen presumed that spirituous liquors made in the province were for the use of the owner. *History of the Insurrection*, 26.

3. Findley, *History of the Insurrection*, 27; Pennsylvania, *Statutes at Large*, 9:297-299, 414-417; 10:175.

4. Findley, *History of the Insurrection*, 30; *Pennsylvania Archives,* first series, 4:633.

5. Findley, *History of the Insurrection*, 29, 30; Pennsylvania, *Statutes at Large*, 11:53-63; *Review of the Revenue System*, 58.

6. *Pennsylvania Archives,* first series, 10:594.

7. Findley, *History of the Insurrection*, 31-34; H. H. Brackenridge, *Incidents of the Insurrection*, 3:6-8.

8. *Pennsylvania Archives,* first series, 10:757; H. H. Brackenridge, *Incidents of the Insurrection*, 3:7, 13; Findley, *History of the Insurrection*, 33.

9. H. H. Brackenridge, *Incidents of the Insurrection*, 3:7, 13; Findley, *History of the Insurrection*, 34; *Pennsylvania Archives*, first series, 12:1.

10. Maclay, *Journal*, 387.

11. United States Continental Congress, *Journals*, 1:109.

12. *Annals of Congress*, 2:1848.

13. *Annals of Congress*, 2:1850.

14. *Annals of Congress*, 2:1846.

15. *Annals of Congress*, 2:1740.

16. *Annals of Congress*, 2:1842, 1846.

17. *Annals of Congress*, 2:1844, 1846, 1857, 1860.

18. *Annals of Congress*, 2:1870, 1872, 1876, 1880.

19. Maclay, *Journal*, 396; Pennsylvania, *House Journal*, 1790-91, p. 94, 104, 108-111, 142-149; Adams, *Gallatin*, 87; *Annals of Congress*, 2:1859; *Pennsylvania Archives*, second series, 4:19; H. H. Brackenridge, *Incidents of the Insurrection*, 3:9; Findley, *History of the Insurrection*, 39; North Carolina, *Senate Journal*, January 11, 1792; North Carolina, *House Journal*, January 11, 1792.

20. *Annals of Congress*, 2:1884.

21. Maclay, *Journal*, 387, 389.

22. Hamilton, *Works*, 6:457.

23. United States, *Statutes at Large*, 1:199-214, 267-271, 378-381.

24. Coxe, *A View of the United States*, 52 n. (Philadelphia, 1794).

25. On the causes of the insurrection, see Ward, "Insurrection," in the Historical Society of Pennsylvania, *Memoirs*, 6:119-182; Findley, *History of the Insurrection*, passim; Carnahan, "Pennsylvania Insurrection," in the New Jersey Historical Society, *Proceedings*, 6:115-120; H. H. Brackenridge, *Incidents of the Insurrection*, 1:85-90, and his "Thoughts on the Excise Law," in the *National Gazette* (Philadelphia), February 9, 1792; H. M. Brackenridge, *Western Insurrection*, 16-30; Gallatin, *Speech ... 1794*, 4-6; White's speech in the Pennsylvania legislature, in the *Virginia Gazette* (Richmond), September 22, 1794; "M. S.," in the *Oracle of Dauphin* (Harrisburg), January 28, 1793; Addison, *Charges*, passim, and in Creigh, *Washington County*, appendix 90-107; "J. R. Distiller," in

the *Pittsburgh Gazette,* March 22, 1794; "Uniontown Meeting," in the *Pittsburgh Gazette,* October 4, 1794; Hamilton, "Spirits, Foreign and Domestic," in his *Works,* 2:368-408, and in the *American State Papers, Finance,* 1:151-158; "Republican," in the *Pittsburgh Gazette,* April 26, 1794; and the following in the *Pennsylvania Archives,* second series, 4:20-22, 29-31, 159-161, 180, 269, 350.

26. The chief refutations of the western arguments are found in the writings of Alexander Hamilton. See especially his *Works,* 2:368-408, 427-472; 6:410-426.

Notes to Chapter IV

The Beginning of Direct Action

1. Findley, *History of the Insurrection,* 79; H. H. Brackenridge, *Incidents of the Insurrection,* 1:122.

2. Maclay, *Journal,* 391.

3. Pennsylvania, *Senate Journal,* September, 1791; Pennsylvania, *House Journal,* September, 1791; H. H. Brackenridge, *Incidents of the Insurrection,* 3:9-12.

4. H. H. Brackenridge, *Incidents of the Insurrection,* 3:132.

5. Findley, *History of the Insurrection,* 41, 263-266; H. H. Brackenridge, *Incidents of the Insurrection,* 3:16; *Pennsylvania Archives,* second series, 4:84.

6. H. H. Brackenridge, *Incidents of the Insurrection,* 3:17; Findley, *History of the Insurrection,* 43.

7. H. H. Brackenridge, *Incidents of the Insurrection,* 3:18, 148; Findley, *History of the Insurrection,* 43; *Pennsylvania Archives,* second series, 4:20-22.

8. Neville to Clymer, September 8, 1791, Wolcott Papers, vol. 19.

9. H. H. Brackenridge, *Incidents of the Insurrection,* 3:11; *Pennsylvania Archives,* second series, 4:36-39, 60, 291, 530.

10. H. H. Brackenridge, *Incidents of the Insurrection,* 3:22.

11. Findley, *History of the Insurrection,* 267; *Pennsylvania Archives,* second series, 4:48-51.

12. H. H. Brackenridge, *Incidents of the Insurrection,* 3:22;

American Daily Advertiser (Philadelphia), September 15, 1794.

13. Findley, *History of the Insurrection,* 79-81.

14. *Pennsylvania Archives,* second series, 4:86; Findley, *History of the Insurrection,* 68; letter from Neville, September 15, 1791, and a clipping of unidentified origin signed by "A Citizen" and warning Johnson's attackers that the processes were forged, Wolcott Papers, vol. 19. Findley, in his account of the outrages, usually followed Hamilton.

15. *Pennsylvania Archives,* second series, 4:37, 44, 88; Neville to Clymer, November 17, 1791, Wolcott Papers, vol. 19; Findley, *History of the Insurrection,* 58; H. H. Brackenridge, *Incidents of the Insurrection,* 3:23.

16. Letter from Neville, December 11, 1791, Wolcott Papers, vol. 19; Findley, *History of the Insurrection,* 58.

17. Neville to Clymer, November 17, 1791, Wolcott Papers, vol. 19; deposition of Captain William Faulkner, September 28, 1792, "Pennsylvania Insurrection," vol. 1.

18. Depositions of Captain William Faulkner, September 28, William Goudy, September 29, Peter Myers, September 29, and Margaret Chambers, October 4, 1792; and Clymer to Randolph, October 4, 1792, "Pennsylvania Insurrection," vol. 1; Neville to Clymer, August 23, 1792, Wolcott Papers, vol. 19; *Pennsylvania Archives,* second series, 4:230, 293; Addison, *Charges,* 50.

19. Neville to Clymer, December 22, 1791, Wolcott Papers, vol. 19; *Review of the Revenue System,* 69.

20. *Pennsylvania Archives,* second series, 4:29-31, 230.

21. *Pennsylvania Archives,* second series, 4:32; Gallatin, *Speech . . . 1794,* 6; H. H. Brackenridge, *Incidents of the Insurrection,* 3:20-22; Findley, *History of the Insurrection,* 44.

22. Hamilton to Coxe, September 1, 1792; Addison to Clymer, September 27, 1792; Clymer to Hamilton, September 28, October 4, 1792, Wolcott Papers, vol. 19; Findley, *History of the Insurrection,* 69-72; H. H. Brackenridge, *Incidents of the Insurrection,* 3:24; *Pennsylvania Archives,* second series, 4:38; *National Gazette* (Philadelphia), November 28, December 1, 5, 1792.

23. Clymer to Hamilton, Oct. 10, 1792, Wolcott Papers, vol. 19.

24. H. H. Brackenridge, *Incidents of the Insurrection,* 3:135; Neville to Clymer, June 21, 1793, Wolcott Papers, vol. 19.

25. Findley, *History of the Insurrection,* 59-61; *Pittsburgh Gazette,* March 15, 1794; affidavit of Benjamin Wells, January 29, 1794, Wolcott Papers, vol. 19; *Pennsylvania Archives,* second series, 4:95, 290.

26. Gallatin, *Speech . . . 1794,* 8; *Pennsylvania Archives,* second series, 4:96.

27. Adams to Jefferson, June 30, 1813, in John Adams, *Works,* 10:47 (edited by Charles F. Adams—Boston, 1850-56).

28. *National Gazette* (Philadelphia), July 17, 1793.

29. Further information on the politics of this period is in: Charles D. Hazen, *Contemporary American Opinion of the French Revolution* (Johns Hopkins University, *Studies in Historical and Political Science,* extra volume 16—Baltimore, 1897); Claude Bowers, *Jefferson and Hamilton* (Boston, 1925); Meade Minnigerode, *Jefferson, Friend of France* (New York, 1928).

30. Washington, *Writings,* 12:454.

31. *Virginia Chronicle* (Norfolk), July 17, 1794.

32. H. H. Brackenridge, *Incidents of the Insurrection,* 3:25, 77, 148; Findley, *History of the Insurrection,* 56. The papers of both the Mingo Creek and Washington Democratic societies seem to have disappeared; probably they were destroyed upon the approach of the army.

33. H. H. Brackenridge, *Incidents of the Insurrection,* 3:25; *American State Papers, Miscellaneous,* 1:929; committee of correspondence of the Washington Democratic Society to John Breckinridge, April 8, 1794, Innes Papers, 19:114; *American Daily Advertiser* (Philadelphia), July 29, 1794. Brackenridge says that the Washington Democratic Society was founded in April, 1794, but the letter to John Breckinridge cited above states that "on the 24th ultimo, a form of a Remonstrance drawn up by the Democratic Society of Kentuckey, was laid before the Democratic Society of this place, by David Bradford, our Vice-President."

34. *American Daily Advertiser* (Philadelphia), July 29, 1794; Innes Papers, 19:126; *Virginia Centinel* (Winchester), August 11, September 29, 1794.

35. In *Pittsburgh Gazette,* April 26, 1794, and in *Gazette of the United States* (Philadelphia), May 5, 1794.

36. *Pennsylvania Archives,* second series, 4:292.

37. Findley, *History of the Insurrection,* 107.

38. *Pittsburgh Gazette,* February 8, 1794. The seizure of the liquor of Andrew Monroe of Canonsburg led to a long newspaper controversy between him and John McGill; Monroe accused the latter of desiring an excise office and finally presented an affidavit by Robert Johnson as proof. See *Pittsburgh Gazette,* June 28, July 5, 19, 26, 1794. "J. R. Distiller" of Fayette County entered into a controversy with Neville through the columns of the *Gazette* over the terms of the excise laws, but though there may have been some grounds for misapprehension of the laws, "J. R. Distiller" was probably quibbling. See issue of February 8, 15, March 22, 1794.

39. *Pennsylvania Archives,* second series, 4:97.

40. Findley, *History of the Insurrection,* 63-65; *Pennsylvania Archives,* second series, 4:62, 146, 292.

41. *Pennsylvania Archives,* second series, 4:97; Neville to Clymer, received March 21, 1794, Wolcott Papers, vol. 19.

42. *Pennsylvania Archives,* second series, 4:65; Findley, *History of the Insurrection,* 65.

43. Neville to Clymer, received March 21, 1794, Wolcott Papers, vol. 19; Findley, *History of the Insurrection,* 59; *Pennsylvania Archives,* second series, 4:97.

44. H. H. Brackenridge, *Incidents of the Insurrection,* 1:78; 3:148; *Historical Magazine of Monongahela's Old Home Coming Week,* 97.

45. H. H. Brackenridge, *Incidents of the Insurrection,* 1:176.

46. *Pittsburgh Gazette,* June 7, 1794.

47. Findley, *History of the Insurrection,* 60; Carnahan, "Pennsylvania Insurrection," in New Jersey Historical Society, *Proceedings,* 6:120; Neville to Clymer, June 13, 20, 1794, Wolcott Papers, vol. 19; *Pittsburgh Gazette,* June 21, 28, 1794; *Pennsylvania Archives,* second series, 4:98.

48. *Carlisle Gazette,* August 21, 1793.

49. The *Oracle of Dauphin* (Harrisburg), February 11, 1793, carried a dialogue between a distiller and a pettifogger that illustrates

the specious reasoning of those who evaded the law.

50. Justin Winsor, *The Westward Movement,* 485 (Boston, 1897); "M. S." in the *Oracle of Dauphin* (Harrisburg), January 28, 1793. The details of the movement against the excise in Ohio County, Virginia, are unknown, but that there were indictable offenses committed is shown by the correspondence between the representatives of that county and the United States commissioners in *Pennsylvania Archives,* second series, 4:201-203.

51. *Ante,* chap. 3; Hamilton, *Works,* 6:343; *American State Papers, Finance,* 1:279, 558.

52. The Treasury's statistics are of doubtful value in estimating the importance of western Pennsylvania's distillation of domestic products in comparison with that of the rest of the country. In addition to being fragmentary, they were somewhat contradictory and did not always use the same bases of estimation from year to year. Sometimes liquors distilled from foreign and domestic materials were lumped together under domestic distillation and again they were separated. The fact that most of the country stills utilized domestic materials, however, aids in estimating the revenue received from the distillation of domestic products. The statistics and conclusions that follow are, it is hoped, better than guesses, but they are not advanced as complete or accurate. A reliable analysis of the subject must await the opening of the Tench Coxe Papers to research.

A table of the revenues from the distillation of domestic products follows. The fiscal year ended in June.

YEAR	U. S.	PENNA.	FOURTH SURVEY OF PA.
1792	$114,334	....	......
1793	134,565	....	......
1794	....	....	$40,056
1795	218,036	$ 53,504	20,000 net
1796	192,087	60,788	26,500
1797	296,960	114,208	38,271
1798	371,508	122,551	27,183
1799	349,071	99,576	......
1800	372,561	114,477	......

(The figures for the United States and Pennsylvania are drawn from *American State Papers, Finance,* 1:250, 279, 280, 350, 390, 562, 593, 618, 683, 714, 721. Those for the fourth survey of Pennsylvania are from Neville to Miller, September 30, 1796, December 8, 1797, Neville's "Abstract of Duties," 1797-98, Carnegie Library Manuscripts, and from Findley, *History of the Insurrection,* 325.) By these figures it is seen that the revenue from the distillation of domestic products more than trebled in less than a decade, in spite of a reduction in duties. How far this proportion applied to Pennsylvania is a matter of conjecture, as statistics of returns in the early years are fragmentary. The increase may also have been in part the result of improved efficiency of excise collections. Creigh (*Washington County,* appendix 112, 113) gives some statistics that he took from the "original records," now unidentifiable. In 1787 Washington County had 228 licensed stills, in 1788 there were 280, in 1790, 262, and in 1791, 272. It would seem that these figures must have been gathered by the state excisemen, who were admittedly unable to enforce the law in the West. In the fiscal year of 1791-92 Pennsylvania, exclusive of the fourth survey, had 831 stills, and the United States, exclusive of Virginia, North Carolina, and parts of South Carolina and Pennsylvania, had 2,389. The omitted sections were the very ones where distillation of domestic products was most important, so it is probable that there were in the United States double the number stated, or about five thousand. This conclusion is drawn from a study of the comparative rank of the states in yielding revenue on distillation of domestic products.

The scattered data in the Carnegie Library Manuscripts show for the years from 1794 to 1798 surprisingly little variation in the number of stills in the various counties of Pennsylvania's fourth survey. If the estimates given above for Washington County can be reckoned only as the stills whose owners compounded with the state excise collectors, it seems fair to assume that the total number of stills in the survey remained fairly constant all through the decade. By 1797 Washington and Greene counties (Greene had been recently set apart from Washington) had 618 stills and Allegheny County had 200 (Neville to Miller, September 22, December 29, 1797, letter book of John Neville, Carnegie Library Manuscripts). In 1798 Neville's "Abstract of Duties" gave Washington and Greene 542 stills, Allegheny 216, Fayette 202, Westmoreland

284, and Bedford (probably including Somerset) 113. This was a total of 1,357 stills, with a capacity of 108,428 gallons and with a revenue of $27,183, of which Washington and Greene counties paid $10,448. It is thus seen that these two counties with twenty-seven per cent of the population of the survey (in 1800), possessed forty per cent of the stills and paid thirty-eight per cent of the revenue of the survey. It is a striking fact that fifty-eight per cent of Allegheny County's stills were in the section that had once belonged to Washington County and that during the insurrection was exceeded in its violence only by the latter county. See a notebook of Neville's, probably of 1797, in the Carnegie Library Manuscripts, that lists Allegheny County's stills by townships.

If the number of stills in Pennsylvania's fourth survey remained fairly constant during the decade, as seems reasonable, they must have numbered in 1791 about twenty-five per cent of all those engaged in the distillation of domestic products in the United States, and Washington County alone must have had ten per cent of the national total. By 1800 when there were 22,527 stills in this business with a capacity of 1,834,371 gallons *(American State Papers, Finance,* 1:714) the Monongahela country could have operated no more than about six per cent of the stills and furnished about the same percentage of the volume of capacity. It must be borne in mind, of course, that the number of stills furnished no certain index to capacity or production and that the stills in the East were probably larger than those in the West. The point remains, however, that a greater distribution of stills in the West would lead to more resistance to the excise.

Notes to Chapter V

Bower Hill

1. *Annals of Congress,* 4:113, 115, 118, 437, 560, 720, 742, 758, 1457; *Pennsylvania Archives,* second series, 4:99.

2. *Pennsylvania Archives,* second series, 4:99; Findley, *History of the Insurrection,* 75, 224-225, 299-300, 312-313; U. S. District Court Docket in Pennsylvania. No. 1, pages 1-37; Ward, "Insurrection," in Historical Society of Pennsylvania, *Memoirs,* 6:155-165. The last is the best discussion of the problem involved in the issu-

ance of the processes. Findley best sets forth the western view.

3. Hamilton, *Works*, 6:341; Washington, *Writings*, 12:186; Findley, *History of the Insurrection*, 75, 224-226, 261; Madison, *Writings*, 6:221 (edited by Gaillard Hunt—New York and London, 1906); *Review of the Revenue System*, 65-69. The last work, reputed to have been written by Findley, developed at great length the thesis that Hamilton had used St. Clair as an instrument in an alleged plot to make an army necessary. St. Clair, the argument ran, had been induced to pick a war with the Indians and the expense involved in prosecuting the war had been used as an argument to gain the votes of those Congressmen who did not favor the other scheme of the dominant party. Joel Barlow was impressed by the idea that Hamilton may have deliberately fostered a revolt, as is shown by the following quotation from a letter to Jefferson. "Are there any facts to be come at, besides what have been published, which will show the secret springs and exciting causes of the Insurrection in the west of Pennsylvania in 1794? I am imprest with a strong belief that Hamilton, probably Washington, wished for an opportunity of that sort to make a military parade and to show what was called the force of the government, but can it be shown that any underhand thing was done by them with a view to produce such a case?" See Barlow to Jefferson, August 1, 1808, in Jefferson Papers, vol. 179. In his reply of August 5 Jefferson avoided an answer to Barlow's question, but as Barlow was on his way to Monticello, they may have discussed it there.

4. H. H. Brackenridge, *Incidents of the Insurrection*, 1:5, 121; 3:26; Findley, *History of the Insurrection*, 77-79; Lenox to Hamilton, September 8, 1794, Wolcott Papers, vol. 19.

5. H. H. Brackenridge, *Incidents of the Insurrection*, 1:122; 3:133, 136; *Pennsylvania Archives*, second series, 4:181.

6. The description of Bower Hill is drawn from observation and from the United States topographic and geological survey map of the Carnegie quadrangle, Pennsylvania. For the manor house see Felton, *General John Neville*, 21-24 and appendix G, and McCook, *The Latimers*, 199.

7. The discrepancies are apparently irreconcilable. Neville said that he had made arrangements for defense with his domestics but that at the time of Holcroft's attack they had just gone to the fields

to work. He also stated that there were a hundred in the attacking party, sixty with firearms and the rest with sticks and stones; Holcroft said that they had thirty-seven guns; and William Miller said that there were thirty men with fifteen guns, only six of them in order. Neville's account is in his letter to Coxe, July 18, 1794, in the Carnegie Library Manuscripts, in the *Magazine of Western History*, 6:514 (September, 1887), and in *Notes and Queries*, third series, 2:94. Miller's and Holcroft's accounts are in H. H. Brackenridge, *Incidents of the Insurrection*, 1:122; 3:133, 136. See also *Pennsylvania Archives*, second series, 4:181, and *The Neville Memorial*, 12.

8. H. H. Brackenridge, *Incidents of the Insurrection*, 1:17; 3:133-135; Neville to Coxe, July 18, 1794, in the Carnegie Library Manuscripts, and in *Notes and Queries*, third series, 2:94. The effective force of the expedition was over "300 guns." In addition there were enough unarmed men to bring the total number to five or six hundred.

9. Neville to Coxe, July 18, 1794, in Carnegie Library Manuscripts, and in *Notes and Queries*, third series, 2:94; Kirkpatrick to Washington, July 28, 1794, Wolcott Papers, vol. 19; H. H. Brackenridge, *Incidents of the Insurrection*, 1:17-19; 3:133-135; H. M. Brackenridge, *Western Insurrection*, 48-51; Findley, *History of the Insurrection*, 86-91; *Pennsylvania Archives*, second series, 4:73-75, 100-102; Carnahan, "Pennsylvania Insurrection," in New Jersey Historical Society, *Proceedings*, 6:121. Henry C. McCook, in *The Latimers* (p. 199-224), has given what is probably the best account of the attack on Bower Hill, basing the narrative partly on local tradition. The number of casualties resulting from the siege will probably never be known. One account has it that a soldier who had been killed during the battle was burned in the house. Major Thomas Butler reported that three soldiers had been slightly wounded and that two were missing. He suspected, however, that the two had seized the opportunity to desert. One of the assailants in addition to McFarlane was killed and an indeterminate number were wounded, of whom some may have died. H. M. Brackenridge, *Western Insurrection*, 49 n., quotes the following epitaph taken from the tombstone of James McFarlane in Mingo Creek Cemetery. "Here lies the body of Captain James M'Farlane, of Washing-

ton County, Pa., who departed this life the 17th of July, 1794, aged 43 years. He served during the war with undaunted courage in defense of American independence, against the lawless and despotic encroachments of Great Britain. He fell at last by the hands of an unprincipled villain, in the support of what he supposed to be the rights of his country, much lamented by a numerous and respectable circle of acquaintance."

10. H. H. Brackenridge, *Incidents of the Insurrection*, 1:6-11; 3:67.

11. Lenox to Hamilton, September 8, 1794, Wolcott Papers, vol. 19; H. H. Brackenridge, *Incidents of the Insurrection*, 1:19-21; 3:134, 135.

12. H. H. Brackenridge, *Incidents of the Insurrection*, 1:23-29; 3:78-80; Lenox to Hamilton, September 8, 1794, Wolcott Papers, vol. 19.

13. H. H. Brackenridge, *Incidents of the Insurrection*, 1:25-27; 3:80.

14. H. H. Brackenridge, *Incidents of the Insurrection*, 1:27; Lenox to Hamilton, September 8, 1794, Wolcott Papers, vol. 19.

15. *Pennsylvania Archives*, second series, 4:71.

16. H. H. Brackenridge, *Incidents of the Insurrection*, 1:33, 60; 2:40. Brackenridge's attempts to cloud the issue as to his responsibility for the incident are not convincing. The method used for getting rid of the notice, however, was certainly characteristic of him.

17. *Pittsburgh Gazette*, July 26, 1794; H. H. Brackenridge, *Incidents of the Insurrection*, 1:84; *Pennsylvania Archives*, second series, 4:70.

Notes to Chapter VI
The Mingo Meeting

1. H. H. Brackenridge, *Incidents of the Insurrection*, 1:29.

2. H. H. Brackenridge, *Incidents of the Insurrection*, 1:29-36; 3:71, 74-77, 81, 85-87, 93-96. Findley, *History of the Insurrection*, 91-93, probably based his account on that of Brackenridge.

3. H. H. Brackenridge, *Incidents of the Insurrection*, 1:41.

4. *Pennsylvania Archives,* second series, 4:111.

5. H. H. Brackenridge, *Incidents of the Insurrection,* 1:38-42; Findley, *History of the Insurrection,* 93-97; *Pennsylvania Archives,* second series, 4:78, 522; Carnahan, "Pennsylvania Insurrection," in New Jersey Historical Society, *Proceedings,* 6:125.

6. H. H. Brackenridge, *Incidents of the Insurrection,* 1:42-44; 3:82, 112, 121; Findley, *History of the Insurrection,* 103; Carnahan, "Pennsylvania Insurrection," in New Jersey Historical Society, *Proceedings,* 6:125.

Notes to Chapter VII

Braddock's Field

1. H. H. Brackenridge, *Incidents of the Insurrection,* 85-87; Conway, *Edmund Randolph,* 243.

2. H. H. Brackenridge, *Incidents of the Insurrection,* 1:43.

3. H. H. Brackenridge, *Incidents of the Insurrection,* 1:45-48; 3:72-75, 83, 87-90, 96-99, 102, 104, 122; *Pennsylvania Archives,* second series, 4:79-81, 168-171.

4. H. H. Brackenridge, *Incidents of the Insurrection,* 1:49-51; H. M. Brackenridge, *Western Insurrection,* 99.

5. Gallatin, *Speech . . . 1794,* 12; *Pennsylvania Archives,* second series, 4:172; H. H. Brackenridge, *Incidents of the Insurrection,* 1:66; Findley, *History of the Insurrection,* 98. Since Washington County, which furnished most of the men who went, then had a population of twenty-four thousand, the number estimated by Wilkins could have been drawn from that county alone.

6. H. H. Brackenridge, *Incidents of the Insurrection,* 2:64; H. M. Brackenridge, *Western Insurrection,* 44 n.; Gallatin, *Speech . . . 1794,* 11.

7. Concerning the possibility of successful revolt see Collot, *Journey in North America,* 1:28.

8. The account in this and the following paragraphs of the muster at Braddock's Field is based upon Carnahan, "Pennsylvania Insurrection," in New Jersey Historical Society, *Proceedings,* 6:126-128; H. H. Brackenridge, *Incidents of the Insurrection,* 1:52-59;

3:101, 135; *Pennsylvania Archives,* second series, 4:171; and Findley, *History of the Insurrection,* 98-101. Brackenridge gives the most extended and graphic account of the muster, perhaps colored somewhat to suit his current objects, but there is no reason to believe that it is not essentially fair and correct.

Notes to Chapter VIII
The Whiskey Boys in Sodom

1. H. H. Brackenridge, *Incidents of the Insurrection,* 1:59-66, 68; 3:100, 110; *Pennsylvania Archives,* second series, 4:172.

2. H. H. Brackenridge, *Incidents of the Insurrection,* 1:66, 69, 79; 2:36; 3:148; *Pennsylvania Archives,* second series, 4:172.

3. H. H. Brackenridge, *Incidents of the Insurrection,* 1:66-70, 71; Carnahan, "Pennsylvania Insurrection," in New Jersey Historical Society, *Proceedings,* 6:128; *Pennsylvania Archives,* second series, 4:172. The *Pittsburgh Gazette* of August 2, 1794, contained an apology for the attempt on Kirkpatrick's house and the burning of his barn, signed by Cook, McFarlane, Marshall, Meetkerke, and David and John Hamilton.

4. H. H. Brackenridge, *Incidents of the Insurrection,* 1:69, 81; *Pittsburgh Gazette,* August 2, 1794; Findley, *History of the Insurrection,* 269.

5. Rupp, *Early History of Western Pennsylvania,* appendix 274; Findley, *History of the Insurrection,* 107-109.

6. H. H. Brackenridge, *Incidents of the Insurrection,* 1:71-76, 79-85; *Pennsylvania Archives,* second series, 4:157, 173.

7. H. H. Brackenridge, *Incidents of the Insurrection,* 1:75-78; 3:92, 96, 103, 107, 128-131; *Notes and Queries,* third series, 2:96; *Pennsylvania Archives,* second series, 4:140-144, 262.

Notes to Chapter IX
The First Parkinson's Ferry Meeting

1. H. H. Brackenridge, *Incidents of the Insurrection,* 1:80-83; 3:117, 120; Findley, *History of the Insurrection,* 112, 271.

2. H. H. Brackenridge, *Incidents of the Insurrection,* 3:132.

3. Findley, *History of the Insurrection,* 112.

4. By far the best account of the first Parkinson's Ferry meeting is in H. H. Brackenridge, *Incidents of the Insurrection,* 1:87-100, 104. It is true that he made himself prominent in his account; but, as he explained, it was in self defense, for he wrote the book while under fire for his actions during the insurrection. His story, however, is probably correct for it checks well with other sources and with the vouchers written by reputable western citizens and published in *Incidents of the Insurrection,* 3:106, 111, 113, 117-121, 132, 137-139. So far as can be found none of those whose vouchers were published ever complained that he had been misquoted, and some of them were Federalists, politically opposed to Brackenridge. Other accounts of the meeting are in Findley, *History of the Insurrection,* 113-117; Gallatin, *Speech . . . 1794,* 13-17; and *Pennsylvania Archives,* second series, 4:163-166.

5. H. H. Brackenridge, *Incidents of the Insurrection,* 1:88-91; Gallatin, *Speech . . . 1794,* 15; Adams, *Gallatin,* 133; Findley, *History of the Insurrection,* 113-115; Ward, "Insurrection" in Historical Society of Pennsylvania, *Memoirs,* 6:201. It was during the debate on the resolutions, says Brackenridge, that Gallatin, "though he did not venture to touch on the resistance to the marshal, or the expulsion of the proscribed, yet he strongly arraigned the destruction of property; the burning of the barn of Kirkpatrick, for instance. What! said a fiery fellow in the committee, do you blame that? The secretary found himself embarrassed; he paused for a moment.—If you had burned him in it, said he, it might have been something; but the barn had done no harm. Ay, ay, said the man, that is right enough." Gallatin, however, denied the story in a notation on the margin of his copy of *Incidents of the Insurrection.*

6. H. H. Brackenridge, *Incidents of the Insurrection,* 1:91; 3:138.

7. H. H. Brackenridge, *Incidents of the Insurrection,* 1:92.

8. H. H. Brackenridge, *Incidents of the Insurrection,* 1:93.

9. H. H. Brackenridge, *Incidents of the Insurrection,* 1:99; 3:148; Findley, *History of the Insurrection,* 115.

10. H. H. Brackenridge, *Incidents of the Insurrection,* 1:94.

11. H. H. Brackenridge, *Incidents of the Insurrection,* 1:95-97.

12. H. H. Brackenridge, *Incidents of the Insurrection,* 1:97; 3:139; Gallatin, *Speech . . . 1794,* 16.

13. H. H. Brackenridge, *Incidents of the Insurrection,* 1:97-99; Gallatin, *Speech ... 1794,* 16.

Notes to Chapter X

The Commissioners to the White Indians Come and Go

1. *Pennsylvania Archives,* second series, 4:144-146. Unfortunately the minutes of the conference are not complete. The date of the conference is in some doubt but August 2 is probably correct, since the judicial certificate had not yet been obtained. Hamilton's report, which was officially dated the fifth, may have been submitted to Washington in draft before the second.

2. *Pennsylvania Archives,* second series, 4:82-109, 112-122; Hamilton, *Works,* 6:1-17; 7:719.

3. *Pennsylvania Archives,* second series, 4:122-137.

4. Bradford to Randolph, August 8, 10, 12, 15, 1794, and minutes of United States commissioners, "Pennsylvania Insurrection," vol. 1.

5. H. H. Brackenridge, *Incidents of the Insurrection,* 1:100-104.

6. William Bradford to Washington, August 17, 1794, "Pennsylvania Insurrection," vol. 1.

7. *Pennsylvania Archives,* second series, 4:167, 180.

8. *Pennsylvania Archives,* second series, 4:182-211; H. H. Brackenridge, *Incidents of the Insurrection,* 1:104-107.

9. H. H. Brackenridge, *Incidents of the Insurrection,* 3:95.

10. *Pennsylvania Archives,* second series, 4:545-549.

11. H. H. *Brackenridge, Incidents of the Insurrection,* 1:110; 3:107.

12. H. H. Brackenridge, *Incidents of the Insurrection,* 1:108.

13. H. H. Brackenridge, *Incidents of the Insurrection,* 1:108-121; 3:28, 150; Findley, *History of the Insurrection,* 121-129.

14. H. H. Brackenridge, *Incidents of the Insurrection,* 1:110-112; Findley, *History of the Insurrection,* 123; United States commissioners to Randolph, August 30, 1794, "Pennsylvania Insurrection," vol. 2.

15. H. H. Brackenridge, *Incidents of the Insurrection,* 1:112-116.

16. H. H. Brackenridge, *Incidents of the Insurrection,* 1:116; Findley, *History of the Insurrection,* 124-126; United States commissioners to Randolph, August 30, 1794, "Pennsylvania Insurrection," vol. 2.

17. H. H. Brackenridge, *Incidents of the Insurrection,* 1:117; Findley, *History of the Insurrection,* 127; *Pennsylvania Archives,* second series, 4:218.

18. H. H. Brackenridge, *Incidents of the Insurrection,* 1:120; Findley, *History of the Insurrection,* 127-130; *Pennsylvania Archives,* second series, 4:211, 218.

19. H. H. Brackenridge, *Incidents of the Insurrection,* 1:120.

20. United States commissioners to Randolph, August 30, 1794, "Pennsylvania Insurrection," vol. 1; letter of William Bradford, August 30, 1794, "Pennsylvania Insurrection," vol. 2; *Pennsylvania Archives,* second series, 4:219.

21. *Pennsylvania Archives,* second series, 4:212-215, 233-237, 259-261, 354.

22. Findley, *History of the Insurrection,* 130; *Pittsburgh Gazette,* September 6, 1794.

23. H. H. Brackenridge, *Incidents of the Insurrection,* 2:5; 3:153; Findley, *History of the Insurrection,* 160; Addison, *Reports,* 277; United States commissioners to Randolph, September 5, 1794, "Pennsylvania Insurrection," vol. 2.

24. Minutes of United States commissioners, "Pennsylvania Insurrection," vol. 1; Randolph to Ross, September 29, 1794, Ross Papers.

Notes to Chapter XI

The Solemn Promise

1. Addison, *Charges,* 100-112. Also in *Pennsylvania Archives,* second series, 4:237-247.

2. H. H. Brackenridge, *Incidents of the Insurrection,* 2:11-13.

3. *Pittsburgh Gazette,* September 13, 1794; H. H. Brackenridge, *Incidents of the Insurrection,* 2:9.

4. H. H. Brackenridge, *Incidents of the Insurrection,* 2:20;

Gazette of the United States (Philadelphia), September 29, 1794; Redstone Presbytery, *Minutes*, 111; Ohio Presbytery, "Records," October 29, 1794.

5. *Pennsylvania Archives,* second series, 4:201-203, 269-271.

6. *Pittsburgh Gazette,* September 13, 1794; *Virginia Centinel* (Winchester), August 18, September 8, 1794; *Gazette of the United States* (Philadelphia), September 3, 1794; Gallatin, *Speech ... 1794,* 13; *Calendar of Virginia State Papers,* 7:29, 267.

7. *Baltimore Daily Intelligencer,* September 16, 20, 1794; *Virginia Gazette* (Richmond), September 15, 1794.

8. *Virginia Centinel* (Winchester), September 8, 29, 1794.

9. Thomas to Gale, September 3, 1794, Wolcott Papers, vol. 19; *Baltimore Daily Intelligencer,* September 20, 1794.

10. *Baltimore Daily Intelligencer,* September 20, 1794; *Carlisle Gazette,* September 24, 1794; *Virginia Gazette* (Richmond), September 29, 1794; *Pittsburgh Gazette,* October 18, 1794.

11. *Baltimore Daily Intelligencer,* September 10, 1794; Findley, *History of the Insurrection,* 322; *Pennsylvania Archives,* second series, 4:167, 340, 380, 404.

12. John F. Meginness, *Otzinachson; or, A History of the West Branch of the Susquehanna,* 327 (Philadelphia, 1857).

13. *Baltimore Daily Intelligencer,* September 5, 1794; *Virginia Gazette* (Richmond), September 29, 1794; affidavits of Samuel Castlethwait, George Rowan, Robert Guthrie, and Ephraim Blaine, September 15, 16, 1794, Mifflin Documents.

14. *Pittsburgh Gazette,* September 6, 1794; Findley, *History of the Insurrection,* 129-137; lists of signers of the oath of submission, "Pennsylvania Insurrection," vol. 2.

15. Smith to Ross, September 15, 1794, "Pennsylvania Insurrection," vol. 2; *Pennsylvania Archives,* second series, 4:343; Findley, *History of the Insurrection,* 133; *Virginia Gazette* (Richmond), October 2, 1794; Findley to Ross, September 16, 1794, Wallace Papers, 3:39; H. H. Brackenridge, *Incidents of the Insurrection,* 2:21.

16. *Pittsburgh Gazette,* October 11, 1794; H. H. Brackenridge, *Incidents of the Insurrection,* 2:20; 3:148; Veech, "Secular His-

tory," in *Centenary Memorial of . . . Presbyterianism,* 395; Findley, *History of the Insurrection,* 133.

17. H. H. Brackenridge, *Incidents of the Insurrection,* 2:23.

18. H. H. Brackenridge, *Incidents of the Insurrection,* 2:14-20.

19. *Pennsylvania Archives,* second series, 4:348-359.

20. H. H. Brackenridge, *Incidents of the Insurrection,* 2:24-27; *Pennsylvania Archives,* second series, 4:315. The *Albany Register* had already published in August a diatribe against Brackenridge, which, reprinted, occupied a column and a half in the *Gazette of the United States* (Philadelphia), September 4, 1794.

21. *Pennsylvania Archives,* second series, 4:342-344; Findley to Ross, September 16, 1794, Wallace Papers, 3:38.

22. *Pittsburgh Gazette,* September 13, October 4, 11, 1794; Findley, *History of the Insurrection,* 110; *Pennsylvania Archives,* second series, 4:319; Ward, "Insurrection," in Historical Society of Pennsylvania, *Memoirs,* 6:165.

23. H. H. Brackenridge, *Incidents of the Insurrection,* 2:28-31.

24. H. H. Brackenridge, *Incidents of the Insurrection,* 2:32-35; Findley, *History of the Insurrection,* 138; *Pittsburgh Gazette,* October 11, 1794; *Pennsylvania Archives,* second series, 4:389.

25. H. H. Brackenridge, *Incidents of the Insurrection,* 2:36, 44.

26. H. H. Brackenridge, *Incidents of the Insurrection,* 2:44; Veech, "Secular History," in *Centenary Memorial of . . . Presbyterianism,* 396; *Pittsburgh Gazette,* October 18, November 1, 1794.

Notes to Chapter XII

The Watermelon Army Marches

1. *Gazette of the United States* (Philadelphia), September 15, 1794; *North Carolina Journal* (Halifax), September 17, 1794; Elizabeth Drinker, *Extracts from the Journal of . . . from 1759 to 1807,* 237 (Philadelphia, 1889).

2. Hamilton, *Works,* 6:410-426.

3. Quoted in the *Kentucky Gazette* (Lexington), October 18, 1794.

4. *Pennsylvania Archives,* second series, 4:280-285, 326-328, 502-527.

5. *Pennsylvania Archives,* second series, 4:306, 550. Among other gems of patriotic poetry inspired by the occasion was one published in the *Gazette of the United States* (Philadelphia), November 26, 1794, beginning,

> Since the Eagle of Freedom is roused from her nest
> Let us chace her fell fiends o'er the hills of the west.

6. *Virginia Gazette* (Richmond), September 18, 1794; Foote, *Sketches of Virginia, Historical and Biographical,* 476, 560 (Philadelphia, 1850).

7. Ford, "Journal," in New Jersey Historical Society, *Proceedings,* 8:5, 9; *Baltimore Daily Intelligencer,* September 10, 1794.

8. Quoted in the *Virginia Gazette* (Richmond), September 22, 1794.

9. *Pennsylvania Archives,* second series, 4:122.

10. Gould, "Journal," in New Jersey Historical Society, *Proceedings,* 3:178; *American Daily Advertiser* (Philadelphia), October 17, 1794.

11. Gould, "Journal," in New Jersey Historical Society, *Proceedings,* 3:179.

12. *Carlisle Gazette,* February 11, 18, 1795; Ford, "Journal," in New Jersey Historical Society, *Proceedings,* 8:11.

13. Findley, *History of the Insurrection,* 143; Ford "Journal," in New Jersey Historical Society, *Proceedings,* 8:10; *General Advertiser* (Philadelphia), October 27, 1794.

14. *Pennsylvania Archives,* second series, 4:429; Ford, "Journal," in New Jersey Historical Society, *Proceedings,* 8:11; *North Carolina Journal* (Halifax), October 27, 1794.

15. *American Daily Advertiser* (Philadelphia), October 17, 1794; Humrich, "Relations Which the People of Cumberland and Franklin Counties Bore to the Whiskey Insurrection," in Kittochtinny Historical Society, *Papers,* 1901-03, p. 241; Dallas, *Life and Writings,* 35.

16. Ford, "Journal," in New Jersey Historical Society, *Proceedings,* 8:11.

17. Findley, *History of the Insurrection*, 140-145, 169-189; Ford, "Journal," in New Jersey Historical Society, *Proceedings*, 8:12; Washington, *Diaries, 1748-1799*, 4:212-216 (edited by J. C. Fitzpatrick—Boston and New York, 1925).

18. Wellford, "Diary," in *William and Mary College Quarterly Historical Magazine*, 11:7-10; Washington, *Writings*, 12:481-483; *Pennsylvania Archives*, second series, 4:411-415. There is a strange similarity between Wellford's account of the review at Bedford and the account in the *American Daily Advertiser* (Philadelphia), October 9, 1794, of the review at Carlisle. For Washington's exact dates and routes on this journey, see *Notes and Queries*, first-second series, 1:224-226. The four prisoners from Bedford were Husband, Filson, Wisecarver, and Lucas. Lucas had been involved in the mutiny of the Pennsylvania line during the Revolution.

19. Washington, *Writings*, 12:487.

20. *Virginia Gazette* (Richmond) November 17, 1794; Wellford, "Diary," in *William and Mary College Quarterly Historical Magazine*, 11:10-15.

21. *General Advertiser* (Philadelphia), October 25, 1794; *Pennsylvania Archives*, second series, 4:432.

22. Michael, "Journal," in *Historical Register*, 1:69; Dallas, *Life and Writings*, 39; *Pennsylvania Archives*, second series, 4:428-434; letter from officers of the right wing of the army, October 8, 1794, Mifflin Documents; Findley, *History of the Insurrection*, 151.

23. *American Daily Advertiser* (Philadelphia), November 18, 1794.

24. Findley, *History of the Insurrection*, 148; Wiley, *Whisky Insurrection*, 42; Gould, "Journal," in New Jersey Historical Society, *Proceedings*, 3:182, 184; Washington, *Writings*, 12:480.

25. Findley, *History of the Insurrection*, 190-199, 227; *Pennsylvania Archives*, second series, 4:435-439.

26. Wiley, *Whisky Insurrection*, 38-41; *Pennsylvania Archives*, second series, 4:439; Findley, *History of the Insurrection*, 228.

27. H. H. Brackenridge, *Incidents of the Insurrection*, 2:38, 46, 51-57.

28. H. H. Brackenridge, *Incidents of the Insurrection*, 1:71.

Notes to Chapter XIII

The Watermelon Army among the White Indians

1. H. H. Brackenridge, *Incidents of the Insurrection*, 2:59-61.

2. H. H. Brackenridge, *Incidents of the Insurrection*, 2:61.

3. H. H. Brackenridge, *Incidents of the Insurrection*, 3:148; petition of Alexander Fulton for pardon, "Pennsylvania Insurrection," vol. 1; *Notes and Queries*, third series, 2:100. These facts are hard to reconcile with Jefferson's statement that, though the westerners let the army pass, it was the object of their laughter, not of their fear. Thomas Jefferson, *Writings*, 9:295 (definitive edition —Washington, 1907).

4. H. H. Brackenridge, *Incidents of the Insurrection*, 2:59; 3:32; *Pennsylvania Archives*, second series, 4:450. According to a note in the *Federal Intelligencer and Baltimore Daily Gazette*, November 24, 1794, the troops found a list of the leaders of the insurrection in Bradford's house as well as letters proving that the insurrection had been in agitation for three years with the purpose of placing the region under the British Crown. The truth of the note is doubtful, since such papers, had they been found, would have been produced as evidence in the trials that followed the insurrection.

5. *Pennsylvania Archives*, second series, 4:435, 443-447, 467.

6. H. H. Brackenridge, *Incidents of the Insurrection*, 2:68-71; Findley, *History of the Insurrection*, 203. Brackenridge gives a list of the Pittsburghers imprisoned.

7. H. H. Brackenridge, *Incidents of the Insurrection*, 2:79; H. M. Brackenridge, *Western Insurrection*, 329; Findley, *History of the Insurrection*, 205-210; Carnahan, "Pennsylvania Insurrection," in New Jersey Historical Society, *Proceedings*, 6:144-146. A tradition in the Mingo Creek district has it that several men who were warned of their danger in time hid behind a waterfall near the meetinghouse and were thus enabled to elude the soldiers. Forrest, *Washington County*, 1:982.

8. Carnahan, "Pennsylvania Insurrection," in New Jersey Historical Society, *Proceedings*, 6:146.

9. Crumrine, *Washington County*, 300; Smith, *Old Redstone*, 262.

10. Crumrine, *Washington County*, 885. Creigh, *Washington*

County, appendix 111, 112, gives two lists with a total of forty-four stills seized on November 14 and 15 and names David Hamilton's still as having been stolen. No source is given for the information.

11. Findley, *History of the Insurrection,* 231-233, 235.

12. Findley, *History of the Insurrection,* 228-230.

13. Carnahan, "Pennsylvania Insurrection," in New Jersey Historical Society, *Proceedings,* 6:150; H. H. Brackenridge, *Incidents of the Insurrection,* 2:80. Three prisoners escaped from the Pittsburgh jail on November 24, and General Lee offered a reward of two hundred dollars for the apprehension of each. *Pennsylvania Archives,* second series, 4:476.

14. H. H. Brackenridge, *Incidents of the Insurrection,* 2:73-82. The controversy over Brackenridge's loyalty was never settled to the mutual satisfaction of his descendants and those of the Nevilles. Brackenridge loaded his third volume with the affidavits of those who claimed to have understood his attitude during the troublous days; and, in the face of such witnesses as Ross, Addison, Purviance, John Hoge, and others, some of whom had no reason to be sympathetic to him, it is hard to accuse him of more than playing a double game with the intention of avoiding bloodshed. In the eighteen-fifties the controversy was revived by Henry Marie Brackenridge, the son of the lawyer, and Neville B. Craig, son of the deputy quartermaster-general and grandson of General Neville. Brackenridge wrote a *History of the Western Insurrection* based largely on his father's account, and Craig countered with a booklet entitled *Exposure of a Few of the Many Misstatements in H. M. Brackenridge's History of the Whiskey Insurrection.* Both works were ill-tempered and somewhat inaccurate.

15. Michael, "Journal," in *Historical Register,* 1:136, 138.

16. H. H. Brackenridge, *Incidents of the Insurrection,* 2:82.

17. *Pennsylvania Archives,* second series, 4:452-456, 460, 466.

18. *Pittsburgh Gazette,* November 15, 1794; *Pennsylvania Archives,* second series, 4:479, 500-502.

19. H. H. Brackenridge, *Incidents of the Insurrection,* 3:30-32, 35, 37-39, 145, 153; Findley, *History of the Insurrection,* 321.

20. Findley, *History of the Insurrection,* 213; H. H. Brackenridge, *Incidents of the Insurrection,* 3:33; *Pennsylvania Archives,* second series, 4:500-502.

21. H. M. Brackenridge, *Western Insurrection*, 328-332; *American Daily Advertiser* (Philadelphia), December 26, 1794; *North Carolina Journal* (Halifax), December 22, 1794. The Reverend John Corbley, soon after the arrival in Philadelphia, published on behalf of the prisoners a letter of thanks to Captain John Dunlap for the "polite usage" received by the prisoners whom he had escorted in Washington County. In the same letter Corbley expressed "sincere thanks" to General White for "his friendly and moving address on the road" and praised Dunham for his "kind and tender treatment." The tone of the letter suggests to the reader that either Corbley was a diplomat or the accounts of the maltreatment of prisoners were overdrawn. *Independent Gazetteer* (Philadelphia), December 31, 1794.

Notes to Chapter XIV

The Aftermath

1. *Carlisle Gazette,* January 7, 28, 1795; *Virginia Gazette* (Richmond), November 17, 1794.

2. *American State Papers, Miscellaneous,* 1:83; *Gazette of the United States* (Philadelphia), August 26, 1794; *American Daily Advertiser* (Philadelphia), August 9, 1794; *Baltimore Daily Intelligencer,* September 4, 1794; *Virginia Gazette* (Richmond), November 13, 1794; *Virginia Chronicle* (Norfolk), September 22, 1794.

3. *Aurora* (Philadelphia), November 24, 29, December 22, 27, 1794.

4. *Annals of Congress,* 4:787, 895-945. Edmund Randolph, in a series of newspaper letters "To the Citizens of the United States" signed "Germanicus," endeavored to prove that the Democratic societies had been guilty of instigating the insurrection. The letters were reprinted as a pamphlet with the title *Germanicus.*

5. James Madison, *Writings,* 6:221-223 (edited by Gaillard Hunt —New York and London, 1906).

6. Pennsylvania, *Senate Journal,* December 18, 1794—February 18, 1795; Pennsylvania, *House Journal,* December 16, 1794—February 14, 1795; Gallatin, *Speech . . . 1794,* passim.

7. Minute Book of the U. S. Circuit Court, April 11, 1795—

October 23, 1795; Adams, *Gallatin*, 147-149; Wharton, *State Trials*, 164-184; H. H. Brackenridge, *Incidents of the Insurrection*, 3:41-61; William Bradford's opinion upon the western combinations, Wallace Papers, 3:13.

8. Minute Book for the U. S. Circuit Court, April 11, 1795—October 23, 1795; *Pennsylvania Archives*, second series, 4:500-502, 533-539; Adams, *Gallatin*, 147-151; H. M. Brackenridge, *Western Insurrection*, 330-332; Wharton, *State Trials*, 164-184; Creigh, *Washington County*, appendix 113-121; *Pittsburgh Gazette*, November 7, 1795; Helmuth and Hendel to Washington, June 12, 1795, and three petitions for the release of John Mitchell and Philip Weigel, June 13, 1795, "Pennsylvania Insurrection," vol. 2.

9. The later history of the excise can be followed in the papers of General Neville in the Carnegie Library Manuscripts. Excise suits in Allegheny, Fayette, and Bedford counties had been discontinued during the winter of 1794-95 in cases where offenders came forward and paid a year's arrears. See *Pittsburgh Gazette*, December 27, 1794. It is interesting to note that as late as November, 1797, the returns from Kentucky were two years behind, and a year later the commissioner of the revenue could write that "by the vigilance and exertion of the present supervisor, order has been introduced" in the district of Ohio. *American State Papers, Finance*, 1:558, 592.

10. Addison, *Charges*, 149; *Pittsburgh Gazette*, May 9, 1795, April 6, 1799; Ohio Presbytery, "Records," April 29, 1795; Forrest, *Washington County*, 1:992.

11. Craig, *Pittsburgh*, 273; Forrest, *Washington County*, 1:992; H. H. Brackenridge, *Incidents of the Insurrection*, 1:116.

12. Randolph, *Vindication*, passim; Conway, *Edmund Randolph*, 270-357; Turner, "Correspondence of the French Ministers to the United States, 1791-1797," in American Historical Association, *Report*, 1903, vol. 2, p. 372-377, 411-418, 444-455; George Gibbs *Memoirs of the Administrations of Washington and John Adams, Edited from the Papers of Oliver Wolcott*, 1:232-280 (New York, 1846). A few details included in this account for explanatory purposes are found in Dispatch No. 6.

13. H. H. Brackenridge, *Incidents of the Insurrection*, 2:84.

BIBLIOGRAPHY

Bibliography

PRINTED works that were used only once or twice, and then incidentally, and are not essential to an understanding of the background or events of the insurrection are not included in the following bibliography. Bibliographical data for such works are given in the footnotes.

SOURCE MATERIAL

MANUSCRIPTS

AYRES, ROBERT. "Diary," 1785-1845. In the possession of Mr. William Ayers Galbraith, Edgeworth, Pa. Ayres was a minister successively in the Methodist and Episcopal churches. His later years were spent as a farmer and teacher near Franklin, Pa.

CARNEGIE LIBRARY MANUSCRIPTS. The Carnegie Library of Pittsburgh has some of the papers of General John Neville, including a letter book, an "Abstract of Duties," a notebook, and some miscellaneous memoranda and correspondence.

GALLATIN PAPERS. In the custody of the New York Historical Society. Volume 3 contains a few letters bearing upon the events of the insurrection and upon the trials that followed.

INNES, HARRY, PAPERS. Library of Congress. Contain some material on the Washington, Pa., Democratic society.

JEFFERSON PAPERS. Library of Congress. Contain a few letters to Jefferson expressing opinions about the insurrection.

MIFFLIN DOCUMENTS. Pennsylvania State Library, Harrisburg. Listed as "Documents of Mifflin's Administration, 1790-1799." They contain some of the official papers and correspondence of Mifflin and the Pennsylvania commissioners to the western counties relating to the insurrection.

OHIO PRESBYTERY. "Records," 1793-1806. Western Theological Seminary, Pittsburgh. The Ohio Presbytery was composed of the

Presbyterian churches in the region around the headwaters of the Ohio.

"PENNSYLVANIA INSURRECTION." Library of Congress. Two volumes composed largely of the papers of the federal commissioners to the western counties.

ROSS, JAMES, PAPERS. Historical Society of Western Pennsylvania, Pittsburgh. Contain a few letters bearing on Ross's activities during the insurrection.

UNITED STATES. District Court of Pennsylvania. *Docket, Civil Actions, No. 1.* Customs House, Philadelphia.

UNITED STATES. Circuit Court for the Pennsylvania District of the Middle Circuit. *Minute Book, 1793-95.* Customs House, Philadelphia.

WALLACE PAPERS. Historical Society of Pennsylvania. Volume 3 contains some correspondence relating to the insurrection and the draft of William Bradford's opinion upon the treasonable nature of the western combinations.

WOLCOTT, OLIVER, JR., PAPERS. Connecticut Historical Society, Hartford. Volume 19 is entitled: "Papers Chiefly concerning the Insurrection in Pennsylvania in 1794 and Letters Written during the Yellow Fever in Philadelphia in 1793."

NEWSPAPERS

The newspapers listed here were consulted only for the years noted and to the extent of the facilities provided by the Historical Society of Western Pennsylvania, the Carnegie Library of Pittsburgh, the Historical Society of Pennsylvania, the Pennsylvania State Library, the American Antiquarian Society, and the Library of Congress. The holdings of these depositories can best be ascertained by consulting Clarence S. Brigham's *Bibliography of American Newspapers, 1690-1820,* published in the American Antiquarian Society's *Proceedings,* 1913-27, and the Western Pennsylvania Historical Survey's manuscript "Inventory of Files of American Newspapers in Pittsburgh and Allegheny County, Pennsylvania." The files of many other newspapers than those listed below were consulted, but the material pertinent to the movement against the excise was found to be much the same in all of them because of the then common habit of copying news items verbatim from other papers.

Baltimore Daily Intelligencer, 1793-94. Continued as the *Federal Intelligencer* (Baltimore).

BALTIMORE. *Federal Intelligencer, and Baltimore Daily Gazette,* 1794-95. Successor to the *Baltimore Daily Intelligencer.*

BALTIMORE. *Maryland Journal,* semi-weekly and tri-weekly, 1791-94.

Carlisle (Pa.) *Gazette,* weekly, 1791-95.

HALIFAX. *North Carolina Journal,* weekly, 1792-95.

HARRISBURG, PA. *Oracle of Dauphin,* weekly, 1792-95.

LEXINGTON. *Kentucky Gazette,* weekly, 1791-95.

NORFOLK. *Virginia Chronicle,* weekly and semi-weekly, 1792-95.

PHILADELPHIA. *Aurora. General Advertiser,* daily, 1794-95. Continuation without change of numbering of the *General Advertiser.*

PHILADELPHIA. *Dunlap and Claypoole's American Daily Advertiser,* 1791-95.

PHILADELPHIA. *Gazette of the United States,* semi-weekly and daily, 1791-95. Established in 1790 in New York by John Fenno, but soon moved to Philadelphia. Fenno strove to make his paper the organ of the "republican court" of President Washington, and succeeded to a considerable extent: the Federalists gave him moral and financial support and Hamilton frequently contributed articles.

PHILADELPHIA. *General Advertiser,* daily, 1791-94. Edited by Benjamin Franklin Bache, grandson of Benjamin Franklin, and a violent partisan of Jacobin principles. The *General Advertiser* became the *Aurora. General Advertiser* in 1794.

PHILADELPHIA. *Independent Gazetteer,* weekly and semi-weekly, 1791-95.

PHILADELPHIA. *National Gazette,* semi-weekly, 1791-93. Established under the patronage of Jefferson by Philip Freneau, the poet of the Revolution and of the Jeffersonian movement. Ardently democratic in its sympathies.

Bibliography

Pittsburgh Gazette, weekly, 1791-95. Published by John Scull. The first newspaper established west of the Allegheny Mountains. Federalist in its sympathies.

RICHMOND. *Virginia Gazette and Richmond and Manchester Advertiser,* semi-weekly, 1793-95. Samuel Pleasants, editor.

WINCHESTER. *Virginia Centinel,* weekly, 1794-95.

OTHER PRINTED SOURCES

ADDISON, ALEXANDER. *Charges to Grand Juries of the Counties of the Fifth District in the State of Pennsylvania.* Washington, Pa., 1800. viii, 318 p.

ADDISON, ALEXANDER. *Reports of Cases in the County Courts of the Fifth Circuit, and in the High Court of Errors and Appeals, of the State of Pennsylvania.* Washington, Pa., 1800. x, 396, xxiv p.

American State Papers. Documents, Legislative and Executive, of the Congress of the United States. Washington, 1832-61. 38 vols. *Miscellaneous,* 1: 83-113, contains official papers relating to the insurrection and titled "Opposition to the Excise Law in Pennsylvania. Communicated to Congress by the President of the United States, November 20, 1794." *Finance,* vol. 1, has statistics and correspondence relating to the excise.

Annals of Congress; the Debates and Proceedings in the Congress of the United States . . . from March 3, 1789 to May 27, 1824. Compiled by Joseph Gales, Sr., and W. W. Seaton. Washington, 1834-56. 42 vols.

BRACKENRIDGE, HENRY M. *Recollections of Persons and Places in the West.* Philadelphia and Pittsburgh, 1868. 331 p. Interesting account of the author's life as boy and young lawyer in Pittsburgh and elsewhere.

BRACKENRIDGE, HUGH H. *Gazette Publications.* Carlisle, 1806. 348 p. Collected poems, essays, and polemic writings.

BRACKENRIDGE, HUGH H. *Incidents of the Insurrection in the Western Parts of Pennsylvania, in the Year 1794.* Philadelphia, 1795. 3 vols. in 1. A hasty and disjointed account of the author's activities during the insurrection, written to prove that he had no share in the movement save to play a prominent part in blocking its development into a serious revolt.

Bibliography

BRACKENRIDGE, HUGH H. *Modern Chivalry: Containing the Adventures of a Captain and Teague O'Regan, His Servant.* Pittsburgh, R. Patterson & Lambdin, 1819. 2 vols. A satirical romance in the manner of *Don Quixote,* that appeared in several instalments, went through many editions, and was very popular in the United States and Great Britain around 1800. Brackenridge's political philosophy here found its clearest expression.

Calendar of Virginia State Papers. Richmond, 1875-93. 11 vols. Includes some letters relating to disturbances in western Virginia.

CARNAHAN, JAMES. "The Pennsylvania Insurrection of 1794, Commonly Called the 'Whiskey Insurrection.' A Paper Read before the New Jersey Historical Society, September 8th, 1852," in New Jersey Historical Society, *Proceedings,* 6:115-152 (1853). Carnahan was a student at Canonsburg Academy in 1794 and witnessed some of the events he described. He exhibited a better understanding of the western viewpoint than have many writers of general accounts of the insurrection.

COLLOT, GEORGES H. V. *A Journey in North America, Containing a Survey of the Countries Watered by the Missisipi* [sic], *Ohio, Missouri, and Other Affluing Rivers.* Paris, 1826. 2 vols. in 1 and atlas.

[*Colonial Records of Pennsylvania.*] Harrisburg, 1851-53. 16 vols. The *Minutes of the Provincial Council,* constituting the first ten volumes of this set, contain data with regard to the excise laws of the colonial period.

DALLAS, ALEXANDER J. *Life and Writings of Alexander James Dallas.* Edited by George Mifflin Dallas. Philadelphia, 1871. 487 p. Contains some of the letters of the elder Dallas written while with the army that marched to put down the insurrection.

DEWEES, SAMUEL. *A History of the Life and Services of Captain Samuel Dewees.* Compiled by John Smith Hanna. Baltimore, 1844. 360 p. Dewees was a fifer with a Harrisburg company; p. 294-321 deal with the Whiskey Insurrection.

ELLIOT, JAMES. "Sketches, Political, Geographical, &c. Extracted from the Journal of James Elliot, during a Period of Three Years Service in the Legion of the United States," in *Poetical and Mis-*

Bibliography

cellaneous Works of James Elliot. Greenfield, Mass., 1798. Elliot was with the army that marched to suppress the insurrection.

FINDLEY, WILLIAM. *History of the Insurrection, in the Four Western Counties of Pennsylvania; in the year M.DCC.XCIV. with a Recital of the Circumstances Specially Connected Therewith; and an Historical Review of the Previous Situation of the Country.* Philadelphia, 1796. 328 p. Written to exculpate the author from blame for promoting or directing the insurrection. Findley laid the onus for the insurrection directly upon Hamilton's political and economic policies.

FINDLEY, WILLIAM. "William Findley of Westmoreland, Pa., Author of 'History of the Insurrection in the Western Counties of Pennsylvania.'—an Autobiographical Letter," in *Pennsylvania Magazine of History and Biography,* 5: 440-450 (1881).

FORD, DAVID. "Journal of an Expedition Made in the Autumn of 1794, with a Detachment of New Jersey Troops, into Western Pennsylvania, to Aid in Suppressing the 'Whiskey Rebellion.'" Reprinted from New Jersey Historical Society, *Proceedings,* vol. 8 (1859).

GALLATIN, ALBERT. *The Speech of Albert Gallatin . . . Touching the Validity of the Elections Held in the Four Western Counties of the State, on the 14th Day of October, 1794.* Philadelphia, 1795. 66 p. An interpretation and defense of the western point of view.

GOULD, WILLIAM. "Journal of Major Wm. Gould of the New Jersey Infantry, during an Expedition into Pennsylvania in 1794," in New Jersey Historical Society, *Proceedings,* 3:173-191 (1848-49).

HAMILTON, ALEXANDER. *Works.* Edited by Henry Cabot Lodge. New York and London, 1904. 12 vols.

LEE, HENRY. "Orders Issued by General Henry Lee during the Campaign against the Whiskey Insurrectionists," in *Western Pennsylvania Historical Magazine,* 19:79-111 (June, 1936). Edited by Leland D. Baldwin.

MACLAY, WILLIAM. *Journal of William Maclay, United States Senator from Pennsylvania, 1789-1791.* Edited by Edgar S. Maclay. New York, 1890. xiv, 438 p. The democratic view of events during the first two years under the Constitution.

Bibliography

MICHAEL, WILLIAM. "A Journal of the 'Whiskey Insurrection,'" in *Historical Register: Notes and Queries, Historical and Genealogical, Relating to Interior Pennsylvania*, 1:64-74, 134-147 (January, April, 1883).

Pennsylvania Archives. First series, Philadelphia, 1852-56. 12 vols. Second series, first edition, Harrisburg, 1874-93. 19 vols. "Papers Relating to What Is Known as the Whiskey Insurrection in Western Pennsylvania, 1794," is in the second series, 4:1-550. This collection is drawn from official reports, private correspondence, and newspapers, and while reasonably complete is poorly edited and contains many mistakes in dates and copying.

PENNSYLVANIA. *House Journal*, 1790-95.

PENNSYLVANIA. *Senate Journal*, 1790-95.

PENNSYLVANIA. *The Statutes at Large of Pennsylvania from 1682 to 1809*. Harrisburg, 1896-1915. 18 vols.

[RANDOLPH, EDMUND.] *Germanicus*. [Philadelphia? 1794?] 77 p. Reprint of a series of newspaper letters addressed "To the Citizens of the United States." Endeavors to prove that the Democratic societies were responsible for the insurrection.

RANDOLPH, EDMUND. *A Vindication of Edmund Randolph, Written by Himself, and Published in 1795*. Richmond, 1855. xi, 82 p. The attempt of a bewildered statesman to vindicate himself. The complete vindication, however, did not come until the publication of Moncure D. Conway's *Edmund Randolph*.

REDSTONE PRESBYTERY. *Minutes of the Presbytery of Redstone, of the Presbyterian Church in the U. S. A. From the Organization of Presbytery, September 19, 1781, to December, 1831*. Cincinnati, 1878. 424 p.

A Review of the Revenue System Adopted by the First Congress under the Federal Constitution: Wherein the Principles and Tendency of the Funding System and the Measures Connected with It to the End of the Second Congress Are Examined. In Thirteen Letters to a Friend. By a Citizen. Philadelphia, 1794. 130 p. First appeared in the *Independent Gazetteer* of Philadelphia in 1794. The work was attributed to William Findley but he categorically denied the authorship in his *History of the Insurrection*, 276-278.

Bibliography

Long and dull, but of value for its analysis of the democratic objections to Hamilton's program.

TURNER, FREDERICK J., ed. "Correspondence of the French Ministers to the United States, 1791-1797," in American Historical Association, *Report,* 1903, vol. 2. Contains the dispatches of Fauchet that caused the resignation of Edmund Randolph from the office of secretary of state.

UNITED STATES. *The Public Statutes at Large of the United States of America from the Organization of the Government in 1789, to March 3, 1845.* Boston, 1845. 6 vols.

UNITED STATES. Continental Congress. *Journals of the Continental Congress, 1774-1789.* Edited by Worthington C. Ford. Washington, 1904+ Vol. 1+

WASHINGTON, GEORGE. *Writings.* Edited by Worthington C. Ford. New York, 1892. 14 vols.

WELLFORD, ROBERT. "A Diary Kept by Robert Wellford, of Fredericksburg, during the March of the Virginia Troops to Fort Pitt to Suppress the Whiskey Insurrection," in *William and Mary College Quarterly Historical Magazine,* 11:1-19 (1902-03). Wellford was surgeon general of the army sent against the insurgents.

WHARTON, FRANCIS. *State Trials of the United States during the Administrations of Washington and Adams with References, Historical and Professional, and Preliminary Notes on the Politics of the Times.* Philadelphia, 1849. 727 p.

SECONDARY MATERIAL

ADAMS, HENRY. *The Life of Albert Gallatin.* Philadelphia, 1879. v, 697 p. The only important biography of Gallatin. Inadequate on his activities before he entered the field of national politics.

ALBERT, GEORGE D., ed. *History of the County of Westmoreland, Pennsylvania.* Philadelphia, 1882. 727 p. Has some excellent chapters on the general history and conditions of Westmoreland County before 1800.

BRACKENRIDGE, HENRY M. "Biographical Notice of H. H. Brackenridge," in Hugh H. Brackenridge, *Modern Chivalry,* 2:151-189 (Philadelphia, c1846). Originally published in the *Southern Literary Messenger,* 8:1-19 (January, 1842).

{ 312 }

Bibliography

BRACKENRIDGE, HENRY M. *History of the Western Insurrection in Western Pennsylvania, Commonly Called the Whiskey Insurrection*. Pittsburgh, 1859. 336 p. Written in defense of the author's father as the result of a newspaper controversy between Henry M. Brackenridge and Neville B. Craig over the rôles played by their respective families during the Whiskey Insurrection. Based upon the elder Brackenridge's account.

BROWNSON, JAMES I. *The Life and Times of Senator James Ross*. Washington, Pa., 1910. vi, 52 p. The most useful account of Ross yet published.

BUCK, SOLON J. and ELIZABETH H. *The Planting of Civilization in Western Pennsylvania*. Pittsburgh, 1939.

CONWAY, MONCURE D. *Omitted Chapters of History Disclosed in the Life and Papers of Edmund Randolph*. New York, 1888. vi, 401 p. Conway effectually defended Randolph from the slurs cast upon him because of the circumstances of his resignation from the office of secretary of state.

CRAIG, NEVILLE B. *Exposure of a Few of the Many Misstatements in H. M. Brackenridge's History of the Whiskey Insurrection*. Pittsburgh, 1859. 79 p. Defense of the Neville connection and impeachment of the elder Brackenridge. The author was a son of Major Isaac Craig and a grandson of General John Neville.

CRAIG, NEVILLE B. *The History of Pittsburgh, with a Brief Notice of Its Facilities of Communication and Other Advantages for Commercial and Manufacturing Purposes, with Two Maps*. Pittsburgh, 1851. 312 p. The account of the insurrection shows little understanding of the underlying causes of the movement against the excise.

CRAIG, NEVILLE B. *Sketch of the Life and Services of Isaac Craig*. Pittsburgh, 1854. 70 p. Laudatory.

CREIGH, ALFRED. *History of Washington County from Its First Settlement to the Present Time*. Harrisburg, Pa., 1871. 375 and 132 p. Has a good chapter on the insurrection and some pertinent statistics in the appendix.

Bibliography

CRUMRINE, BOYD. *The Courts of Justice, Bench, and Bar of Washington County, Pennsylvania.* Washington, Pa., 1902. xii, 352 p. Considerable information on men prominent at the time of the insurrection.

CRUMRINE, BOYD, ed. *History of Washington County, Pennsylvania, with Biographical Sketches of Many of Its Pioneers and Prominent Men.* Philadelphia, 1882. 1002 p. Has a good chapter on the insurrection and is of value in the other portions for information about persons and places connected with the insurrection.

EATON, S. J. M. "Ecclesiastical History, with Biographical Sketches," in *Centenary Memorial of the Planting and Growth of Presbyterianism in Western Pennsylvania,* 205-250 (Pittsburgh, 1876).

FELTON, MARGARET M. "General John Neville." University of Pittsburgh, MS. thesis, 1932. [7] 78 [27] p. A clear and concise account of one of the chief figures in western Pennsylvania during the insurrection.

FERGUSON, RUSSELL J. "Albert Gallatin, Western Pennsylvania Politician," in *Western Pennsylvania Historical Magazine,* 16: 183-195 (August, 1933). The most adequate account of Gallatin's connection with western Pennsylvania politics.

FERGUSON, RUSSELL J. *Early Western Pennsylvania Politics,* Pittsburgh, 1938. xvi, 300 p.

FORREST, EARLE R. *History of Washington County, Pennsylvania.* Chicago, 1926. 3 vols. Offers some information on the insurrection not found elsewhere and reproduces photographs of local scenes connected with the movement.

Historical Magazine of Monongahela's Old Home Coming Week, Sept. 6-13, 1908. N. p., n. d. 312 p.

HUMRICH, C. P. "The Relations Which the People of Cumberland and Franklin Counties Bore to the Whiskey Insurrection of 1794," in Kittochtinny Historical Society, *Papers Read before the Society from March 1901, to February 1903,* 221-247 (Chambersburg, Pa., 1904).

JUNKIN, DAVID X. "Life and Labors of the Rev. John McMillan, D. D.: The Gospel He Preached and Its Influence on the Civilization of Western Pennsylvania," in *Centenary Memorial of the*

Bibliography

Planting and Growth of Presbyterianism in Western Pennsylvania, 11-34 (Pittsburgh, 1876).

LINK, EUGENE P. *The Democratic-Republic Societies, 1790-1800.* New York, 1942.

McCOOK, HENRY C. *The Latimers, a Tale of the Western Insurrection of 1794.* Philadelphia, 1898. 593 p. Excellent portrayal of pioneer life and psychology in western Pennsylvania and of the chief events of the insurrection.

MILLER, WILLIAM. "Democratic Societies and the Whiskey Insurrection," in *Pennsylvania Magazine of History and Biography,* 62:324-349 (July, 1938).

"The Neville Memorial" Services and Addresses. N. p., n. d. 19 p. Report of services held November 2, 1912, in St. Luke's Church, Woodville, Pa., in memory of General John Neville.

NEWLIN, CLAUDE M. *The Life and Writings of Hugh Henry Brackenridge.* Princeton, 1932. vi, 328 p. Devoted mostly to Brackenridge's literary career.

Notes and Queries, Historical, Biographical and Genealogical, Relating Chiefly to Interior Pennsylvania. Edited by William H. Egle. Harrisburg, Pa., first-second series, 1894-95, 2 vols.; third series, 1895-96, 3 vols.; fourth series, 1893-95, 2 vols. Miscellaneous notes collected by Egle and reprinted from his column in the *Harrisburg Daily Telegraph.*

RUPP, ISRAEL D. *Early History of Western Pennsylvania.* Pittsburgh and Harrisburg, 1846. 352 and 406 p.

SCHARF, JOHN T. *History of Western Maryland.* 2 vols. Philadelphia, 1882.

SMITH, JOSEPH. *Old Redstone: or, Historical Sketches of Western Presbyterianism, Its Early Ministers, Its Perilous Times, and Its First Records.* Philadelphia, 1854. 459 p. Contains a sympathetic general account of the insurrection.

TURNBULL, ARCHIBALD D. *William Turnbull, 1751-1822, with Some Account of Those Coming After.* Binghamton, N. Y., 1933. vii, 175 p.

VEECH, JAMES. *The Monongahela of Old; or, Historical Sketches of Southwestern Pennsylvania to the Year 1800.* Pittsburgh, 1858-

92. 259 p. One of the best treatments of the early history of the region.

VEECH, JAMES. "The Secular History, Its Connection with the Early Presbyterian Church History of Southwestern Pennsylvania," in *Centenary Memorial of the Planting and Growth of Presbyterianism in Western Pennsylvania*, 287-409 (Pittsburgh, 1876). One of the best general accounts of the development of the Monongahela country to 1794.

WARD, TOWNSEND. "The Insurrection of the Year 1794, in the Western Counties of Pennsylvania," in Historical Society of Pennsylvania, *Memoirs*, 6:117-203 (1858). Clear and competent treatment of the circumstances of the origin of the insurrection.

WESTERN PENNSYLVANIA HISTORICAL SURVEY. *Guidebook to Historic Places in Western Pennsylvania*. Pittsburgh, 1938. x, 186 p.

WILEY, RICHARD T. *The Whisky Insurrection: A General View*. Elizabeth, Pa., 1912. 59 p. The best of the many short accounts of the insurrection.

WILSON, ERASMUS, ed. *Standard History of Pittsburg, Pennsylvania*. Chicago, 1898. 1074 p. Carelessly edited, but valuable for the immense body of information it presents.

INDEX

Index

Index

Index

Index

Marie, Jean, tavern, 29
Marshall, James, 79, 86, 89, 118, 189; at Mingo meeting, 131, 133, 134, 136, 138; and Braddock's Field crisis, 140, 142, 153, 163; at Parkinson's Ferry meetings, 175-182, 190
Martinsburg, 207
Maryland Journal, 62, 63
Maryland, 66, 185, 207
Meetkirk, William, 143
Methodist church, 17
Meyerstown, 225, 226
Middletown, 207
Mifflin, Gov. Thomas, 35, 183, 185, 186, 263, 267; and the militia army, 221, 222, 225, 226, 228, 237
Mifflin Township, 173
Militia, western: 11, 14, 73, 102; at Bower Hill, 113-124; during Braddock's Field crisis, 139-165; army: called out, 100, 112, 184, 185, 259; enlistments, 221-225; route, 225-235; activities, 240, 253-258
Miller, James, 153, 154
Miller, Oliver, 116
Miller, William, 113, 116, 225
Mingo Creek, attack on Faulkner, 85; and oath of submission, 211, 213; arrests, 245
Mingo Creek Democratic Society, 52, 95, 108, 113, 129-137, 165, 213
Mingo meeting, 129-137
Mississippi River commerce, 3, 39, 40, 73, 97, 108, 109, 189
Mitchell, John, mail robber, 138, 255, 257, 264
Modern Chivalry, 25, 41
Monongahela country, described, 1-8; settlers, 20-23; opposition to excise, 106-109, 169
Monongalia County (Va.), 137, 206
Monroe, James, 262
Morgan, Gen. Daniel, 45, with federal army, 188, 233, 240; remains in West, 255-258
Morgan, George, 49

Morgantown (Va.), 206
Morris, Robert, 35, 39, 58
Morris, Gov. Robert Hunter, 56
Morrison, Robert, 84
Morton, Thomas, 186, 190, 234
Murray, Capt.——, 158
Murphy, Molly, tavern, 187

Nationalities, in western Pa., 19-23
Neville, John, 5, 95, 98, 99, 241, 242, 252; sketch, 44-47; as excise inspector, 66, 68, 76, 80, 82, 84, 85; growth of opposition to, 101-104, 186; during Bower Hill crisis, 113-132
Neville, Presley, 115, 186, 219, 240, 250, 256, 258; early activities, 45, 47, 90, 99; and Bower Hill attack, 120, 121, 123, 125; and Mingo meeting, 129-132, 138; and Braddock's Field crisis, 143-145, 158, 159, 162, 166-169
Neville family, 44; country estates, 48; opposition to Brackenridge, 188, 236-238
New England, 66
New Jersey, 66; militia, 185, 222, 225, 228
New state movement, 16, 38, 169, 177, 178, 195, 202
New York, 66
North Carolina, 66, 105
Northumberland County, 57, 58
Northwest Territory, 73
Nottingham Township, 210

Oath of allegiance, 243
Oath of submission, 209-217
O'Hara, Col. James, 163
Ohio County (Va.), 175, 190, 206
Ormsby, John, 121, 151

Parker, Josiah, 65
Parkinson, Benjamin, 86, 109, 174, 179, 212, 245, 247, 255; at Bower Hill,

Index

Index

Westbay, Henry, 138
Western Pennsylvania, described, 1-4; democracy, 11-16
Westmoreland County, 2, 9, 16, 38, 51, 57, 58, 68, 102, 103, 165, 175, 190; federal reports on, 89, 198
Whiskey, social and economic importance, 10, 25-28, 69, 105; rise of distilleries, 57; seized by collectors, 99
Whiskey boys, 128, 172-174, 189, 192, 195
Whiskey Insurrection, causes, 69-75, 91-101, 106-114; results, 264-272
Whiskey Point, 174
White, Gen. Andrew, 245, 257, 258
White Indians, origin, 192
Wilkins, John, Sr., 167, 168, 169, 173, 189
Wilkins, Gen. John, 117, 137, 170, 173,

189, 204, 237; and Bower Hill crisis, 121; and Braddock's Field crisis, 143, 145, 147, 149, 156, 163
Wilkinson, Gen. James, 3
Wilson, James, 184
Wilson, Robert, 83
Wolcott, Oliver, 266, 268
Woods, John, 47, 49; and Brackenridge, 215, 237, 241, 242, 252; election of *1794*, 217-219
Woods family, 51
Woodville, 45, 115, 119
Woolf, Henry, 167
Wright, Edward, 263
Wright, Zedick, 151

Yeates, Judge Jasper, 187, 226; as U. S. commissioner, 185